ARTTALK

ARTTALK

ROSALIND RAGANS

ASSOCIATE PROFESSOR
MARVIN PITTMAN LABORATORY SCHOOL
SCHOOL OF EDUCATION
GEORGIA SOUTHERN COLLEGE

GLENCOE

Macmillan/McGraw-Hill

New York, New York
Columbus, Ohio
Mission Hills, California
Peoria, Illinois

Send all inquiries to:
GLENCOE DIVISION
Macmillan/McGraw-Hill
15319 Chatsworth Street
P.O. Box 9609
Mission Hills, CA 91346-9609

ISBN 0-02-667700-8

Printed in the United States of America.

10 11 12 13 14 15   AGK   99 98 97 96 95 94

Cover

Pat Steir. *Drawing Lesson with Chrysanthemum.* 1983. Oil
on canvas. 121.9 x 121.9 cm (48 x 48″). Collection General
Electric Company. Courtesy Harcus Gallery, Boston.

Photography

With the exception of the photographs listed below, all photographs of student works and studio techniques were taken by
Patricia Meisel.

The photographs on pages 51, 75 (Figure 5-29B), 83 (Figure
5-38), 108, 145, 230, 300, and 341 (Figure 12-35) were taken
by Frank Fortune.

Photographs on pages 296, 341 (Figure 12-36), and 342
were provided courtesy of the Fulton County Schools,
Fulton County, Georgia.

Illustration

Sally Shimizu, pages 66, 67, 68, 96, 97, 98, 101, 112, 115, 116,
117, 141, 142, 143, 144, 147, 149, 150, 153, 198, 203, 245,
248, 256, 275 and 276.
Larry Hughston, pages 104, 141, 276, 283, 285 and 286.
Gretchen Schields, pages 51 and 55.

Design and Production

Design Office, San Francisco
Bruce Kortebein, Marilyn Perry

Art educators have paid a great deal of lip service to the ideal of teaching art history, criticism and aesthetics along with artistic performance. For a long time we have claimed that studio *activities* and art appreciation *subject matter* are combined in our classrooms. And sometimes they are. Usually, however, we concentrate on making art while dropping a few artists' names and titles of works as a bow in the direction of art appreciation. Finally, in *Art-Talk*, we have a book that puts it all together. Rosalind Ragans makes good on our educational claims and demonstrates conclusively that art appreciation and art skills can be taught effectively in a mutually reinforcing manner.

Dr. Ragans is an experienced classroom teacher—she knows young students and knows how to talk to them. The lessons in this book are based on years of classroom practice, plus a long career in the training of art teachers. At the same time, she is fully conversant with the theory and techniques of art criticism and knows how to present her material in a form that makes sense to students. The linguistic model that she has chosen for her book reflects a sure grasp of what students can understand, what administrators can learn (if they try), and what teachers need.

Readers of this book will feel that they are in the hands of a professional—one who speaks in concrete terms, offers no advice unless it has been tested first, and has a realistic idea of what can be accomplished within the constraints of today's schools. Her teaching practices are designed to be used by beginners and more advanced students, and by the artistically and academically gifted, as well as those whose skills and aptitudes are less developed. I think users of this book will be helped, too, by the abundance of reproductions of art works by students and by major artists. These are meant to stimulate artistic growth as well as to provide images for the practice of art criticism.

I must confess to a strong sense of pride in seeing Rosalind Ragans' book come before the public. She was my graduate student some years ago, and, as this text testifies, she went on to do what we hope all our doctoral advisees will do: write an important book. She has done this under often trying circumstances, and with unfailing courage and good humor. This book was not easily conceived nor instantly written and published: it has gone through the crucible of much personal and professional struggle. For these and other reasons, *ArtTalk* deserves the attention of teachers. Rosalind Ragans is above all a teacher. As you read on I think you will agree.

Edmund Burke Feldman
ALUMNI FOUNDATION PROFESSOR OF ART
THE UNIVERSITY OF GEORGIA

PART THREE   *The Principles of Design*

N.C. Wyeth. *Invocation to the Buffalo Herds.* c. 1910. Oil on canvas. 88.7 x 63.7 cm (35½ x 25½"). Permanent collection of the High Museum of Art, Atlanta, Georgia. Gift of the Armand Hammer Foundation.

PART ONE

Appreciating the Visual Arts

In *ArtTalk* you will be learning about the **visual arts**. These are the arts that produce beautiful objects to look at. The visual arts include all objects created for visual appeal—including those that serve a useful purpose.

When they think of visual arts, most people first think of painting, sculpture, and architecture. Some people might add photography and filmmaking to the list. But today, the world of visual art also includes the crafts; industrial, fashion, and interior design; landscape architecture; television production; and the new computer arts.

Why should you read about and learn how to make visual art? Because the visual arts serve the same purposes today that they've served since the early history of humanity. They satisfy human needs—both personal needs and group needs. They satisfy our needs for display and celebration. They also satisfy our physical needs for useful objects and shelter.

Among the strongest needs satisfied by the visual arts are our needs for personal expression and communication. We use the visual arts to express our innermost feelings and to communicate our ideas. Whether we create a painting to hang on the wall or a decorated food container, we are communicating our feelings and ideas to others, through the visual arts.

In this first part of *ArtTalk* you will learn about the language of visual art. You will begin to learn how to look at art in new ways. You will also learn about the many different kinds of art created through history and the career opportunities in art today. After completing Part One, you will be ready to begin creating your own art. You will also be on your way toward developing a fuller appreciation for the visual arts.

Figure 1.1 This painting tells more than a simple story of a hero rescuing a helpless maiden. How is the scene in the painting different from a modern movie about monsters, heroes, and helpless victims?

Raphael. *Saint George and the Dragon.* c. 1506. Oil on wood. 28.5 ×21.5 cm (11⅛ × 8⅜"). National Gallery of Art, Washington, D.C. Andrew W. Mellon Collection.

The Language of Art

LEARNING OBJECTIVES

After reading this chapter and doing the exercises, you will be able to

- □ understand the purpose of this book.
- □ realize there is a language of art that can be learned and practiced.
- □ name and describe the parts of a work of art.
- □ name the elements of art and the principles of design.

WORDS TO LEARN

In this chapter you will learn the meanings of the words listed below.

content

elements of art

form

media

medium

principles of design

subject

symbol

When you talk to someone or write a letter, you *communicate*. You share your ideas and feelings with someone. You use words—either spoken or written—to communicate a message.

You can also communicate through the arts. The arts offer you a very special type of communication. They are languages for expressing ideas and feelings that everyday words cannot explain. The arts talk in ways that go beyond simply describing something or telling a story.

The arts can cross the language barriers of different countries. You do not need to speak French to understand a painting by Renoir. You don't need to speak German to appreciate a Beethoven symphony. Mikhail Baryshnikov may speak English with a Russian accent, but when he dances, the language of his movement is understood all around the world.

The arts may even help us communicate with beings from other planets. For example, in 1972 the National Aeronautics and Space Administration (NASA) officials attached a special plaque to Pioneer 10, the first rocket sent beyond our solar system. On the plaque were drawings of earthlings and a diagram of our solar system. NASA thought that these objects of visual art had the greatest possibility of successfully communicating with whatever beings the rocket probe might encounter.

The Elements and Principles

You know that there are many different languages. English, Spanish, and French are just a few.

Each language has its own system of words, phrases, and rules. To learn a new language you need to learn a whole new set of words and a new set of rules for putting those words together.

It is the same with the language of visual art. All of the objects we look at are made up of certain common elements. They are arranged according to certain basic principles. As you learn these basic elements and principles, you will learn the language of art.

Being able to speak the language of visual art will help you in many ways. It will increase your appreciation and enjoyment of art. It will help you talk about art with other people. It will even help you produce more beautiful and meaningful works of your own.

The Elements of Art

Symbols are visual images that stand for, or represent, something else. In the English language we use words, which are symbols, to communicate with others. In the language of art we communicate through visual symbols other than words.

The basic visual symbols in the language of art are known as the **elements of art**. Just as there

Figure 1.2 Using a variety of lines, Dürer created shiny, fuzzy, and smooth textures. Can you find them? He also controlled the lines to create the impression of different fabric weights. Can you guess what kinds of fabrics were used to make the woman's clothes?

Albrecht Dürer. *Young Woman in Netherlandish Dress.* 1521. Brush drawing in water and body color. 28.3 × 21 cm (11⅛ × 8¼"). Syma Busiel Fund.

are basic kinds of words—such as nouns, verbs, adjectives, and so on—there are basic kinds of art elements. These are *line, shape* and *form, space, value, color,* and *texture*. These elements are the visual "pieces" that artists put together to build a work of art. No matter how a visual image is made, it will contain some or all of these elements.

It is difficult to separate one element from another when you are looking at a visual image. When you look at a painting, for instance, you may see a rough, red square outlined with a dark black line. But rather than seeing the elements of texture (rough), color (red), shape (square), and line (dark black) separately, you see them all at once. You see the object as a whole. You will visually "read" the elements together.

Sometimes, however, the differences are not clear-cut. A line may be so wide that it looks like a shape. Or a line may be placed so close to the other lines that, together, they create a texture, such as you see in Figure 1-2.

When you first learned to read, you did not begin with a full-length novel. You started to read one word at a time. That is how you will start to read the language of art: one element at a time.

Because the elements of art are so important, several chapters of *ArtTalk* are devoted to them. After you have studied them in depth, you will have learned a large share of the art language vocabulary.

Principles of Design

After you have learned to recognize the elements of art, you will learn the ways in which the elements can be put together. When you learn a language, you learn the rules of grammar by which words are organized into sentences. Without these rules people would find it very difficult to communicate.

Visual images are also organized by means of rules. These rules are called the **principles of design.** These rules are guides that artists developed as they saw how people reacted to visual images.

The principles of design help artists organize the elements of art for certain effects. The principles are closely related to the way art communicates, and they are the subject of several chapters in *ArtTalk*. The principles you will learn about are *rhythm, movement, balance, proportion, variety, emphasis,* and *unity* (Figure 1-3).

The Media of Art

The material used to make an art object is called the **medium.** The medium can be something such as paint, glass, metal, or fibers. If a sculptor takes copper and welds it into a piece of sculpture, the copper is the medium. What was the medium used in the sculpture shown in Figure 1-9 (page 10)?

You should know that the word medium has an unusual plural form. It is **media.** You should also know that some people confuse different types of art with art media. Sculpture, for example, is a type of art. The metal used by the sculptor is the medium. Architecture is a type of art; concrete is a medium used by the architect.

Figure 1.3   The ancient Greek artist who created this vase used the principles of design. The artist organized the elements of line, shape, value, color, and texture to create a design that complements the basic form of the vase.

The Pan Painter. *Young Hunter with Dog* (Attic Red Figure Lekythos). 5th century B.C. 0.392 m (1'3½") high. The Museum of Fine Arts, Boston, Massachusetts. The Francis Bartlett Fund.

Figures 1.4 and 1.5   The images you see in these two works by Winslow Homer are almost exactly alike. The difference is that one is painted with thin, wet, flowing watercolor paint, while the other is painted with thick, creamy oil paint. Can you describe the different effects these two materials have on the same subject?

Figure 1.4 (above)   Winslow Homer. *Sketch for Hound and Hunter.* 1892. Watercolor. 35.4 × 50.3 cm (13⅞ × 19⅞"). National Gallery of Art, Washington, D.C. Gift of Ruth K. Henschel in memory of her husband, Charles R. Henschel.

Figure 1.5 (below)   Winslow Homer. *Hound and Hunter.* 1892. Oil on canvas. 71.8 × 122.3 cm (28¼ × 48⅛"). National Gallery of Art, Washington, D.C. Gift of Stephen C. Clark.

The Work of Art

Every work of art, whether it is a painting to hang on the wall or a chair to sit in, has three main parts. These parts are the *subject*, the *form*, and the *content*.

Subject

The **subject** of a work of art is the part of the work that the viewer can easily recognize. The subject might be a person, a tree, or a house. In some paintings nothing is really recognizable. The subjects of these paintings will be discussed later. The subject of a work of art that has a function, such as a chair, is the chair itself.

What is the subject of the painting in Figure 1-6?

Form

The second part of a work of art is the **form** of the work. The form is the artist's unique way of using the elements, principles, and media. For example, suppose that an architect designs a house

so that the bottom part only is to be covered in brick. The architect's decisions about the material—brick—and how it is to be used—on the bottom only—have to do with the form the architect has chosen.

Content

The third, and most important, part of a work of art is the **content.** The content is the message that the artist is trying to communicate using the language of art. The content may be an idea or

Figure 1.6 This large historical painting records one event in the siege of Gibraltar, when the British defended the huge rock from the Spaniards in 1784. Everyone in the scene is carefully posed to create a scene of dignity. You have probably seen real war on the evening news. Did the people in the news stories have immaculate uniforms and pose in such pleasing arrangements?

John Trumbull. *The Sortie Made by the Garrison of Gibraltar.* 1789. Oil on canvas. 180.3 × 271.8 cm (71 × 107"). The Metropolitan Museum of Art, New York, New York. Purchase.

Figure 1.7 These paintings are from the NASA space art collection. Each artist painted the same subject: a Saturn rocket with its service tower and gantry. Yet each artist has created an individual statement by using different arrangements of elements, principles, and media.

Figure 1.7A Kingman interpreted the subject in terms of his Oriental heritage. He transformed the rocket into a pagoda form. Why do you think he included the birds, hot air balloon, and single-engine plane? Notice the many areas of clear white paper.

Dong Kingman. *Higher, Faster, and Farther.* 1969. Watercolor on paper. 71.1 × 91.4 cm (28 × 36″). Courtesy of NASA.

Figure 1.7B Fernandez saw the launch as a graceful leap from the earth's surface. He bathed his work in the glowing colors of the morning sun. If you look closely, you can see the audience along the bank of the Banana River, almost hidden in the brilliance of the light.

Julio Fernandes. *Apollo 11.* 1969. Watercolor on paper. 34.3 × 40.6 cm (13½ × 16″). Courtesy of NASA.

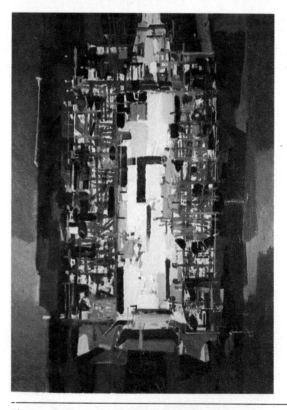

Figure 1.7C Dodd captures the glowing Saturn rocket encased in its web of red supports. He sees beyond the mechanical forms to portray for us the effect it has on his emotions.

Lamar Dodd. *Night Before Launch.* 1969. Oil on canvas. 127.5 × 91.4 cm (50 × 36″). Courtesy of NASA.

Figure 1.8 Frank Lloyd Wright has organized the shapes and spaces of this house to be beautiful, as well as to shelter people from the weather.

Frank Lloyd Wright. The David Wright House. 1951. Scottsdale, Arizona. Photography by Sandak, Inc., Stamford, Connecticut.

theme, such as patriotism or family togetherness, or it may be an emotion, like love or anger.

For example, in the 1960s NASA took photographs of the space program. However, NASA officials felt that they needed artists to tell people in the future about the wonder and excitement everyone felt about moving into space. They asked the artists to capture these emotions. The emotions the artists put into the paintings made up the content. Three of these paintings are shown in Figure 1-7.

The Purpose of *ArtTalk*

You may have heard people say, "I don't know anything about art, but I know what I like." These people were reacting to the way a work of art made them feel when they looked at it. If you are one of these people, you may have already formed ideas about the kinds of art you like or don't like.

It may be hard to let go of your old ideas when you are faced with something completely new and different. But *ArtTalk* will help you understand many different kinds of artworks. You will also understand why you like certain ones. You may even find yourself liking works of art that you didn't like in the past.

When you have completed *ArtTalk*, works of art will mean much more to you. You will understand why an artist does certain things and what he or she is trying to accomplish. The painting in Figure 1-1, for example, will tell you more than its obvious story about a hero rescuing a helpless maiden.

Figure 1.9   This sculpture is Henry Moore's personal expression about the idea of family. He created the sculpture just before his first child was born. Does the sculpture tell you anything about how he felt the child would affect his relationship with his wife?

Henry Moore. *Family Group.* 1948–49. Bronze (cast 1950). 150.5 × 118.1 cm (59¼ × 46½"). The Museum of Modern Art, New York, New York. A. Conger Goodyear Fund.

What you learn will affect your everyday life. For example, you will have a better understanding of architecture, such as the house in Figure 1-8 on the preceding page. You may choose such things as clothes and hairstyles differently. Everything around you will have more meaning because you will look at it with different eyes.

How will *ArtTalk* accomplish all of this? It will do so by helping you learn the language of art. It will help you develop your skills of observing and thinking about what you observe. You will then be better able to express your ideas and feelings through your own art. You will also be better able to understand your visual environment and the feelings and ideas of others. Learning the language of art may even help you learn more about your own feelings and ideas.

Chapter 1 Review: Talking about Art

USING THE LANGUAGE OF ART

For each new art term below, choose a work of art from this chapter. Then write a sentence about that work using the new term correctly in the sentence.

content
elements of art
form
media

medium
principles of design
subject
symbol

LEARNING THE ART ELEMENTS AND PRINCIPLES

1. What will you learn as you learn the basic elements and principles of art?
2. With what kind of symbols do we communicate in the language of art?
3. Name the elements of art.
4. Name the principles of art.
5. Name at least three purposes of *ArtTalk*.
6. What skills will *ArtTalk* help you develop?
7. Which is the most important component of a work of art?

INCREASING YOUR ART AWARENESS

1. Look at Figure 1-2. What is the subject matter of this work?
2. What is the subject of the work of art shown in Figure 1-3? What makes this type of subject matter different from that of Figure 1-2?
3. Look carefully at Figures 1-4 and 1-5. Which of the three main parts of a work of art—subject, form, or content—is the same in both works?
4. Describe how your impressions of the Saturn rocket launch change as you look at the three different paintings in Figure 1-7.
5. The subject of Moore's sculpture in Figure 1-9 is the family. Look through the rest of this book to see if you can find another artwork with this same subject. How do the two works differ in media? How do they differ in content? Which work do you prefer? Why?

UNDERSTANDING ART CULTURE AND HERITAGE

1. What is the title of the oldest work of art shown in this chapter? When was it created?
2. Name the two works of art in this chapter that were created in the 16th century.
3. Look at Figure 1-6. On what historical event is this painting based?
4. The painting in Figure 1-6 was created eight years after the event it portrays took place. Photography had not been invented yet. How do you think the artist would have known about this scene since he wasn't at the battle?
5. Do you think the painting in Figure 1-6 is a valuable recording of an historical event? Why or why not?

JUDGING THE QUALITY OF ART

Works of art are composed of many parts that are "read" together. But often people decide how they feel about a work of art without really knowing why they feel as they do.

You may already have a fairly clear idea about what kinds of art you like. For instance, how do you feel about Figure 1-1? Write a paragraph about your first reaction to this work. When you have completed your paragraph, look at the work again and list the subject and content of the work.

When you have finished all the chapters in this book, examine Figure 1-1 again. Use what you will have learned about the language of art and the art criticism process to describe the form of the work and to judge whether it is a success or a failure.

LEARNING MORE ABOUT ART

Find out how music and dance communicate. Is there a language of music? Is there a language of dance? Look this up in the library or interview a friend or teacher who is involved with music or dance. Write a report in which you discuss the "words" and "grammar" of either of these art forms.

Figure 2.1 Mary Cassatt was an American artist who went to Europe to study. The subjects of her Impressionistic paintings were mostly mothers and children. Many of the models for her early works were family members.

Mary Cassatt. *The Bath.* c. 1891. Oil on canvas. 99.1 × 66 cm (39 × 26"). Courtesy of The Art Institute of Chicago, Chicago, Illinois. Robert A. Waller Fund. 1910.2.

Art Criticism and Aesthetic Judgment

After reading this chapter and doing the exercises, you will be able to

☐ explain the purpose of art criticism.

☐ begin to criticize works of art yourself.

☐ explain three theories of art.

☐ know what to look for when judging functional objects.

WORDS TO LEARN

In this chapter you will learn the meanings of the words listed below.

aesthetic judgment

art criticism

emotionalism

formalism

imitationalism

Have you ever been so involved in watching a movie that you felt as if you were part of the action? Have you ever gone to one movie you really liked so many times that you knew the dialogue by heart? If so, you have been deeply involved with a work of art. You have had an *aesthetic experience*.

After you see a new movie, you probably discuss it with your friends. You probably tell them what you thought of the movie. You might even recommend that they go to see the movie—or advise them to save their money. In either case you are evaluating the movie and making decisions about why it was a failure or a success. You are *criticizing* the movie.

In this chapter you will learn about **art criticism**—the skill of judging a work of art. The judgment you will use is called **aesthetic judgment.** Aesthetic judgment has to do with the reasons why we find a work of art beautiful or satisfying.

Why Study Art Criticism?

You may think criticism means saying that you don't like something. This is not true. A criticism can also mean saying that you *do* like something. It is a method of judging both the successful and unsuccessful parts of a work of art. But how do you know what is successful and what isn't?

Do you feel confused when you look at a painting like *Zirchow VII* in Figure 2-2? If you are like most people, you don't know whether it is a successful painting or not. You are afraid that you will say the wrong thing.

But art criticism doesn't need to be difficult. In fact, it can be a lot of fun. At the very least, it can make the study of art less mysterious and more logical.

The system of criticism that you will learn in this book can be used by anyone. You do not need to be an art expert. All you really need are eyes to see and a brain to think about what you see.

If you look at art without thinking, nothing can happen. But if you look and think carefully about what you see, you will learn a great deal.

No one has done or seen exactly the same things that you have. So no one will see exactly what you see in a work of art. No one will think exactly the way you think.

You will use your own experience to help you understand each work of art. You may see ideas in a painting that were never dreamed of by the artist. This does not mean that you are wrong. It simply means that a work of art is so powerful that it has special meanings for everyone.

Learning art criticism will give you the confidence to discuss a work of art without worrying about what other people might think. It will help

Figure 2.2   This painting may make you feel uncomfortable because you cannot recognize familiar objects. If so, do you think the painting is a "bad" painting?

Lyonel Feininger. *Zirchow VII*. 1918. Oil on canvas. 80.7 × 100.6 cm (31¾ × 39⅝"). National Gallery of Art, Washington, D.C. Gift of Julia Feininger.

Figure 2.3 If you are a cat lover, you will have a positive reaction to the tiger cat resting luxuriously on the cushion. If you do not like cats, however, you will probably have a completely different response to this work.

Théophile-Alexandre Steinlen. *Winter: Cat on a Cushion.* Unknown date. Color lithograph. 50.8 × 61 cm (20 × 24"). The Metropolitan Museum of Art, New York, New York. Gift of Henry J. Plantin, 1950.

you organize your thoughts. You will develop the courage to speak your mind and make sound aesthetic judgments.

As you learn the language of art, you will be able to "dig deeper" into each art object. The deeper you dig, the more important your feelings for that work of art will become. This will make your reaction, your aesthetic experience, more meaningful and memorable. The work of art will then become a permanent part of your memory. From that point on it will make a difference in how you feel and think about all visual objects. It may even make a difference in your entire outlook on life.

DEVELOPING YOUR SKILLS

1. Show the cat in Figure 2-3 to at least three people outside of class. Ask each one to describe this work of art. Then ask each person how he or she feels about cats. Did the words used to describe the painting match the person's feelings about cats?

How to Criticize a Work of Art

Doing art criticism is like playing detective. You must assume that the artist has a secret message hidden inside the work. Your job is to solve the mystery and find the message.

In this chapter you will learn a special, four-step system that will help you find the hidden messages in art. The four steps, which must be taken in order, are *description, analysis, interpretation,* and *judgment.* By taking these steps you will be able to answer the following questions:

- ☒ "What do I see?" (description)
- ☒ "How is the work organized?" (analysis)
- ☒ "What is happening?" and "What is the artist trying to say?" (interpretation)
- ☒ "What do I think of the work?" (judgment)

First you will collect facts and clues. Then you will make guesses. You will decide what you think the artist is trying to say. Finally, you will express your personal likes and dislikes.

Step One: Description

To begin art criticism, make a list of all the things you see in the work. This step is meant to slow your pace. Slowing down helps you notice things you might otherwise miss.

During this step you must be objective. In other words, give only the facts. For instance, if you describe Mary Cassatt's painting entitled *The Bath* in Figure 2-1, you must say that you see a woman holding a baby. Do not say that you see a mother with her child. That would be a guess. You do not know that the woman is the child's mother. Save guessing for later. If you see some figures and you cannot tell whether they are women or men, simply list them as people.

Every description should include the size of the work and the medium used. You will find dimensions given near each work. The first number listed is always the height and the second is always the width. If there is a third dimension, it is the depth. Listing these sizes will help you visualize the actual work of art. Describe what you see in Figure 2-4 on the next page.

Let's look at Figure 2-5, the statue entitled *The Visitation* by Jacob Epstein, on the next page. Note that the figure is 66 inches (167.6 cm) tall. How does that compare to your own height? If you were standing face to face with the statue, about where would its eyes be?

The medium of this statue is cast bronze. Do you know what bronze looks like when it is new? Do you know what happens to bronze when it ages?

DEVELOPING YOUR SKILLS

2. Watch a sports program on TV. Pretend that you are an explorer from another planet and that you don't know anything about the game. Describe what the athletes are doing, but remember you

know nothing about the game itself. Read your description in class. Can your classmates guess what game you were watching?

Step Two: Analysis

During step two you are still collecting facts. Now, however, you will pay attention to the elements and principles, which you read about in Chapter 1. You will study how the artist has used each element and principle.

For example, look again at Figure 2-5. Notice the shape of the figure; the lines formed by the skirt folds; the surface texture of the hair, skin, and fabric; and so on. In this step you would list the ways that Epstein used each of these elements. You would also list the ways in which he used rhythm, movement, balance, proportion, variety, emphasis, and unity. Of course, you will learn more about both the elements and principles later in this book.

Step Three: Interpretation

During step three, you have two questions to answer: "What is happening?" and "What is the artist trying to say?" You will *interpret* (explain or tell

Figure 2.4 What do you see in this painting? Note everything you see. Do not guess.

Winslow Homer. *Breezing Up (A Fair Wind)*. 1876. Oil on canvas. 61.5 × 97 cm (24⅛ × 38⅛"). National Gallery of Art, Washington, D.C. Gift of the W. L. and May T. Mellon Foundation.

the meaning of) the work. It is here that you can make guesses.

Interpretation is the most difficult art criticism step for some people. But it can also be the most creative and the most rewarding.

You must use your intelligence, imagination, and courage. You must not be afraid to make an interpretation that is different from someone else's. After all, you are different from anyone else.

How you interpret a work of art will depend on what you have done and seen in your life. However, your interpretation should be based upon the facts and clues you collected during the first two steps. Your interpretation can express your feelings, but your feelings must be backed up by observation.

DEVELOPING YOUR SKILLS

3. Show the painting in Figure 2-6 to three people outside of class. Ask them what they think the meaning of this painting is. Tell them that it doesn't matter whether they like the work or not. You just want to know what they think it means. Then write two or three sentences telling what each person says. Compare your results with those of your classmates. Are there any similar answers? Do adults see different meanings than people your age?

Figure 2.5 Imagine standing next to this figure. How would it look? What do you think your first reaction would be?

Sir Jacob Epstein. *The Visitation*. 1926. Bronze. 167.6 × 48.3 × 44.5 cm (66 × 19 × 17½"). Hirshhorn Museum and Sculpture Garden, Smithsonian Institution, Washington, D.C. Gift of Joseph H. Hirshhorn, 1966.

Figure 2.6 What kind of responses did you receive to this painting? Were these responses similar to your own response?

Leo Twiggs. *The Blue Wall*. 1969. Batik painting. 61 × 76.2 cm (24 × 30"). Private collection.

Step Four: Judgment

In step four you will judge whether or not the work succeeds or fails. This is the time to give your opinions. No one can ever tell you what to like or dislike. You must make up your own mind.

To make a good judgment you need to be honest with yourself. You need to know why you feel the way you do. For example, look at Figure 2-3 on page 15. How do you feel about this picture? The artist loved cats. Do you? How do you think the way you feel about cats might affect your reaction to this work?

Theories of Judging Art

People who study or judge art sometimes use certain theories that say how a work should be considered. Critics regularly use three of these theories—*imitationalism*, *formalism*, and *emotionalism*.

Some people think art should imitate what we see in the real world. Using this theory to judge art is called **imitationalism.**

Others feel that the most important part of a work is the use of the principles and elements of art. According to this theory, called **formalism,** the work is successful if the textures, colors, lines, and so on are organized properly.

Still others believe that art must speak to the viewer through her or his emotions. This theory says that the most important part of the work is the mood the artist communicates. This last theory is called **emotionalism.**

Look below at Margareta Haverman's painting, *A Vase of Flowers*, in Figure 2-7. You may like it because she has painted everything very realistically (imitationalism). You can see drops of water sparkling on the leaves. Someone else may like this painting because of the flow of light sweeping in a

Figure 2.7 Which theory of art would you use to judge this painting?

Margareta Haverman. *A Vase of Flowers.* 1716. Oil on wood. 79.4 × 60.3 cm (31-1/4 × 23-3/4"). The Metropolitan Museum of Art, New York, New York. Purchase. 1871.

Figure 2.8 This teapot has a sculptured, geometric form. It is beautifully crafted, but if it didn't pour properly, it would be useless.

Marianne Brandt. *Teapot.* 1924. Nickel silver and ebony. 17.8 cm (7") high. Collection, The Museum of Modern Art, New York, New York. Phyllis B. Lambert Fund.

curve from the large tulip at the top, through the other flowers and down to the bunch of grapes (formalism). A third person may like the painting simply because he or she like flowers (emotionalism).

You can judge art using one theory, or more than one, depending upon the type of art and your own purposes. If you stick to one theory, however, you may miss some exciting discoveries in a work. Perhaps the best method is to use all three. Then you will be able to discover as much as possible about a particular piece of art.

Judging Functional Objects

You can use art criticism to make aesthetic judgments about functional objects, as well as objects of fine art. The objects in Figures 2-8 and 2-9 are examples.

In criticizing functional objects, you do the first three steps as described earlier. But during the fourth step, judgment, you must consider how the object works when it is used. A chair may look beautiful, but if it is uncomfortable to sit in, it does not function properly.

Some people buy a car based on looks alone. Other people may buy clothing with no regard for the way it looks on them. Neither method is wise. When judging functional objects, attention must be given to both beauty and usefulness.

Judging Your Own Work

Art criticism will help you analyze your own works of art. The four steps of art criticism will help you be as honest and unbiased as possible. The analysis step will probably be the most useful. It will help you perceive how you have used the elements and principles of art. When you analyze your work, you should find out why your work either needs improvement or is a total success.

DEVELOPING YOUR SKILLS

4. Look through this book and find one work that you like. Show the picture to at least three people outside of class. Ask them whether or not they like that work. Then ask them to tell you why they like or dislike it. Classify their answers according to the three theories of art. Was one of the theories used more than the others?

Figure 2.9 Sitting on this beautiful chair would make you feel as if you were sitting on a pedestal. But the chair would not be considered a successfully made chair unless you were comfortable.

Eero Saarinen. *Armchair.* 1957. Molded plastic reinforced with fiberglass; painted aluminum base. 81.3 cm (32") high. Collection, The Museum of Modern Art, New York, New York. Gift of Knoll Associates, Inc.

Art Criticism: Getting Started

There is only one way to learn art criticism: to do it. This is why you will be given many opportunities to develop your criticism skills in *ArtTalk*.

At the end of each chapter in Parts Two and Three, you will criticize a work of art. To help you begin, we will now look at, and criticize together, *Christina's World* by Andrew Wyeth.

When you finish this exercise, read the short biography, which follows. It may help you understand a little more about Wyeth's painting. Each of the criticism activities in Parts Two and Three is also followed by a biography of the artist.

Description

Look at the painting in Figure 2-10. Record the size of the painting and the medium. Try to imagine the actual size of the painting.

Now study the painting very carefully. List everything you see. Try to be objective. Don't make guesses and don't let your feelings about the painting influence you. Write down every fact that you observe.

When you finish describing the work, read through the following questions. These questions will show you the types of details you should have noticed. Don't feel upset if you missed some details. Remember, this is your first attempt at art criticism.

What facts about the girl's dress did you list? Did you notice the faded pink of her dress? Does it look new? What kind of fabric do you think it is made of, heavy or light? Look at the folds. What do they tell you? What does the belt look like? What color is it?

What matches the belt color? Her hair. Look at her hairdo. Notice all the individual hairs. Does the way she wears her hair match the style of her dress? What about those strands of hair flying loosely around her head?

Next, notice her shoes. What do you think they are made of? Is there any sign of wear on the shoes? Look closely at her legs. What color are they? Is the color quality the same as that of her arms? Do you notice anything unusual about her arms? About her

hands? Look closely at her left hand. Is it at the same level as the rest of her body?

Try to imitate her posture. Look carefully at the picture as you try. As you imitate, where is all your weight resting?

Where is the girl located? What facts can you gather from the background and grass? What color are they? In what direction do the blades of grass bend? What is the difference between the area where she is sitting and the top of the hill? Do you see the road? Did you notice what material the road is made of?

How many buildings do you see? How are they different? What are they made of? What color are they? Do they look well maintained? Do you see the birds flying around the barn and the fence posts? Look at the piece of farm equipment. How modern is it? How many chimneys do you see? Is there any smoke coming out of them? Do all the windows look the same?

What color is the sky and from where is the light coming? Look at the shadows—is all the light coming from the same direction? How much of the picture is sky and how much is ground? Was the artist looking down from above or up from below the scene?

Try not to make guesses yet. Save your clues.

Analysis

Since you have not yet learned very much about the elements and principles, you are not ready to analyze the painting. For now we will skip to interpretation. Later on, when you know more about the language of art, come back to *Christina's World* and look again. You will then see many more things in it.

Interpretation

Review the clues you have collected. What do you think the artist is telling you about the relationship between the girl and her environment? What do you think is happening in this painting?

Hold a ruler along the left slope of the roof on the main house. Do you see how that line leads your eyes to the girl? And notice how the girl is straining toward the house. She is wearing faded

Figure 2.10   Andrew Wyeth. *Christina's World.*
1948. Tempera on gesso panel. 81.9 × 121.3 cm
(32¼ × 47¾"). Collection, The Museum of Modern
Art, New York, New York. Purchase.

colors, and the house is gray and unpainted. Why do you think such a large area of ground is visible? Why has the artist shown separate blades of grass? When you acted out the girl's pose, did you feel the pressure on your arms? Did you feel the tension? Did you notice that your legs were not carrying any weight?

Can you guess what the artist is trying to say about the relationship between the girl and that house? Do you sense any special feelings? What do you think he is saying about being a part of things?

Other than its title, can you think of a word or phrase that describes this work? What title would you give it?

Try to go beyond the events that appear to be taking place in this painting. Seek the general idea, or theme, that you believe the artist was trying to express. If you put together the facts and your own ideas about the world, you will probably discover the meaning of the painting for you.

Judgment

Finally you are ready to decide if you like *Christina's World*. As you judge the work, be ready to give your reasons for liking or disliking it.

Do you like the way Wyeth has imitated reality? Why? Why not?

Do you like the way he has used and organized the elements? Why? Why not?

Do you think Wyeth has been successful in expressing feelings and ideas? Why? Why not?

Does this painting make you think? Give the reasons for your answer.

Would you like *Christina's World* in your home? Give your reasons.

A B O U T   T H E   A R T I S T

Andrew Wyeth

Figure 2.11 Andrew Wyeth, American, 1917—

© Peter Ralston, 1986

Andrew Wyeth is one of today's most famous painters. He likes to paint people—the ordinary country people he sees every day.

Andrew Wyeth was born in 1917, the youngest of five children. His father was N. C. Wyeth, a successful illustrator of adventure stories. Andrew's son is also a famous artist, which makes Andrew part of an artistic "dynasty."

Wyeth was a sickly child. His father did not believe in public schools, so he was taught at home. Until he was 15, he amused himself drawing and painting with water colors.

When N. C. Wyeth brought Andrew into the studio to work, he gave him a real pirate flintlock pistol to draw. For five months he had to draw this pistol over and over, from different views, using only charcoal. The strange result of this was that the longer he spent drawing the pistol, the more interested in it he became.

In 1937, when Andrew was 20, he had his first show in New York. Every painting in the show was sold.

Andrew Wyeth is much more than a photographic realist. He studies his subject first and makes many, many sketches in pencil and watercolor. He tries to go beyond illusion and tricks to express the feelings he has about a place, an object, or a person.

Christina Olson, the subject of the painting you just studied, was a friend of the Wyeth family. Christina was disabled from polio, and her legs were paralyzed.

One day he saw her out in the field gathering vegetables. She pulled herself back to the house with her arms. The memory of what Wyeth saw haunted him. He felt he had to paint it.

He worked on his painting of Christina every day for weeks. He was afraid to ask Christina to pose, so his wife posed instead to help him get the position just right. As it turned out, Christina knew about the painting and did not mind.

After painting *Christina's World*, Wyeth said that he painted more than a portrait. He said that he had included her entire life and the things she liked in it.

Wyeth uses watercolors to put down ideas quickly. Watercolors are the free side of his nature. But when he wants to get deeply involved with his subject, he works with egg tempera and a dry brush. His tempera paintings take him several months to complete. The paint he uses is not like school tempera. He uses pure earth pigments from all over the world. He mixes the pure pigments with distilled water and egg yolk. Then he builds layer upon layer of transparent colors.

Chapter 2 Review: Talking about Art

USING THE LANGUAGE OF ART

For each new art term below, choose a work of art from this chapter. Then write a sentence about that work using the new term correctly in the sentence.

aesthetic judgment formalism
art criticism imitationalism
emotionalism

LEARNING THE ART ELEMENTS AND PRINCIPLES

1. What will learning art criticism help you develop?
2. Name the four steps of art criticism in the order in which they must be followed.
3. Which of the art criticism steps will help you answer the question "How is the work organized?"
4. Which of the criticism steps will help you answer the question "What do I think of the work?"
5. Which art criticism step will help you answer the question "What do I see?"
6. Which criticism step will help you answer the questions "What is happening?" and "What is the artist trying to say?"
7. When three dimensions for a work are given, in what order are they listed?
8. When criticizing functional objects, what must you consider, besides beauty, during interpretation?

INCREASING YOUR ART AWARENESS

1. Describe one aesthetic experience you have had involving a movie, a TV show, or a concert.
2. Which theory of judging art would be the *least* useful in understanding Figure 2-2?
3. If you could choose one painting in this chapter for which all the theories of art seem equally useful, which painting would it be? Give reasons for your answer.
4. What theory of judging art do you think would be most helpful in understanding Figure 2-5? Give reasons for your answer.

5. Compare Figures 2-6 and 2-7. Which one appeals more to your emotions? Which one appeals more to your recognition of life-like subject matter?
6. Do you think the objects in Figures 2-8 and 2-9 have been judged a success? Why or why not?

UNDERSTANDING ART CULTURE AND HERITAGE

1. Without looking at the dates, tell which work of art in this chapter you think was created first. Explain your guess.
2. No date is given for Figure 2-3. Look at the list of artists in the back of the book and tell when you think Figure 2-3 might have been created.
3. Name three women artists represented in this chapter.
4. Give the artist and title of the color lithograph shown in this chapter.
5. Give the artist, title, date, medium, and dimensions of the sculpture shown in this chapter.

JUDGING THE QUALITY OF ART

Use the four steps of art criticism to study one of your favorite possessions. Does this change your perception of that familiar object? If so, how?

Now look at the painting in Figure 2-1. The artist has taken a familiar, everyday event and created a work of art. Do you feel that common, everyday objects and events are suitable subjects for an artwork? Why or why not?

LEARNING MORE ABOUT ART

Compare the four steps of art criticism to the scientific method you use in science class. Ask your science teacher for help if you need it. Are there any similarities between the two procedures? Write a report in which you explain your findings or give an oral report in the form of a skit. If you choose the latter, you may wish to enlist the help of a friend to act out the two procedures.

Figure 3.1 Judith Leyster was a Dutch woman who dared to break rules. In the early seventeenth century women artists were expected to paint delicate still lifes, but Leyster chose to do portraits and genre paintings (scenes and subjects from everyday life).

Judith Leyster. *Self-Portrait.* c. 1635. Oil on canvas. 72.3 × 65.3 cm (29⅜ × 25⅝″). National Gallery of Art, Washington, D.C. Gift of Mr. & Mrs. Robert Woods Bliss.

Art History

LEARNING OBJECTIVES

After reading this chapter and doing the exercises, you will be able to

☐ understand the credit lines attached to art reproductions.

☐ understand how historical events influence artists' work.

☐ briefly discuss movements in the history of art, from prehistoric through modern times.

WORDS TO LEARN

In this chapter you will learn the meanings of the words listed below.

Abstract Expressionism

Baroque

Byzantine

Cubism

Gothic

Impressionists

Post Impressionists

Realists

Renaissance

Romanesque

Surrealism

Ever since there have been human beings, there has been art. The need to create has always been a part of human nature. Even before people kept written records, they made drawings, paintings, and carvings.

You can look at visual images from our past to learn what the people who lived before us were like. The art they made reveals a great deal about their feelings, their beliefs, their ideas, and the way they lived. This combination of behaviors and ideas of a group of people is called *culture*. Someday people will learn about our culture by studying the art objects that we are producing now.

The history of visual art is as broad and complex as the history of the world itself. This chapter is just a peek into the overflowing treasure chest that makes up your visual *heritage* (something inherited). It will help you understand how works of art are all linked together.

You will learn how the major periods and artistic styles came into being, and how one led to another. In learning about artistic styles you will learn about the distinct, identifying methods and features of a group of artists. This knowledge will provide a foundation for your growing appreciation of the visual arts.

The Prehistoric and Ancient World

Let's look briefly at some of the earliest known works of art. The art discussed in this section was produced over a period of thousands of years. Many of these works tell us a great deal about the first great Western civilizations.

Prehistoric Cultures

In Figure 3-2 is a painting left by Stone Age cave dwellers. The colors are so bright, and the animals so realistic that for a long time experts refused to believe paintings such as these were really created by prehistoric artists.

No one really knows the true purpose of the paintings. They were found deep inside caves, far from the entrances and living areas. Because of their location we know they were not created for decoration. Some people believe the paintings were part of a hunting ritual. They may have been painted by the shaman, or medicine man, who believed that the magical image of the animal could help hunters capture the animal. It could be that the paintings were visual prayers that animals would appear during the next hunt. Another theory is that the paintings were created to celebrate a successful hunt.

Egypt

Ancient Egypt developed along the banks of the Nile River over three thousand years before the birth of Christ. The Egyptian civilization continued for almost three thousand years after that. The arts of Ancient Egypt express the endurance and solidity of that culture.

Religion influenced every part of Egyptian life. The Pharaohs, or rulers, were worshiped as gods, and along with the priests held complete authority over the kingdom. Egyptians believed in life after death and preserved the bodies of the dead for use in the afterlife. The famous pyramids of Egypt are the tombs of the Pharaohs.

Egyptian artists who decorated temples and tombs had to follow very strict rules made by the priests. In wall sculpture and painting, figures were represented in an unnatural way. Look at Figure 3-3. The head, eyes, shoulders, arms, legs, and feet were shown from an unusual point of view, not as they actually appeared. For instance, artists set a front view of the eye in a profile view of the face. The aim was to show features of the body in a clear and complete way.

We have learned a great deal about everyday life in Egypt from the paintings found on the walls inside the tombs. Scenes from the buried person's life were painted on these walls. The scenes were intended to remind the spirit of its life on earth.

Figure 3.2 What do you think the purpose of this cave painting was?

Horses with Black Manes. c. 15,000 B.C. Cave painting. France. Art Resource, New York, New York.

Figure 3.3 This artist has followed a strict rule: a front view for the eye set in a head shown in profile; the upper chest in front view; hips and legs in profile.

Egyptian, from El Bersheh. *Coffin (Detail).* XI Dynasty. Painted wood. 2.62 × 1.15 m (8.6 × 3.8'). Courtesy, Museum of Fine Arts, Boston, Massachusetts.

Greece

Greece was the birthplace of our Western civilization. The influence of ancient Greek culture can still be seen today. Almost every city in our country has at least one building with features that resemble the architecture of the classic Greek temple.

The Greeks built temples in honor of their gods. The most outstanding example is the Parthenon in Athens. Inside was a huge statue of the goddess Athena in ivory and gold.

The Greeks believed in a logical, harmonious world. They sought perfect proportions in buildings, sculpture, and music by following formulas. Their artists produced statues that represented the Greek ideal of a perfect body. According to one story, athletes used statues, like the statue in Figure 3-4, as models for building their own muscle structure.

When they were new, Greek temples and statues were not the pure white they are today. The Greeks loved color, and they painted their sculpture and buildings. Time has worn the paint away.

We know very little about Greek wall paintings because only a few traces remain. However, we have an idea of what such paintings might have shown from the scenes Greek artists painted on ceramic vases. See Figure 1-3 on page 5.

Figure 3.4 All of the original sculptures by the great Greek artists have been lost to us. What we have are copies that the Romans made.

Lancillotti. *Discobulus (Discus Thrower).* c. 450 B.C. Roman copy of Greek sculpture. Life size. Museodelle Terme, Rome. Art Resource, New York, New York.

Rome

Even though the Romans conquered Greece in 146 B.C., they did not conquer Greek culture. Romans adopted Greek culture and changed it to suit their own needs. Greek sculptors, painters, architects, philosophers, and teachers had a great influence on the Roman Empire, and at one time the Roman Empire included almost all of the civilized Western world.

Earlier, the Romans had absorbed the culture of the Etruscans in Italy. The Romans adopted Etruscan arts and engineering skills. Two outstanding Etruscan developments were a system of drainage and improved use of the arch in building. So what we call Roman art is in many ways a blend of the ideal Greek and the practical Etruscan arts.

The Romans added much to what they adopted from the Greeks and Etruscans. They used concrete and the arch to build large-scale structures, including huge vaulted and domed inner spaces. The Romans also developed beautiful interior decoration, excellent roads, and honest, rather than ideal, portrait sculpture. The man in Figure 3-5 looks like someone you might meet today.

In the fourth century a Roman emperor legalized Christianity, which until that time was against the law. Before the fourth century Christians could not practice their religion in public. They met in the catacombs, which were tunnels under the streets and hills of Rome.

The need for secrecy gave rise to art using Christian symbols, the meaning of which only the Christians knew. They used symbols such as a cross, a lamb, and a fish to express their ideas in paintings on the catacomb walls. After Christianity was made legal, the Christians were able to build churches.

Figure 3.5 The Romans were not concerned with the Greek ideal of human perfection. They wanted accurate, realistic portraits that looked like the people they represented. Notice the wrinkles and loose skin of the man in this portrait.

Graeco-Roman. *Man of the Republic.* c. 50 B.C. Terracotta. 35.7 cm (14.1″) high, face 18 cm (7.1″) long. Courtesy, Museum of Fine Arts, Boston, Massachusetts. Purchase of E. P. Warren.

Their churches were based on a Roman design and the interiors were decorated with *mosaics* (pictures made with small pieces of a material such as glass).

In the eastern part of the Roman Empire, a style of art known as **Byzantine** thrived. This style developed around the city of Constantinople (now Istanbul) and spread to towns such as Ravenna in

---

TECHNIQUE TIP

Decoding a Credit Line

Look at Figure 3-1. The credit line beneath the caption is full of information. Here is what each part means:

Judith Leyster   The artist's name

Self Portrait   The title of the work always appears in italics.

c. 1635   The year the work was completed. "c" stands for circa, which means "about." It is used before approximate dates.

Oil on canvas   The medium used.

72.3 × 65.3 cm (29 3/8 × 25 5/8″)   The size. The first number is always the height, the second number is the width, and, if the work is three dimensional, a third number indicates the depth.

The National Gallery of Art   The museum, gallery, or collection where the work is kept.

Washington, D.C.   The location of the museum, gallery, or collection.

Gift of Mr. and Mrs. Robert Woods Bliss   The names of the donors.

the Western Empire. Byzantine art was a blend of Roman, Greek, and Oriental art, usually with a religious theme. See Figure 3-6.

Pictures on the walls inside Byzantine churches were mosaics set unevenly so that they glittered in the reflected light of church candles. Byzantine art was extremely colorful and was done in a flatter and stiffer style than that of early Christian art. In Byzantine mosaics, the viewer often can read a familiar religious story.

DEVELOPING YOUR SKILLS

1. Look through this chapter to find and copy the credit lines of the following:
   • Three works from the National Gallery of Art.
   • Three works that were created in different countries during the same century.
   • Three works that were created using media other than oil paint.

Figure 3.6 This painting is a good example of the Byzantine blending of Western realism and Oriental decorative patterns. The heads and graceful hands are shaded to give the illusion of roundness. The Oriental influence is seen in the flat bodies and the patterns of gold lines.

Byzantine. *Madonna and Child on a Curved Throne*. 1480. Tempera on wood. 81.5 × 49.0 cm (32⅛ × 19⅜″). National Gallery of Art, Washington, D.C. Andrew W. Mellon Collection.

The Middle Ages

The Middle Ages began with the conquest of Rome in 476 A.D. by barbarian invaders from the north. (*Barbarian* was a name given to all non-Greek-speaking peoples.) The Middle Ages lasted about one thousand years, and the period is also called the *Age of Faith* because religion was a dominant force. Monasteries grew in number, and monks created finely decorated religious manuscripts. Churches grew in size and importance.

In the newly built churches of western Europe, a style of architecture and sculpture called **Romanesque** developed. Increased size; solid, heavy walls; wide use of the rounded Roman arch; and many sculptural decorations were its features.

In the twelfth century, more and more European people moved from the countryside into towns. Workers such as stone carvers and carpenters organized into craft guilds (unions), and apprentices learned their craft from masters. A wealthy new middle class, city pride, and religious faith led to the building of huge cathedrals.

Two developments—the pointed arch and the flying buttress—brought about changes in architecture. Buildings began to soar upward, like the cathedral in Figure 3-7. This new style was called **Gothic.** The Gothic cathedrals became the world's largest architectural constructions since the Egyptian pyramids.

Gothic builders used stained glass for windows, changing the light that entered into rich, glowing color. Gothic sculpture and painting took on more human qualities. Artists created church altarpieces from wood panels painted with egg tempera and gold leaf.

DEVELOPING YOUR SKILLS

2. Find a picture of a painting or sculpture of people made during the Middle Ages. Do the people look like people of today? Write a short paragraph explaining your answer.

Figure 3.7 Notice how the pointed arches act like arrows pointing toward heaven.

Reims, Cathedral of Notre Dame facade. c. 1225–1299. France. Photography by SEF/Art Resource, New York, New York.

The Fifteenth Through the Eighteenth Centuries

It is difficult to say when the Middle Ages ended. But certainly by the fifteenth century the "Dark Ages" were giving way to a new era. The invention of the printing press and Columbus' discovery of America are just two events that signify this great change. As you would expect, the art of Western civilization also went through many changes.

The Renaissance

Renaissance is a French word that means "rebirth." In Italy the fifteenth century brought new interest, a rebirth, in the philosophy and art of Classical Greece and Rome. This period of awakening and rebirth at the end of the Middle Ages is called the **Renaissance.**

But the Renaissance in Italy, and later much of Europe, was much more than a rebirth of ancient ways. It was a complete change in human awareness. Religion began to lose its tight control over people's lives. People became more aware of the world they lived in and realized that each person had an important part to play. Kings and church leaders had to make room at the top of the power structure for wealthy bankers and merchants.

During the Middle Ages artists had worked not for themselves but for the Church. They were members of the working class. During the Renaissance, however, great artists such as Leonardo da Vinci, Michelangelo, and Raphael mingled socially with nobles.

In both painting and sculpture the solid, realistic appearance of people and things became most important. Figure 3-8 is an example. To show the human figure correctly, Italian artists studied nature as well as the classical art of Greece and Rome. Leonardo studied many subjects in depth. He left about 120 notebooks filled with drawings and notes on subjects that range from human anatomy to plans for machines.

An architect named Filippo Brunelleschi developed a technique called *perspective*, which creates

Figure 3.8 In this work by Michelangelo, the Virgin's face is calm, yet her attitude expresses an inward sorrow. The artist adjusted the size of the Virgin so that she is large enough to hold the body of Christ without strain. But the artist has organized all the elements into such a perfect unity that the viewer never notices the exaggeration.

Michelangelo. *Pietà*. c. 1500. Marble. 174 cm (5'8½") high; base 195 cm (6'4⅘"). Vatican, St. Peter's, Rome. Scala/Art Resource, New York, New York.

the illusion of depth on flat surfaces. Perspective combined geometry and drawing skill to portray the world as it had never been portrayed before.

The art of Venice developed along somewhat different lines from those of other Italian cities. In the late fifteenth and early sixteenth centuries, Venetian artists such as Giorgione (Figure 10-20) and Titian used light and color in new and very effective ways.

The changes in painting seen in Renaissance Italy came later to northern European countries, such as Flanders. Northern artists like Jan van Eyck concentrated mainly on symbols and the surface details of objects. The invention of oil painting (usually credited to van Eyck) allowed artists to work on fine details while the paint was still wet. Later, northern artists combined this attention to detail with an emotional style.

Figure 3.9 Rembrandt lit this scene as if he were using modern spotlights. The areas he wanted to emphasize glow with light; the areas of less importance fade into darkness.

Rembrandt van Rijn. *Portrait of a Lady with an Ostrich-Feather Fan.* c. 1660. Oil on canvas. 99.5 × 83 cm (39¼ × 32⅝"). National Gallery of Art, Washington, D.C. Widener Collection.

Mannerism

The fifteenth century had been a time of peace, and the style of the Italian Renaissance reflected that peace. But in the sixteenth century, the religious unity of Europe was dramatically altered by Martin Luther and the Protestant Reformation. The invasion of Italy by France added to the unrest and tensions. A style of art called *Mannerism* developed. Mannerism featured highly emotional scenes and distorted figures such as those in the works of El Greco (Figure 11-43).

Baroque and Rococo

By the start of the seventeenth century, artists were creating dramatic, theatrical works that burst with energy and strong emotions. The art style that developed is called **Baroque.**

The world was growing through exploration and scientific discoveries. Both the telescope and the microscope changed the way people saw the universe. This new way of seeing was reflected in the arts.

The forms and figures of Baroque art turn, twist, and spiral in space. Baroque artists refined perspective to the point where they could make figures seem to move toward the viewer. They opened up space in the distance toward infinity. In addition to all this movement, they added dramatic lighting effects using dark mysterious shadows and brightly lighted areas. See Figure 3-9.

In the eighteenth century Baroque changed to the delicate, more graceful style called *Rococo.* Rococo was used to decorate the homes of the French aristocracy. Their luxurious and carefree life was often shown in paintings. The Rococo style was carried to the rest of Europe by artists who worked for the wealthy aristocracy.

DEVELOPING YOUR SKILLS

3. Find at the library a picture of Leonardo da Vinci's *Last Supper.* Explain in a short paragraph why you think it is typical of Renaissance art.
4. Find a picture of a Baroque sculpture. Write a brief paragraph describing the emotions you think the artist has portrayed.

The Nineteenth Century

The industrial and democratic revolutions of the late eighteenth century brought about a new, faster way of life. Change was the only thing that was certain. New styles of art developed quickly as reactions to the styles of earlier artists.

Neoclassicism

The French Revolution abandoned the Rococo style because it mirrored the idle, useless life of the aristocracy. Academies, or art schools, which replaced the old apprentice system, taught a new style of art that better suited the new society. The new style was based on Greek and Roman art and was called *Neoclassic* ("new classic"). The Neoclassic style was severely realistic and unemotional.

Romanticism

Romanticism was a reaction against the "coolness" of Neoclassic art. The Romantic artists disliked the many rules and lack of emotion in neoclassic art. Romanticists painted emotional scenes with brilliant colors and loose brush strokes. The Romanticists discovered that the artist's personal impression of an event was more interesting than accurate, historical reports about it. Do you remember from Chapter 1 what NASA said about artists and the exploration of space?

Realism

Another group of French artists, called **Realists,** felt that they should portray political, social, and moral issues. They rejected the rules of Neoclassicism and the drama of Romanticism. They believed that peasants and factory workers shown accurately were suitable subjects for artistic study. In Spain, Francisco Goya's art took a realistic turn as he recorded the ugly truth of war during the Spanish Revolution. French artists like Edouard Manet and American artists like Thomas Eakins also painted everyday subjects realistically (Figure 3-10).

Figure 3.10 There is nothing dramatic about this ordinary, daydreaming young lady as she stares off into space. But Manet has managed to capture just the right pose to express her mood.

Edouard Manet. *The Plum.* c. 1877. Oil on canvas. 73.6 × 50.2 cm (29 × 19¾"). National Gallery of Art, Washington, D.C. Collection of Mr. and Mrs. Paul Mellon.

Impressionism

The Realists had taken a hard look at the real world. The **Impressionists** also were interested in the world outside of the studio and, in fact, did much of their painting outdoors. Scientific discoveries about light and color led the Impressionists to emphasize the effects of sunlight on objects. They concentrated on reflected light rather than the form of objects. They melted solid forms and blurred edges. These artists also used small dabs of pure color that had to be blended together in the eyes

of the viewer. If you stand too close to an Impressionist's painting, all that you can see are colorful dabs and dots. Look at Figure 3-11 at the top of the opposite page. You have to step back from the actual work for the colors to blend and take form.

Post-Impressionism

Gradually some artists who had started as Impressionists became dissatisfied. They felt their art was superficial (meaningless). Instead, they wanted to express feelings, intuitions, and ideas, or to reveal basic structures like that in the house in Figure 3-12 (bottom, opposite page). The most outstanding of these **Post-Impressionists** were Paul Cézanne, Vincent van Gogh, and Paul Gauguin. These men all had roots in Impressionism, but each expanded his style to create something so unusual that the styles themselves led to important developments in the art of the twentieth century.

DEVELOPING YOUR SKILLS

5. Choose one of the styles of the nineteenth century. Find a picture of a painting or sculpture in that style. Tell the class why you think your example represents that style.

Figure 3.11 (top, opposite page)   In this work, Monet dissolves all edges and lines in variations of color. The buildings and the water seem to melt together into dabs and dots of flickering violet and blue.

Claude Monet. *Palazzo da Mula, Venice.* 1908. Oil on canvas. 62 × 81.1 cm (24½ × 31⅞"). National Gallery of Art, Washington, D.C. Chester Dale Collection.

Figure 3.12 (bottom, opposite page) Cézanne was concerned with the structure of objects. He used small brushstrokes like little building blocks to make forms look like geometric solids. Notice how the foliage looks as solid as the rocks.

Paul Cézanne. *Le Chateau Noir.* 1900/1904. Oil on canvas. 73.7 × 96.6 cm (29 × 38"). National Gallery of Art, Washington, D.C. Gift of Eugene and Agnes Meyer.

The Beginning of the Twentieth Century

During the first half of this century, the range of art styles grew, and the speed at which changes occurred increased. The influence of rules and the Academy were dead. Artists were free to experiment and explore. It became impossible to separate artists into neat categories. Increased travel and new ways to communicate helped artists compare ideas. One individual or group could influence another. Some artists who lived a long life, such as Picasso, changed their own styles several times.

European Art

In general, art in Europe moved in three major directions and spread to the rest of the Western world. One direction was mainly concerned with expressing emotions. Another emphasized structure or design. Still another stressed imagination and dream-like inventions. Artists experimented with subject matter and materials as well as with form and style.

Expression of Emotion

At the start of the twentieth century, a group of young French painters were creating works that exploded with brilliant colors, bold distortions, and loose brush strokes. They were called *Fauves,* which is French for "wild beasts." The Fauves continued the expressive ideas of van Gogh and Gauguin. The leader of this group, Matisse, was concerned with expressing the feeling he had for life and insisted that his work had but one purpose: to give pleasure.

A different sort of feeling characterized a movement called *German Expressionism.* German artists had always been more involved with personal feelings than mathematical perfection and composition. But the German Expressionists experienced the terrible economic and social conditions in Germany before World War I. Their emotional subjects ranged from fear and anger to concern with death. Figure 3-13 (next page) is an example.

Figure 3.13   Kirchner painted this work just as World War I began. The figures show a phony, strained elegance. In the painting's sharp, closely placed forms, Kirchner suggests that tension lurks just beneath the surface of Berlin life.

Ernst Ludwig Kirchner. *Street, Berlin*. 1913. Oil on canvas. 120.7 × 91.1 cm (47½ × 35⅞"). Collection. The Museum of Modern Art, New York, New York. Purchase.

Structure and Design

Art that emphasizes structure and design is called *Abstract Art*, and **Cubism** is a prime example of Abstract Art. Three factors influenced the development of Cubism, as shown in Figure 3-14. One was the idea that all shapes in nature are based on geometric solids such as the cylinder, the sphere, and the cone. The second was the discovery by scientists that matter was made up of atoms that are constantly in motion. The third factor was the cubical form of African sculpture, which had recently been brought to Paris. The Cubists tried to paint three-dimensional objects as if they were seen from many different points of view at the same time.

A group of Italian artists called *Futurists* took Cubism a step further by placing angular forms in an arrangement to suggest motion. Their paintings and sculpture seem to come to life.

Figure 3.14   Picasso has changed the traditional view of the human form using a style known as *Analytical Cubism*. We see hints of geometric shapes with transparent openings through which colors melt and flow. Can you see how the atomic theory of matter in motion has influenced this stage of Picasso's work?

Pablo Picasso. *Nude Woman*. 1910. Oil on canvas. 187.3 × 61 cm (73¾ × 24"). National Gallery of Art, Washington, D.C. Ailsa Mellon Bruce Fund.

Figure 3.15 Dali has created a strange world in which metal objects that should be firm seem to melt. Realistic details, such as the ants, add to the nightmare-like quality of the scene. Can you recognize the object lying on the ground in the center of the picture?

Salvador Dali. *The Persistence of Memory.* 1931. Oil on canvas. 24.1 × 33 cm (9½ × 13″). Collection. The Museum of Modern Art, New York, New York. Given anonymously.

In Holland, an artist named Mondrian helped develop *De Stijl*, which is Dutch for "The Style." Mondrian used only vertical and horizontal black lines; black, white, and gray rectangles; and the three primary colors. His style was the exact opposite of Expressionism, and he avoided realism completely.

Imagination and Fantasy

Fantasy was not created during the twentieth century. It can be traced back to Greek mythology and to the monsters and devils of the Middle Ages. Later it was used to give free reign to the imagination, often with startling results. After World War I, the *Dadaists*, for example, took aim at the culture they thought had failed them. Their works featured strange objects, such as a fur-lined teacup.

Surrealism offered a slightly saner version of the Dada philosophy. Surrealists presented very realistic, almost photographic images, but created "crazy" situations. Figure 3-15 is an example. The work of the surrealists is strange and dreamlike. Some paintings are nightmares, some are funny, and some are mysterious and frightening. But no surrealist art is supposed to make sense to the viewer.

American Art

At the beginning of the twentieth century, a group of young artists in the United States turned to the harsh realities of the city for subject matter. They called themselves "The Eight" and organized an exhibit in 1908. But their original name was forgotten when they were quickly labeled the "Ashcan School" by critics who were shocked by the stark tenement buildings, crowded city streets, poor working people, and ragged children.

An even greater impact on the American art world was made when the Armory Show of 1913 was held. Some members of the Ashcan School joined with others to organize the exhibit. This show introduced Americans to the new art being created by Europeans. Most of the American public was totally confused, but many artists were challenged and took the first steps toward making modern art in America.

However, there was one group of artists—the *Regionalists*—with whom Americans felt comfortable. These artists painted the farmlands and cities of America realistically, as in Figure 3-16, and each one had a different style. But their message was more "up-beat" than the message of the Ashcan School. They focused on the vast expanse, beauty, productivity, and abundance of America. American people were shown as happy and hardworking.

Most sculptors at this time worked with traditional materials using traditional methods. Then a few experimented with the new materials of the twentieth century. The most exciting step was taken by the American, Alexander Calder, Figure 3-17, who made sculpture move. He arranged wire and sheet metal into a balanced arrangement that stayed in motion. He called these moving sculptures *mobiles*.

The twentieth century also saw big changes in architecture, as shown in Figure 3-18. New materials and new demands helped develop skyscrapers. Functional structures with steel frames that emphasized simplicity of form replaced heavy, decorated structures. Frank Lloyd Wright believed that form should follow function when he designed buildings that blended with the surroundings.

The strong emotions of the time were also revealed in the art of a group of Mexican artists. As

Figure 3.16 Grant Wood painted American farm scenes. His paintings are full of smoothly rounded trees and hills, and they are painted with great detail.

Grant Wood. *New Road*. 1939. Canvas mounted on hardboard. 33 × 37.9 cm (13 × 14⅞"). National Gallery of Art, Washington, D.C. Gift of Mr. and Mrs. Irwin Strasburger.

Figure 3.17 Calder never named his pieces until they were complete and hanging in their environment. Only when they were moving in the proper setting did they take on their true character. He died before this work was hung, so it has no name.

Alexander Calder. *Untitled.* 1976. Aluminum and steel. 9.1 × 23.2 m (29'10½" × 76'). National Gallery of Art, Washington, D.C. Gift of the Collectors Committee.

the twentieth century started, Mexico was deeply troubled. The tension erupted into the Mexican Revolution, which ended in 1921. Some Mexican artists developed a style with which to express their feelings about the plight of the people. Often called the *Mexican Muralists,* they combined solid forms with the powerful colors of European Expressionism. They covered walls and ceilings with their murals about Mexican history, the suffering of the common people, and the immoral behavior of the ruling class.

DEVELOPING YOUR SKILLS

6. Write a short paragraph explaining what you think the artist in Figure 3-15 was trying to say about memory. Give reasons for your answer.

Figure 3.18 Sullivan believed that "form followed function." He felt that an office building with walls hung on a steel frame should not look like an Ancient Greek temple. In the Wainwright Building, he has omitted any columns or excessive decoration. You can "feel" the lines of the supporting steel beams beneath the brick covering.

Louis Sullivan. Wainwright Building. 1890–91. Photography by Sandak, Inc., Stamford, Connecticut.

From the Fifties into the Future

After World War II the European art world was disorganized. Paris was no longer the center of creativity. Many artists who had fled Hitler's Germany settled in New York City. They began teaching there, and by the 1950s they and their students established a new center for the arts.

What happened next happened with breathtaking speed. There have been more changes in artistic style and technique during the last forty years than there had been since prehistoric times.

Painting and sculpture were not the only art forms affected. A variety of forms once considered minor arts found a place as equals to painting and sculpture, and their creators are constantly exploring new frontiers. Some of these arts include printmaking, weaving, fabrics, ceramics, and jewelry. Craftspeople today create works for pleasure rather than just usefulness.

There are also more artists working today than ever before. Because of increased opportunity and changing attitudes, more women and minority artists have been able to study, exhibit, and be recognized. Artists have developed new ways to express how they feel about space travel, computers, and nuclear energy. Only the major movements will be mentioned here.

Abstract Expressionism

Abstract Expressionism was the first new style to come on the scene in New York in the years following World War II. It was called *abstract* because it emphasized the elements and principles of art as its subject matter. It was expressive because it stressed emotion rather than planned design. This style is also sometimes called *Action Painting*. An example is shown in Figure 3-19.

Pop and Op Art

During the early 1960s artists turned to the mass media, and especially to advertising, for subject matter. Pop artists portrayed Coke bottles, soup cans, Brillo boxes, giant hamburgers, and comic strips in a variety of art forms. These artists made people take a new look at everyday objects.

Figure 3.19 Hofmann came to New York from Germany and opened an art school. He was the father of the abstract expressionist style that grew in New York. He is best known for his heavy use of brilliant colors. In this work several colored rectangles seem to float over a background of loosely brushed, but heavily built-up colors, which suggest water and flowers.

Hans Hofmann. *Flowering Swamp.* 1957. Oil on wood. 122 × 91.5 cm (48⅛ × 36⅛"). Hirshhorn Museum and Sculpture Garden, Smithsonian Institution, Washington, D.C. Gift of Joseph H. Hirshhorn Foundation, 1966.

People have always been fascinated by illusions. They enjoy looking at pictures that fool the eye. *Op,* or "optical" art is based on this interest in illusion. But the Op artist uses scientific knowledge about vision to create optical illusions of movement. Op art has hard edges and smooth surfaces, and every element is planned mathematically. See Figure 7-6.

Color Field Painting

Color Field Painting is concerned only with flat fields of color. But it is done without the mathematical precision of the Op artists and is without emotion. It is color for the pure sensation of color. One example is the work of Mark Rothko. His color areas have hazy edges which seem to float in space. See Figure 7-21.

New Realism

Americans have a love for realism, and some American artists continue to portray subjects realistically. Andrew Wyeth, whose painting you studied in Chapter 2, is one example. Sculpture by Duane Hanson (Figure 3-20) is so real that it fooled a gallery nightwatchman. When he thought that one of Hanson's motionless, seated figures was ill, he called an ambulance. This style has several names: *Photorealism*, *Hyper-realism*, and *Super-realism*.

Figure 3.21   The two towers of this structure rising above the streets of Houston are separated by a narrow ten-foot space. Their tops are slanted at forty-five degree angles.

Philip Johnson. Pennzoil Place. 1976. Photograph courtesy of Pennzoil Company, Houston, Texas.

Directions in Architecture

As with every other visual form, architecture has not followed just one direction. Some buildings, like the glass and metal boxes that fill our cities, are still being designed mainly for function. Some buildings are shaped to take advantage of solar power. Architects are designing buildings that are also giant sculptures, such as Pennzoil Place in Figure 3-21. Landscape architects are teaming up with city architects and planners to design cities that help solve urban living problems. Other teams are redesigning the centers of cities to make them more attractive places to live.

Figure 3.20   Doesn't this man look familiar? If you walked into a dimly lit room, would you mistake him for a real person?

Duane Hansen. *Traveler with Sunburn*. 1986. Bronze, oil painted and mixed media. Life size. OK Harris, New York City, New York.

DEVELOPING YOUR SKILLS

7. Compare Figure 3-20 with Figure 3-5. How are the two sculptures alike? How are they different? Write a short paragraph giving your answers.

Art from Non-Western Cultures

Western culture is only one limb on the human family tree. Western culture is not independent of the other branches. Throughout history there have always been exchanges between cultures, with one influencing another.

The cultures of India, China, Japan, the Pacific, Islamic world, Sub-Equatorial Africa, and the Pre-Columbian Americas all produced beautiful art forms. One way that the art of these cultures is different from Western art is that it is based on different religious beliefs. These beliefs are often difficult for Western people to understand.

Because of limited space we cannot trace the history of each one of the different cultures named here. Only a few examples of art from non-Western cultures are included.

Figure 3.23 Notice what a small space on the scroll is taken up by the people. The hut blends into the natural setting. The fine handwriting in the upper right corner is an important part of the composition. The busy lines of the writing balance the busy lines of the autumn leaves below.

Hua Yen. *Conversation in Autumn.* 1762. Ink and color on paper. 115.3 × 39.7 cm (45⅜ × 15⅝"). The Cleveland Museum of Art, Cleveland, Ohio. Purchase. John L. Severance Fund.

Figure 3.22 Vishnu, The Preserver, holds his symbols: a discus, a conch shell, a mace, and a lotus.

South Indian. *Standing Vishnu.* Early Chola Period, X century, first half. Bronze. 85.7 × 35.6 cm (33¾ × 14"). The Metropolitan Museum of Art. Purchase, 1962. Mr. and Mrs. John D. Rockefeller gift.

The art of *India* has been dominated by the Hindu and Buddhist religions for over 2500 years. Images of the many gods (Figure 3-22) have long played an important role in Indian culture.

The religions of *China* stress meditation, a calm, deep reflection about life. Understanding meditation is important in creating and viewing Chinese painting, such as the examples in Figure 3-23. Chinese painting has always been the artist's personal response to the natural world.

Until the end of the ninth century *Japanese* artists copied the work of China and other Asian cultures. Later, Japanese artists developed their own styles. Many different subjects are shown in Japanese painting and printmaking. Some of the subjects are stories of war, everyday scenes, court life, and nature (Figure 3-24).

Islamic art, the art of the Moslem world, is decorative. Moslems are forbidden to show human figures in sculpture. But miniature paintings illustrating stories about successful rulers have been permitted (Figure 3-25).

Figure 3.25 To the right is a scene from a book about court life in Iran.

Nizami. *Khamseh: Bahram Gur and the Chinese Princess in the Sandalwood Pavilion on Thursday.* 1524–25. Colors and gilt on paper. 32.4 × 22.2 cm (12¾ × 8¾"). The Metropolitan Museum of Art, New York, New York. Gift of Alexander Smith Cochran, 1913.

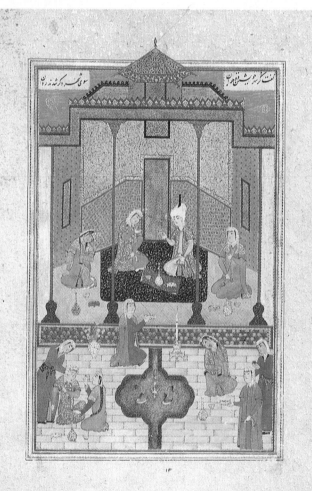

In both *African* art and the art of *Pacific Ocean* peoples, the geometric designs and abstract forms were not meant for beauty. They were created to link the people to unseen forces, such as those of nature or the gods. Figure 3-26 is an example.

The term *Pre-Columbian* refers to all the civilizations in North and South America before the arrival of Christopher Columbus in 1492. Cultures such as the Olmec, Mayan, and Aztec in Central America; the Peruvian in South America; and the North American Indian are examples. They produced art mainly of a functional or religious nature, as in Figures 3-27 and 3-28.

DEVELOPING YOUR SKILLS

8. Look up in an encyclopedia one of the non-Western cultures described here. Find three facts about it that you think might affect the art created by these people. Report your findings to the class.

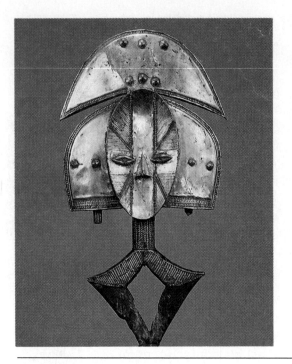

Figure 3.26   This figure was made to stand above a basket of ancestral bones.

Primitive. African, Gabon, Kota. *Reliquary Figure.* XIX–XX century. Wood, brass, copper, iron. 73.3 cm (28⅞") high. The Metropolitan Museum of Art, New York, New York. Purchase, 1983.

Figure 3.28   A corn husk mask made by the Seneca tribe.

Seneca. *Corn Husk Mask.* Woven corn husks. Denver Art Museum, Denver, Colorado.

Figure 3.27   This fat, helmeted baby is thought to be a statue of the ancient Mexican rain god.

Olmec. *Seated Figure.* c. 1000 B.C. Whiteware with traces of cinnabar. 34 × 31.8 cm (13⅜ × 12½"). The Museum of Primitive Art, New York, New York.

Chapter 3 Review: Talking about Art

USING THE LANGUAGE OF ART

For each new art term below, choose a work of art from this chapter. Then write a sentence about that work using the new term correctly in the sentence.

Abstract Expressionism
Baroque
Byzantine
Cubism
Gothic
Impressionists

Post-Impressionists
Realists
Renaissance
Romanesque
Surrealism

LEARNING THE ART ELEMENTS AND PRINCIPLES

1. What are artistic styles?
2. What is meant by the word *culture?*
3. Choose one of the credit lines in this chapter and explain each part.
4. What is perspective and who developed it?
5. What is the meaning of the word *mobile?*

INCREASING YOUR ART AWARENESS

Tell what style is represented in each illustration listed below. Choose your answers from the following list of styles:

Color Field Painting
Fauves
Futurists
Mannerism

Neoclassicism
Pop Art
Romanticism
De Stijl

1. Figure 11-43
2. Figure 8-3
3. Figure 4-1
4. Figure 7-45

5. Figure 9-30
6. Figure 7-36
7. Figure 9-15
8. Figure 7-21

UNDERSTANDING ART CULTURE AND HERITAGE

1. Four works of art in this chapter were definitely created before the birth of Christ. Name the four works. (Clue: no date is given for one of these works.)
2. Art historians are not certain if one work of art in this chapter was created before or after the birth of Christ. Name the work.
3. List one artistic style from each of the following centuries: 17th, 18th, 19th, and 20th. For each style list one work from this chapter that is a good example of that style.
4. In this chapter almost all of the works of art appear in the order in which they were created. Look at the works. What statements can you make about the way art has changed over the years? Consider subject matter, form, content, media, and style.
5. How did the Renaissance change the rank that artists held in society?
6. What historical event brought an end to the Rococo style? Why?
7. Name five artistic styles that emerged after the industrial and democratic revolutions of the eighteenth century.

JUDGING THE QUALITY OF ART

Use the four steps of art criticism to study one work of art from this chapter. You may choose Figure 3-1 or another work that you're interested in. Then read something about the artist who created the work. Does knowing more about the artist help you understand more about the work of art?

LEARNING MORE ABOUT ART

Explore further how artists express meaning, ideas, or themes in works of art. They sometimes use symbols to stand for something else or *allegories,* which tell a story with a meaning that goes beyond what you first see.

Now read about one period in art history that interests you. Find out if artists of that time used symbolism in their works, and, if so, what does it tell us about their world? Prepare an oral report on your findings.

Figure 4.1 Daumier was a Frenchman with a genius for capturing gestures and facial expressions. He spent most of his life creating editorial cartoons that criticized the social and political leaders of the nineteenth century.

Honore Daumier. *Advice to a Young Artist*. Probably after 1860. Oil on canvas. 41 × 33 cm (16⅛ × 12⅞"). National Gallery of Art, Washington, D.C. Gift of Duncan Phillips.

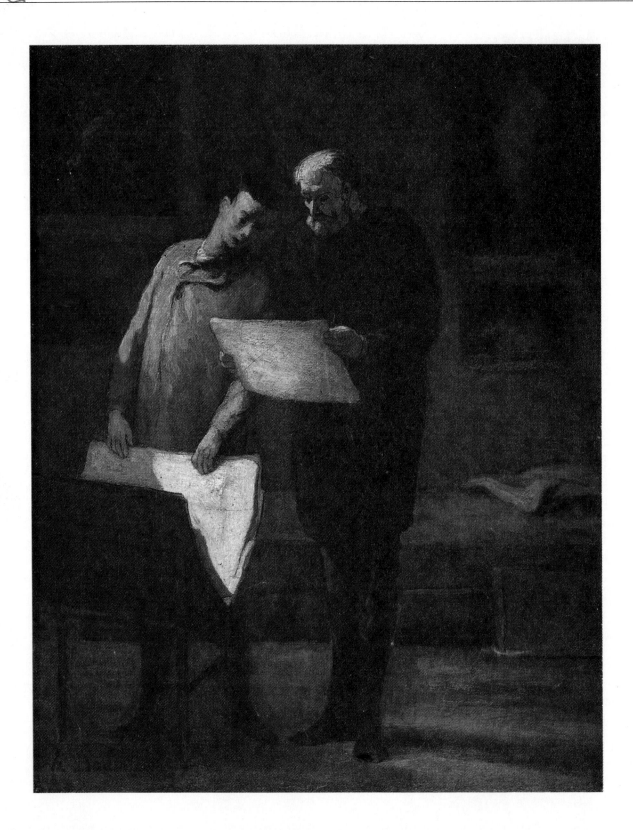

Careers in Art

After reading this chapter and doing the exercises, you will be able to:

- □ name many fields in which an art career is possible.
- □ name some of the skills artists need for various jobs.
- □ make a meaningful decision about your own interest in a career in art.

WORDS TO LEARN

In this chapter you will learn the meanings of the words listed below.

animation
apprentices
layout
storyboards

Now is an exciting time to consider a career in the visual arts. There are many possibilities from which to choose, whether you want to be an artist or work in a related job. The number of jobs in the visual arts is growing. Artists and related workers are needed in almost every area of industry, entertainment, and education.

Some people, however, still follow the traditional path. They choose to work on their own as painters, sculptors, printmakers, weavers, jewelers, and so on. Many of these artists need a second job to help pay expenses. In the visual arts, as in the performing arts, the opportunities for stardom and big salaries are rare. So, even if you think you would like to work on your own, you may have to consider working for someone else at the same time.

In this chapter you will learn how to find out whether or not you might be suited for a career in art. You will also get a taste of the many different types of art careers from which you can choose. If you have been thinking that you might enjoy a career in art, this chapter should help you move closer to a career decision. If you have never considered an art career, this chapter may open the door to some exciting career possibilities.

Thinking About an Art Career

Are you suited for a career in the art world? It may be too soon for you to make a final decision about your future. But, if you have talent and art is something you enjoy, then an art career may be right for you.

Ask yourself the following questions. The more "yes" answers you give, the better your chances of being happy in the art field.

- ☐ Are you sensitive to colors?
- ☐ Do you notice how changes in light affect the things you see?
- ☐ Do you find yourself noticing things that your friends may miss, such as the colors of autumn leaves or the shapes of clouds?
- ☐ Do you like to draw or make things with your hands?
- ☐ Do you get "lost" in an art project and lose track of time?
- ☐ When a work of art turns out wrong, are you willing to throw it out and start again?
- ☐ Are you curious?
- ☐ Do you like to solve problems?
- ☐ Do you keep an open mind about new and unusual forms of art?
- ☐ Do you like to experiment with new materials and techniques?
- ☐ Do you set aside time each day to work on an art project or study someone else's work?
- ☐ Do you keep at a project until it is finished?
- ☐ Can you meet deadlines?
- ☐ Do you try to work even when you don't feel "in the mood"?

In the past, young people who wanted to be artists worked as **apprentices** to master artists. They learned as they assisted the master in the studio. Today, some craftspeople are bringing back the apprentice system. However, the usual way to develop skills is by taking courses in high school and post-secondary school. Training for some art careers can also be gotten in vocational and professional art

Figure 4.2   You can learn many skills and techniques through study and practice at an accredited art school.

schools (Figure 4-2). Other art careers may require four- or five-year college degrees.

If you finally decide you want a career in art, you should begin working toward it in high school. In the meantime, practice your skills on your own. Study the great artists. Ask your teachers for advice. If you really want a career in art, it will be there for you!

DEVELOPING YOUR SKILLS

1. Ask your school or community librarian to help you find art careers in a book titled, *The Occupational Outlook Handbook*. Note what job opportunities are available and in which industries. Report your findings to the class.

Career Fields

Following are descriptions of a number of art careers in different fields. As you read, think about each one and keep those that interest you in mind. It's never too soon to consider career possibilities.

Graphic Design

The field of graphic design began when the printing press was invented in the fifteenth century. Craftspeople who arranged type and illustrations on the printed page were the first graphic designers. They had to plan the **layout** (way items are arranged on a page) or design of each page before it was printed. Today graphic designers use computers, photocopiers, laser scanners, overhead projectors, and duplicating machines to help design a project.

Graphic artists work as members of a team that may include art directors, layout and pasteup artists, letterers, calligraphers, air brush artists, block engravers, sign painters, and typographers. Graphic artists may be employed by outdoor advertising agencies to design billboards, by corporations to design promotional materials, and by advertising agencies to work on advertising campaigns such as the one shown in Figure 4-3.

Graphic designers usually specialize in a certain field, such as publishing, computers, or television. Those fields are mentioned briefly below.

Editorial Design and Illustration

Newspaper, magazine, and book publishers employ graphic designers as art directors, illustrators, layout artists, photographers, and printers.

A designer planned the look of this book. Commercial illustrators drew the special illustrations, such as the viewing frame on page 104. Illustrators may specialize in one area such as cartoons and comics, medical publications, or technical manuals.

Editorial cartoonists must be interested in politics. They present complex ideas in a simple drawing that usually makes a humorous point. Editorial cartoonists try to make people think about current issues. They also try to influence public opinion.

Comic strip artists are entertainers. A comic strip has a story line and characters who keep an audience reading every day.

Most medical illustrators work for medical schools, medical centers, or for publishers of medical journals or textbooks. They must have medical knowledge and be able to work with a variety of media. An illustrator may be asked to make an accurate drawing of such organs as the heart or to prepare diagrams of a medical procedure.

Figure 4.3 The subway riders who whiz past this poster are able to read both the visual and the verbal messages very easily. The artist must get the message across as quickly as possible since no one will be slowing down to read the sign.

Robert Gage. *New York Is Eating It Up! Levy's Real Jewish Rye.* 1952. Offset lithograph. 116.8 × 76.8 cm (46 × 30¼″). Collection, The Museum of Modern Art, New York, New York. Gift of Doyle Dane Bernbach, Inc.

Technical illustrators draw such things as machine parts and must enjoy drawing tiny details. They also need at least a basic understanding of the objects they draw.

Computer Graphics

Computer technology is improving rapidly, and many artists are turning to electronic equipment to create graphic designs. This is the most recent addition to the world of commercial art. A career in this field combines a strong background in design with knowledge of computer technology.

The designer works with tools such as electric light pens on electronic tablets, as in Figure 4-4. With these tools any image may be drawn and colored. Electronic equipment merely speeds up the design process.

Drawings are stored in the computer's memory system and recalled and revised as needed. Some systems let the artist see the finished work in a variety of color and size arrangements. Computers can also send images along telephone lines to customers on the other side of the world.

Figure 4.4 If you like working with computers and you like to draw, computer graphics may be a possible career choice.

Courtesy of Peter Green Design.

Television Graphics

Television graphic designers must be able to use all art, electronic, and computer designing media and techniques. The graphic artist may be the only artist working for a small, local TV station, or one of many employed by a large city station.

The following are just a few of the things a graphic artist working for a TV station might design: sets for local shows, the graphic symbols and pictures that are shown behind news reporters, weather maps, and the symbols for the maps, signs for the station, and newspaper ads.

Industrial Design

Industrial designers design the products of industry. They plan the forms of everything from dinnerware and furniture to automobiles and space vehicles. Designers plan a product based on three requirements. First, it must do the job for which it was designed. Second, it must look like it can do the job. Third, it must be visually pleasing.

Package designers produce boxes, tubes, bottles, shopping bags, and other kinds of containers. They use shape and color to make every package unique and appealing. Package designers must also consider package function. For example, when cassette tapes first came on the market, theft was a problem because the packages were small. Designers had to come up with a package that could not be slipped into a pocket but that was easy to carry and display.

Designers usually specialize in one industry or product, such as furniture, sports equipment, or cars. The design of an automobile is a team effort. Special designers plan the outward shape. Then other specialists who work with fabrics and plastics create new interiors to go with the body shape. Computers help insure that all the parts fit together accurately.

Raymond Loewy is credited with many advances in industrial design. He was born in Paris and became an American citizen in 1938. He started designing when he was asked to improve the look of a duplicating machine. During his career he has designed a NASA space suit, and, most recently, the new Exxon signs.

Loewy is best known for his automotive designs. The 1953 *Starlight Coupe* was chosen for exhibition at the Museum of Modern Art in New York be-

Figure 4.5 Look closely at this *Avanti*. Like many of today's aerodynamic cars, it has no grill. How do you think this design might affect the car's performance?

Raymond Loewy. *Avanti.* 1963. Photography by Frank Fortune.

cause of its unusual design quality. The *Avanti* (Figure 4-5) is a luxury sports car that was made between June 1962 and December 1963. It is such an unusual design that it is still being produced and sold by a small, independent company today. The Smithsonian Institute has the car on display as an outstanding example of industrial design.

Fashion Design

Fashion designers design clothing, hats, handbags, shoes, gloves, jewelry, and other apparel. High-fashion designers set fashion trends. Their designs, such as the one in Figure 4-6, are usually very expensive. Manufacturers select designs to copy for lower-priced clothing. All clothing designers are supported by a team of patternmakers, factory workers, weavers, cutters, tailors, and seamstresses.

Architecture

Architects must design buildings that function properly, are well constructed, and are aesthetically pleasing.

To function properly a building must do what it was planned to do. Private houses and apartments must work as comfortable homes for people. Office buildings, schools, and factories must also be comfortable, efficient, and aesthetically pleasing. The aesthetic effect of a building is extremely impor-

Figure 4.6 Fashion designers must come up with fresh, new ideas every season. Anyone considering a career in this area must be able to work under intense pressure to meet deadlines.

tant. The structure must fit into its environment and improve the community.

An architect must know about such things as building materials, ventilation, heating and cooling systems, plumbing, stairways, and elevators.

Because modern technology is so complex, architects usually specialize in a particular type of building. An architect must be creative, be able to make accurate mechanical drawings, have a strong background in mathematics and drafting, and be able to deal with customers.

City Planning

City planners are trained as architects, but they are mainly concerned with the care and improvement of city environments. Every major American city has a city planner. This person helps control the growth and the development of the city. Some of the responsibilities of the city planner are land use, harbor development, city parks, shopping malls, and urban renewal projects. Reston, Virginia, shown in Figure 4-7, is a planned city.

Figure 4.7   Reston is a planned community that was founded in 1962, with completion expected in the mid 1990s. About 40 percent of the total area has been planned for open space and public use. People can work, shop, attend school, and participate in a variety of leisure activities without leaving the community.

Aerial view of Reston, Virginia—a planned city. Courtesy of the Reston Land Corporation, Reston, Virginia.

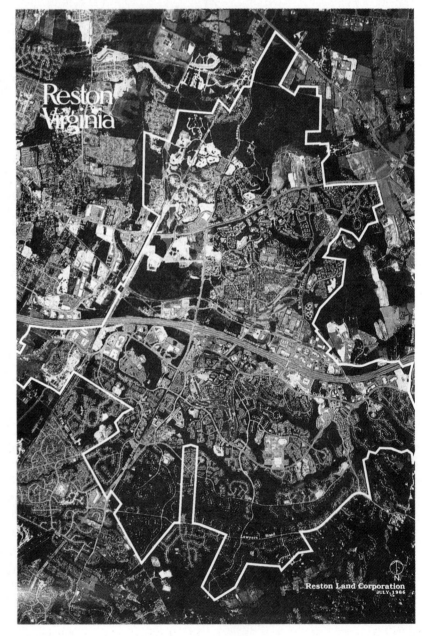

Landscape Architecture

Landscape architects design outdoor areas around buildings, in playgrounds and parks, and along highways. They work closely with architects and other planners to use and improve the natural setting so that it is easy to maintain and beautiful to look at. They create designs using flowers, plants, trees, shrubs, rivers, ponds, lakes, walks, benches, and signs, as shown in Figure 4-8.

Landscape artists work with architectural firms, government agencies, individual home owners, and private companies, such as golf courses.

Interior Design

Interior designers plan the decoration of interior spaces, such as homes and offices. Successful designers use styles and materials that blend with the architecture and that please the client.

Interior designers must understand decorating styles and materials. They must be able to look at an empty room and visualize the finished area. They must know what is new in wallcovering, carpets, furniture, appliances, and lamps.

Since interior designers spend as much time with clients as at the drawing board, they must have patience and the ability to make a client feel comfortable. Some designers plan and coordinate the interiors of department stores or large hotels, while others work for individual home owners.

Exhibit and Display Design

Exhibit designers work for trade shows, department stores, showrooms, art galleries, and museums. They plan presentations of collections, temporary exhibits, and traveling shows of all types. They decide which things should be grouped together and how they should be lit.

Displays attract customers and help persuade them to buy. The display designer is an important member of the sales team. The way the designer makes the merchandise look in a store window helps draw customers into the store.

Photography

In this book Figures 5-2 and 6-2 were created by a fine art photographer, W. Robert Nix, for purely aesthetic purposes. His photographs help us see certain visual ideas in the natural environment.

Photojournalists are visual reporters. They work for newspapers and magazines. Photojournalists understand design, know how to develop and print their own work, and have an eye for what is interesting to look at. See Figure 4-9 above. Other photographers may be able to work in the comfort of a studio, but photojournalists must go where the news is happening.

Other careers in photography include fashion photography, product and food photography, architectural photography, and medical photography.

Animation

Animation, the art of moving cartoons, was invented for film, but it is used on TV as well. Animation needs more visual artists than any other art career area.

When artists create an animated film, they first select a story. They decide what styles of architecture and dress fit the story. Then they develop the story by drawing **storyboards,** still drawings that show the story's progress. They draw about sixty sketches for each board. A short film needs three storyboards, and a full length film needs over twenty-five. The storyboards look like comic books. They provide the outline for the development of the film.

Layout artists are responsible for the total look of the film. Background artists paint the settings

Figure 4.10 Today the more advanced techniques for creating animated films involve computers. Here you see a knight being created on the computer for the animated film "Young Sherlock Holmes."

from the layout artist's sketches. Animators draw the major poses of each character (Figure 4-10), while other artists fill in the many other drawings required to complete each movement. Every second of film requires twenty-four drawings to make the movement look smooth.

Art Direction for the Performing Arts

In the theater the art director works with scenic, costume, and lighting designers, as well as makeup artists and hair stylists, to make all elements of the show fit together. See Figure 4-11. Art directors know art history as well as the special techniques of their craft. If a play is set in the past, the setting, furniture, costumes, and hair styles must correctly reflect that period of history.

Art directors also coordinate all the visual elements involved in the production of a movie or a television program. They work with scenic designers, costume designers, graphic artists, property designers, and location planners.

Special Effects Design

There is no school for special effects. The people who create the magic illusions we love in film and TV have come up through the ranks. Perhaps they started by building theater sets or designing film backgrounds.

Special effects artists are a combination of painter, sculptor, and engineer. They have the ability to imagine and create fantasy scenes or creatures that look real (Figure 4-12). They can make you believe you are watching the Muppets driving a car or a battle scene in a galaxy far, far away. They use papier-mache, plaster, plastic molds, paint, makeup, trick photography and computers.

Figure 4.11 Art directors must make backgrounds, costumes, and other visual elements work together. They coordinate the work of all the creative people who work in the theatre.

Figure 4.12 This motion picture make-up and special effects artist uses sculpture to create the models for many of his movie characters. His characters have appeared in movies such as *A Nightmare on Elm Street, Trick or Treat,* and *Cocoon.*

Photography by Scott Holton.

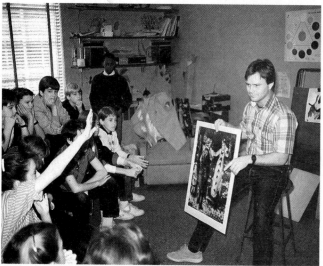

Figure 4.13 In addition to enjoying art, teachers must enjoy working with people and sharing their knowledge.

Art Education

People who like to share their knowledge and skills and have a strong interest in art may choose to teach. Teachers work in elementary, middle, or high schools, museums, and colleges (Figure 4-13). Teachers help their students learn to make aesthetic judgments and to develop their artistic skills and talents.

Art therapists, who are also teachers, use art to help people with their emotional and physical problems. They help patients change behavior in a positive manner. They work in psychiatric hospitals, community centers, drug and alcohol treatment centers, and prisons.

DEVELOPING YOUR SKILLS

2. Compare the 1963 *Avanti* on page 51 to some of the cars sold today. List any differences or similarities you find.
3. Think of one room in your school that looks like it needs an interior designer. List some of the things you would like to change. Then describe how you would change them. Think in terms of color, traffic flow, furniture, and so on.
4. Watch several animated programs on TV. Notice the differences in quality. Then list the programs you watched in order, from best to worst. How did the backgrounds compare? Describe the quality of the movement. Did the programs with the best movement have the best backgrounds?

SOMETHING EXTRA

A. Do some library research or interview an industrial technology teacher to find out how computers are replacing gigantic wind tunnels in the transportation industry. Report your findings to the class.

USING THE LANGUAGE OF ART

For each new art term below, choose an illustration from this chapter. Then write a sentence about that work using the new term correctly in the sentence.

animation   layout
apprentices   storyboards

LEARNING THE ART ELEMENTS AND PRINCIPLES

1. Name three ways to develop skills in art.
2. Name a book that lists art careers.
3. Name at least ten fields in which an art career is possible.
4. Name three fields in which graphic designers may specialize.
5. What kind of knowledge and ability does a medical illustrator need?
6. What art elements do package designers use to make every package unique and appealing? What else must they consider?
7. Name six things an architect must know. What characteristics and abilities should an architect have?
8. With what are city planners mainly concerned? Name three responsibilities of city planners.

INCREASING YOUR ART AWARENESS

1. List ten different types of media used in the works of art in Chapters 1-4.
2. What is the subject of Figure 4-9? What do you think the theme, or message, of this photograph is? How does this theme, or content, differ from the theme of Figure 1-9?
3. Identify the subject and content of Figure 4-1. What can you say about the form?
4. What theory or theories of art would you find helpful in understanding Figure 4-1? Why?
5. Are people in your town or city working in art careers? What works of art have they created?
6. What product would you want to redesign to improve its appearance? Explain.

UNDERSTANDING ART CULTURE AND HERITAGE

1. Modern technology has created ways to make new kinds of art. Name three art forms either shown or discussed in this chapter that could not have been produced at the time Daumier painted *Advice to a Young Artist* (Figure 4-1).
2. What artistic style does Figure 4-1 represent?
3. What was Honoré Daumier's main occupation?
4. When did the field of graphic design begin? What invention made it possible?

JUDGING THE QUALITY OF ART

The painting in Figure 4-1 is entitled *Advice to a Young Artist*, but it could just as easily be entitled *Judging the Quality of Art*. No matter what art career you might enter, the quality of your work will be important to your employer. It will also be important to know what is expected of you in your job and what education and training are necessary.

Working with a partner, find out more information about one of the many visual art careers mentioned in this chapter. What type of education and experience is necessary for this particular career? Develop and present to the class a brief drama about an employer interviewing a prospective employee for that position, but do not actually name the position. Plan questions for the employer to ask and information for the job seeker to offer. Include educational background and experience, and include extra-curricular activities in school. Dress appropriately and prepare a portfolio just as a stage prop to present during the dramatization. When you have finished, ask members of the class to guess which career has been the subject of your drama.

LEARNING MORE ABOUT ART

From the visual art careers listed in this chapter, choose one that seems interesting. Through personal interviews or library research, write a brief biography of one person (famous or not so famous) who has had experience in this career.

Joseph Mallord William Turner. *Slave Ship*. Date unknown. Oil on canvas. 90.8 x 122.6 cm (35¾ x 48¼"). The Museum of Fine Arts, Boston, Massachusetts. Henry Lillie Pierce Fund.

The Elements of Art

The next four chapters are devoted to the elements of art. These elements are *line, value, shape, form, space, color,* and *texture.*

Chapter 5 is devoted to line, but it also discusses value as it relates to line. In fact, you will find value discussed in each of the Part Two chapters. Chapter 6 is about shape, form, and space. But again, you will find that value plays an important role. Chapter 7 is all about color, and Chapter 8 explains texture.

In each chapter you will learn to recognize, identify, and describe the elements. You will also learn to use the elements to express your own ideas and feelings in your own works of art. You will be doing this in a variety of art media.

You will become more aware of the elements of art in your environment. You will study photographs that will help you become more perceptive. As a result, you will begin to notice the elements as they appear in the world around you.

You will also learn to appreciate the use of the elements in works of art. You will study works of art from various periods of history, from prehistoric times to the late 20th century. In this way you will see how artists use the expressive qualities of the elements to enhance their works of art.

In each chapter you will start by examining the elements as concrete, familiar things in your environment. You will then become acquainted with the more abstract, expressive qualities of the elements. After finishing a chapter you will be able to use the element you have studied to uncover the mystery of meaning in a work of art by a master artist.

You will learn to recognize and use the elements one at a time. After completing Part Two, however, you will have a full understanding of all the elements. You will have made one giant step toward learning the language of art.

Figure 5.1 Because he had such a curious mind, Dürer collected and drew all sorts of unusual objects. Notice the many different textures and forms he creates with lines.

Albrecht Dürer. *An Oriental Ruler Seated on His Throne.* c. 1495. Pen and black ink. 30.6 × 19.7 cm (12 × 7¾"). National Gallery of Art, Washington, D.C. Ailsa Mellon Bruce Fund.

Line

LEARNING OBJECTIVES

After reading this chapter and doing the exercises, you will be able to

☐ observe the lines in your environment more closely.

☐ name the different kinds of lines.

☐ tell the five ways lines can vary in appearance.

☐ understand the expressive qualities or meanings of different lines in works of art.

☐ use lines to make contour, gesture, and calligraphic drawings.

☐ use lines to change values.

WORDS TO LEARN

In this chapter you will learn the meanings of the words listed below.

contour lines

crosshatching

dimension

calligraphy

gesture

implied lines

line

static

value

Lines are everywhere. You write words, numbers, and symbols with the help of lines. You use lines to draw pictures. You read lines of printed words. The lines on a map help you find the best route from one place to another. Have you ever had to stand *in line* to get into the movies or to pay for merchandise in a store? And if you cook, you may have *lined up* cookies on a cookie sheet.

How many times a day do you see lines? What about the bare winter trees making lacy line patterns against the sky? Have you ever felt the grain lines in a piece of wood? Did you ever interrupt a line of ants parading from a piece of food to the ant hill?

The photos in Figure 5-2 show just a few examples of lines in our environment. How many lines can you find in each picture?

DEVELOPING YOUR SKILLS

1. Sit in the middle of a room and look slowly around. Make a list of the lines you see. Then identify, locate, and in some way describe each line. For instance, you might list the straight, blue lines on your writing paper or the wrinkles around your knuckles.
2. List the ways other than drawing in which line is a part of everyday things. You might start your list by noting lines of printed words.

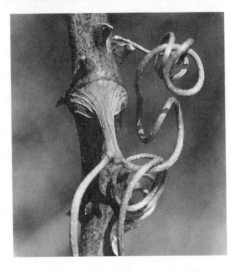

Figure 5.2 What lines do you see around you?

Photography by Robert Nix.

What Is Line?

In geometry, line is defined as an endless series of dots. In drawing, a **line** is a mark drawn with a pointed, moving tool. You can draw a line on paper with a pencil or scratch a line into wet clay with a stick.

A line has width as well as length, but the width of a line is always very small compared with its length. In fact, line is thought of as being one-dimensional. Its one dimension is length. **Dimension** means the amount of space an object takes up in one direction. You will learn more about dimensions in the next chapter, when you study shapes, forms, and spaces.

As mentioned in Chapter 1, line is one of the elements of art. Artists like to think of a line as the path of a dot through space. This definition is a good one to remember because it reminds you that it takes movement to make a line. When you see a line, your eyes usually follow the line's movement.

Artists use lines to control your eye movement. Lines can lead your eyes into, around, and out of visual images, as in Figure 5-3.

Of course the world is full of lines that were not drawn with a tool. Some thin, solid objects look like lines. Examples are flower stems, yarn, spiderwebs, and wires. These items look like lines because length is their most important dimension.

Figure 5.3 In this painting Grant Wood uses the artificially smooth road to pull you into and through this picture story. The fork in the road on the far right acts like an arrow point-ing toward the main area of movement. As your eyes follow the road, you see lights shin-ing from the neat little windows. Then you notice the hero riding toward the darker road ahead. The smooth line of the road has pulled you into, through, and out of this enchanted memory of an American legend.

Grant Wood. *Midnight Ride of Paul Revere*. 1931. Oil on masonite. 76.2 × 101.6 cm (30 × 40″). The Metropolitan Museum of Art, New York, New York. @ Estate of Grant Wood/V.A.G.A., New York. 1987.

Some lines that we think we see in nature do not really exist. For instance, when you look at the edges of shapes, you think of lines. Notice in the photo of the dogwood blossom, Figure 5-4, there are no black lines around the outside of each petal. But in the drawing of that same blossom, Figure 5-5, lines are used to show the edges of each shape.

Look at Figure 5-6 on the next page. The series of white dots representing car lights creates lines that pull your eyes up into the picture. At first the dots are widely spaced, but as you follow them, they get closer and closer together until the line is almost solid. These are called *implied lines*.

Implied lines are a series of points that the viewer's eyes automatically connect. Implied lines are only suggested; they are not real. A dotted line, a line of machine stitches, or a trail of wet footprints can create an implied line. A group of shapes arranged in a row can also create an implied line.

Figure 5.4 What edges do you see?

Photography by Robert Nix.

Figure 5.5 Student work. Are there edges in this picture? How have they been created?

DEVELOPING YOUR SKILLS

3. Draw a rough plan of your school building with a pencil and ruler. With a felt-tip pen, mark the path you follow from room to room on an average day. Invent symbols to mark the locations of the lunchroom, math class, main entrance, principal's office, and so on.
4. Make a map of the route you follow from your home to school each morning. Label important streets and invent symbols for the landmarks you pass. Use a variety of materials, such as water-based markers, cut paper, and magazine cutouts.

SAFETY NOTE

Vapor or fumes from permanent markers can be harmful. Always use water-based markers. Also avoid using rubber cement and airplane glue for your projects. Both contain solvents that are harmful if inhaled or allowed to remain on the skin too long.

Figure 5.6 Can you identify two examples of implied line in this painting?

Yvonne Jacquette. *East River Drive.* 1976. Pastel on paper. 47.6 × 58.4 cm (18¾ × 23″). The Metropolitan Museum of Art, New York, New York. Purchase. Friends of the Department gifts and matching funds from the National Endowment for the Arts. 1978.

SOMETHING EXTRA

A. If you have a camera that can make a time exposure, try this experiment. Mount your camera on a tripod and record the movement of car lights that pass your house during the night. Try different effects with a variety of lens openings and exposure times.

B. If you can get far away from city lights, you can record the movement of the stars. Mount your camera on a tripod and aim it at the sky on a clear, starry night. Open the lens after dark. Try a variety of lens openings and time settings.

Kinds of Lines

There are five main kinds of lines: vertical, horizontal, diagonal, curved, and zigzag.

Vertical lines (Figure 5-7) move straight up and down—they do not lean at all. A vertical line drawn on a piece of paper is perpendicular to the bottom edge. It is also perpendicular to the horizon (where earth and sky seem to meet). When you stand up straight, your body forms a vertical line.

Horizontal lines (Figure 5-8) are parallel to the horizon. They do not slant. When you lie flat on the floor, your body forms a horizontal line.

Diagonal lines (Figure 5-9) slant. Diagonals are somewhere between a vertical and a horizontal line. Diagonals look as if they are either rising or falling. Imagine standing straight up and then, with your body stiff, you fall to the floor. At any point during your fall, your body forms a diagonal line.

Curved lines (Figure 5-10) change direction gradually. When you draw wiggly lines, you are putting together a series of curves. Other kinds of curves form spirals and circles.

Figure 5.8 Horizontal lines lie parallel to the horizon.

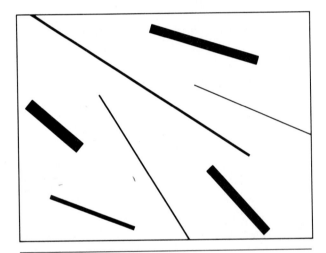

Figure 5.9 Diagonal lines slant.

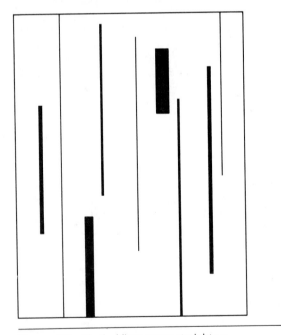

Figure 5.7 Vertical lines move straight up and down.

Figure 5.10 Curved lines change direction gradually.

Figure 5.11 Zigzag lines are combinations of diagonals.

Zigzag lines (Figure 5-11) are made from a combination of diagonal lines. The diagonals form angles and change direction suddenly.

DEVELOPING YOUR SKILLS

5. Choose one of the paintings shown in this book. Using different colors for different kinds of lines, make a rough diagram of the lines in the painting. For instance, you could make all vertical lines red and all diagonal lines green. Do not label your diagram. The colors will be the identification. Ask your friends to guess which painting is represented.

SOMETHING EXTRA

C. Take a series of photographs to illustrate each of the five line types. Mount and label the photos with the type of line each illustrates.
D. If you have access to a computer with graphic capabilities, use it to create a series of drawings to illustrate each of the five line types. Label each drawing.

Line Variation

Lines vary in appearance in five major ways:

☐ Length: Lines can be long or short (Figure 5-12).

☐ Width: Lines can be wide or thin (Figure 5-13).

☐ Texture: Lines can be rough or smooth (Figure 5-14).

☐ Direction: Lines can move in any direction, such as vertical, horizontal, or diagonal (Figure 5-15).

☐ Degree of curve: Lines can curve gradually or not at all, become wavy, or form spirals (Figure 5-16 on the next page).

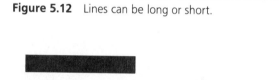

Figure 5.12 Lines can be long or short.

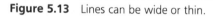

Figure 5.13 Lines can be wide or thin.

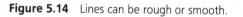

Figure 5.14 Lines can be rough or smooth.

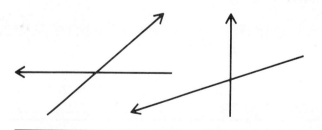

Figure 5.15 Lines can move in any direction.

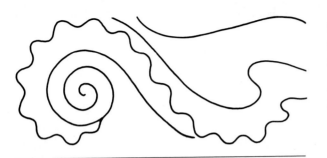

Figure 5.16 Lines can curve gradually, follow reverse curves, or turn inward to form spirals.

Figure 5.17 Roualt created many sad, expressive paintings and prints. In all of these works he used wide, heavy black lines to help create the desired effect.

Georges Roualt. *Man with Glasses*. c. 1948. Etching. 22.9 × 15.2 cm (9 × 6″). Private collection.

These five variations can be combined in many, many ways. You can make long, wide lines; rough, short lines; and smooth, curved lines. The list is almost endless.

The media, tools, and surfaces used to make lines affect the way a line looks. As with the combination of various line types, the possible affects are endless.

Some common materials used by artists to make lines are chalk, crayon, ink, and paint. The material is applied by using a tool. Some tools used

for making lines include pencils, markers, pens, brushes, and scissors. A line drawn with chalk on a chalkboard looks smoother than a line drawn with chalk on a cement sidewalk.

Artists use different tools and materials to create different types of line. Some artists have discovered very unusual ways of using line, as shown in Figures 5-17 and 5-18.

Figure 5.18 This construction of metal rods and wires seems to be held together by pure energy. The thin lines create a shimmering burst of light within a carefully calculated geometric structure.

Richard Lippold. *Variation Number 7: Full Moon.* 1949–50. Brass rods and nickle-chromium and stainless steel wire. 303 cm (119.3″) high. The Museum of Modern Art, New York, New York. Mrs. Simon Guggenheim Fund.

DEVELOPING YOUR SKILLS

6. Using your imagination and as many different media and tools as you can, cover a sheet of paper with a variety of lines. Number the lines. Then, on the back of the paper, list the medium and tool used for each line.

7. Look carefully at a bicycle and think of it as an object made of thin and thick lines. Notice the difference between the thickness of the spokes and the thickness of the handlebars. On a large sheet of paper, make a pencil line drawing of the bicycle. Your drawing should show the different thicknesses of the parts by the use of different line widths. See Figure 5-19 below.

8. On a sheet of paper, do a close-up line drawing in pencil (Figure 5-20) of one of the following:
   • Bare twigs on the limb of a tree
   • Pine needles on the end of a branch
   • A patch of uncut weeds
   • The cracks in one square of pavement
   • The feathers of a bird
   • The bark of a tree
   • The bristles of a toothbrush

Figure 5.19 Student work. Using thin and thick lines.

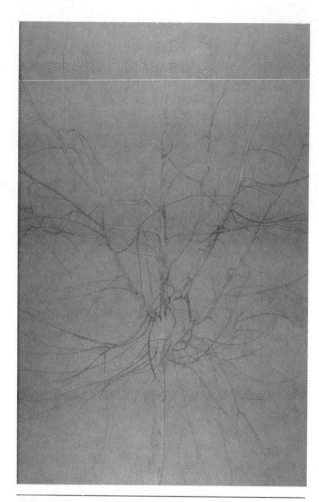

Figure 5.20   Student work. Close-up line drawings.

E. Make a collection of fabrics, wallpaper samples, and wrapping papers that are decorated with lines. The lines may be printed, woven, or knitted. Cut your samples into matching shapes and mount them for display.

F. Take a series of photographs and make a photo essay on one of the following themes:
  • "Lines can be wide or thin."
  • "Lines can be rough or smooth."
  • "Lines vary in degree of curvature."
Mount and display your essay.

What Different Lines Express

Depending upon its direction, a line can say, or express, different ideas or feelings. This is why lines are an important part of the language of art. For instance, vertical lines can make objects look tall. Vertical lines on wallpaper make low ceilings seem higher. Clothing designers use vertical lines to make short people look taller and heavy people look thinner.

Since vertical objects, such as tree trunks and tall columns, pull a viewer's eyes up from the ground toward the heavens, vertical lines have often been connected with religious feeling. See, for example, Figure 3-7 on page 30. The builders of cathedrals in the Middle Ages used many vertical lines in their structures because of the uplifting effect created by these lines.

Vertical lines are **static,** which means that they are inactive. They appear to be at rest. For this reason, they express stability. Vertical lines can also give an impression of dignity, poise, stiffness, and formality, as in Figure 5-21 on the next page.

Horizontal lines are also static. They express feelings of peace, rest, quiet, and stability, as in Figure 5-22. Horizontal lines make you feel comfortable, relaxed, and calm. Modern, casual furniture uses horizontal lines to create an easy, comfortable look.

Unlike vertical and horizontal lines, diagonal and zigzag lines are *active* lines. They give the feeling of action and movement because they seem to be pulled one way or the other. They are not at rest.

Diagonals express instability, tension, activity, and excitement, as in Figure 5-23 on page 72. Since they can appear to be either falling or rising, they sometimes make a viewer feel uncomfortable. Artists use them to add tension or to create an exciting mood. However, when two diagonals meet and seem to hold each other up, as in the roof of a house, they appear more stable.

Zigzag lines create confusion. They are extremely active and express feelings of excitement and nervousness, as in Figure 5-24. Zigzags that move horizontally, such as those at the top of a picket fence, show less activity than the irregular zigzags of a lightning streak.

Figure 5.21 Each thin figure in this sculpture expresses vertical movement, even if the legs are slightly slanted. If this were a photograph, on what do you think the people's eyes would be focusing? What do you think Giacometti is saying about people who live in cities?

Alberto Giacometti. *City Square*. 1948. Bronze. 21.6 × 64.5 × 43.8 cm (8½ × 25⅜ × 17¼"). Collection, The Museum of Modern Art, New York, New York. Purchase.

Figure 5.22 Strong horizontal lines create a sense of calm on this empty street. As you look at this painting, you get the feeling that everyone is sleeping peacefully. How many real and how many implied horizontal lines can you find in this painting?

Edward Hopper. *Early Sunday Morning*. 1930. Oil on canvas. 89.2 × 152.4 cm (35 × 60"). Collection of Whitney Museum of American Art, New York, New York. 31.436.

Figure 5.23 In this print, every line that should be static is diagonal. Look at the window, the lamp, the rug, the floor planks, and the fiddler's bench. The diagonal lines fill the work with a sense of excitement. Not only the people, but every corner of the room seems to be alive and dancing to the music of the fiddler.

Thomas Hart Benton. *I Got A Girl On Sourwood Mountain.* 1938. Lithograph. 31.7 × 23.4 cm (12½ × 9¼″). Courtesy of the Library of Congress, Washington, D.C.

Figure 5.24 (at left) Marin uses zig-zag line movement to create cityscapes that explode with excitement. In this work, everything seems to be in motion. How can this be the same city as that in Figure 5-22?

John Marin. *Lower Manhattan.* 1920. Watercolor. 55.6 × 67.9 cm (21⅞ × 26¾″). The Phillip L. Goodwin Collection. Museum of Modern Art, New York, New York.

Because curved lines change directions, they too express some activity. How much activity they express depends upon the type and direction of the curve. The less active the curve, the calmer the feeling.

Whatever the amount of activity, all curved lines are graceful. Often curved lines are used in interior decoration to suggest a feeling of luxury, as in Figure 5-25. Spiral curves wind around a central point. They are hypnotic and draw the eye to their center.

DEVELOPING YOUR SKILLS

9. Choose two words from the following list:

swimming	burning	praying
sitting	flowing	jumping
rocking	running	growing
marching	crawling	laughing
dancing	writing	tickling
wagging	itching	flying

On separate sheets of paper, illustrate the words you have chosen by using line movement only (Figure 5-26). Do not draw objects. Choose the medium you think will work best. When you are finished, write the word on the back of each paper. Ask your friends to guess which words you have illustrated.

10. Make two line drawings of crowded city buildings. Use static lines in one to express calm stability. Use active lines in the other to express the rush and confusion of a crowded city. Choose the medium you think best for each cityscape. See Figure 5-27.

Figure 5.25 Everything in this luxurious bedroom seems to swirl with curves. How do you think you would feel owning a room like this? Would you be comfortable?

Italian, Venice. Bedroom from the Sagredo Palace. c. 1725–1735. Photograph courtesy of the Metropolitan Museum of Art, Fletcher Fund, 1925.

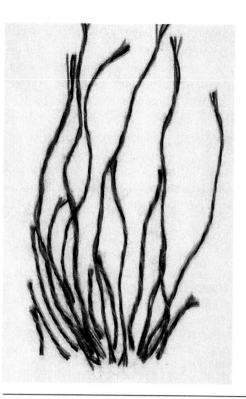

Figure 5.26   Student work. Which title fits this drawing?

Figure 5.27   Student work. What contrasting moods do these two scenes express?

Contour Drawing

Contour lines define the edges and surface ridges of an object. A contour line creates a boundary separating one area from another. Contour drawing will add to your drawing skills, as well as to your ability to observe and understand objects. See the examples in Figures 5-29A and 5-29B.

Figure 5.28   Notice how carefully the artist has created the illusion of shadow and form by simply changing the pressure on his pencil to create thin, light lines and heavier, dark lines. He takes advantage of the curved wrinkles in the fabric of the vest and sleeve to emphasize the roundness of the model's body.

Juan Gris. *Max Jacob*. 1919. Pencil on paper. 36.5 × 26.7 cm (14⅜ × 10½"). The Museum of Modern Art, New York, New York. Gift of James Thrall Soby.

TECHNIQUE TIP

Contour Drawing

When you make a contour drawing, your eye and hand must move at the same time. You must look at the object, not at your drawing. You must imagine that your pencil is touching the edge of the object as your eye follows the edge. Don't let your eye get ahead of your hand. Also, do not pick your pencil up from the paper. When you move from one area to the next, let your pencil leave a trail. If you do pick your pencil up accidentally, look down, place your pencil where you stopped, and continue.

To help you coordinate your eye-hand movement, try this: First, tape your paper to the table so it will not slide around. Then hold a second pencil in your non-drawing hand and move it around the edges of the object. With your drawing hand, record the movement.

If you have trouble keeping your eyes from looking at the paper, ask a friend to hold a piece of stiff paper between your eyes and your drawing hand so the drawing paper is blocked from view. You might also place your drawing paper inside a large paper bag turned sideways. A third method is to put the object on a chair and place the chair on a table. When you are standing, the object should be at your eye level. Then, place your drawing paper on the table directly under the chair. In this way you will be unable to see the paper easily.

When you draw without looking at the paper, your first sketches will look strange. Don't be discouraged. The major purpose of blind contour drawing is to teach you to concentrate on directions and curves. The more you practice, the more accurate your drawings will become.

As you develop your skills, remember that in addition to edges, contours also define ridges. Notice the wrinkles you see at the joints of fingers and at a bent wrist or bent elbow. Those wrinkles are curved lines. Notice the

ridges and dents where the lid joins a glass jar. Those ridges curve around the jar. If you draw them carefully, the lines you use to show these things will add the look of roundness to your drawing.

After you have made a few sketches, add pressure as you draw to vary the thickness and darkness of your lines. Some lines can be emphasized and some made less important through the right amount of pressure from your hand. Notice how Gris has done this in Figure 5-28.

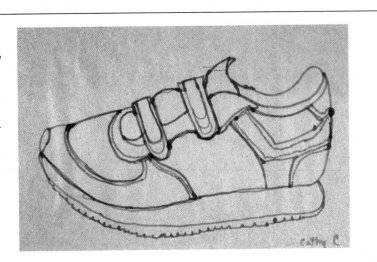

Figure 5.29A Student work. A contour drawing.

Figure 5.29B Student work. Notice how the line flows through this hospital scene. Look at the difference between the busy, zigzag lines that describe the wrinkles in the sheet and the few lines that define the person's face.

When you draw contours, do not lift the pencil from the paper. The line should be continuous. Draw the line slowly and with care. Concentrate in order to draw accurately.

DEVELOPING YOUR SKILLS

11. Use a water-based felt-tip or ballpoint pen and one sheet of paper to make a series of five contour drawings of a single object, such as a pair of scissors, a key, a shoe, or a brush. Change the position of the object for each drawing. Then, using a new sheet of paper, draw the object from memory. See the Technique Tip on the preceding page for help in making contour drawings.

12. Using a felt-tip or ballpoint pen, make a series of five contour drawings of your hand or bare foot on a single sheet of paper. You can indicate roundness by showing the curve of wrinkles around your fingers or toes. Change position for each drawing. Then, on a second sheet of paper, draw your hand or foot from memory.

Gesture Drawing

A **gesture** is an expressive movement. The purpose of drawing gestures is to capture the feeling of motion. A gesture drawing is not a drawing of details (Figure 5-30).

Lines showing gestures are quickly drawn and capture movement. They should be drawn freely and loosely, almost in a reckless manner. Unlike contours, they represent the interior of an object. Your drawing of gestures may look like scribbles at first, but this is acceptable. Concentrate on position and movement.

Figure 5.30   Tintoretto describes the gesture and bulk of this figure with just a few, rough lines. You can sense the movement of the figure through the looseness of the quickly drawn lines.

Jacopo Tintoretto. *Standing Youth With His Arm Raised, Seen From Behind.* Black chalk on laid paper. 36.3 × 21.9 cm (14¼ × 8⅝"). National Gallery of Art, Washington, D.C. Ailsa Mellon Bruce Fund.

DEVELOPING YOUR SKILLS

13. Make a series of gesture drawings (see the Technique Tip below). Classmates should take turns posing for each other. Start with thirty-second poses. Shorten the time by five seconds for each pose until you are down to ten seconds. Since the poses are so short, ask the model to be active. Have her or him twist, turn, bend, kick, or sit—never doing the same thing twice.

14. Play "musical gestures." You will need a record or tape player and a recording of favorite music. Choose at least two people for models and one for a disc jockey. The DJ is in charge of starting and stopping the music and must face away from the models. When the music starts, the models dance; when it stops, the models freeze. As soon as the music stops, the artists draw the models in the positions in which they have frozen, using a single sheet of paper. The DJ may let a pose last from ten to thirty seconds. When the music starts again, the artists stop drawing, and the models resume dancing. This exercise can be repeated as many times as desired. Change crayon or pen color with each pose and feel free to overlap figures.

TECHNIQUE TIP

Gesture Drawing

Unlike contour drawings, which show an object's outline, gesture drawings show movement. They should have no outlines or details. Using the side of a piece of unwrapped crayon or a pencil, make scribble lines that build up the shape of the object. Do not use single lines that create stick figures. Work very quickly. When drawing people, do the head, then the neck, and then fill in the body. Pay attention to the direction in which the body leans. Next, scribble in the bulk of the legs and the position of the feet. Finally, add the arms.

Figure 5.31A (above)   Student work. A page of gesture drawings.

Figure 5.31B (below)   Student work. A page of gesture drawings.

Calligraphic Drawing

The word **calligraphy** means "beautiful handwriting." Calligraphy is often thought of in connection with Oriental writing and art. In China and Japan, calligraphy is used to form *characters* that Oriental writers use in much the same way we use the alphabet. Chinese and Japanese characters are more like pictures, however. They can represent a complete idea, object, or verbal sound—more than just a letter. The Chinese and Japanese use the same types of lines and brush strokes in their paintings (Figure 5-34). In fact, in Chinese the same word is used for writing as for painting.

Calligraphic lines are usually made with brush strokes that change from thin to thick in one stroke. To make a very thin line, use the tip of the brush. As you press on the brush and more of it touches the paper, the line becomes darker and wider.

DEVELOPING YOUR SKILLS

15. Practice making calligraphic lines with ink or watercolor paint. Use round, pointed brushes, both thin and thick. Also, try bamboo brushes.

16. Use a watercolor brush and ink or watercolor paint to make a series of five calligraphic studies of one natural object, such as a leaf or vegetable. See Figure 5-35.

TECHNIQUE TIP

Calligraphic Lines

Mastering the technique of drawing with flowing, calligraphic lines takes practice. You will need a round watercolor brush and either watercolor paint or ink. First, practice making very thin lines (Figure 5-32). Dip your brush in the ink or paint and wipe the brush slowly on the side of the ink bottle until the bristles form a point. Then hold the brush at the metal ferrule so the brush is vertical rather than slanted above the paper. Imagine that the brush is a pencil with a very sharp point—if you press down, you will break the point. Touch the paper lightly with the tip of the brush and draw a line.

When you are able to control a thin line, you are ready to make calligraphic lines. Start with a thin line and gradually press the brush down to make the line thicker. Pull up again to make it thinner (Figure 5-33). Practice making lines that vary in thickness.

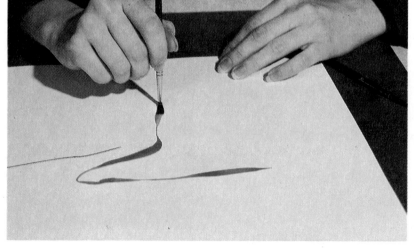

Figure 5.32 (above)   Hold the brush vertically.

Figure 5.33 (at right)   Press down, then pull up.

Figure 5.34 Shojo blends the shapes and colors of the flowers with the flowing lines of the written characters to create a unified visual expression of his idea.

Shōkadō Shōjō. *Hollyhocks.* c. 1615–20. Ink, gold, and silver on colored paper. 20.2 × 17.6 cm (7¹⁵⁄₁₆ × 6¹⁵⁄₁₆"). The Metropolitan Museum of Art, New York, New York. Purchase. Mrs. Jackson Burke Gift, 1979.

Figure 5.35 Student work. A drawing made with calligraphic lines.

G. Research and report to the class on the evolution of the English alphabet. Make drawings to show how some pictures gradually changed into sound symbols.

H. Research and report to the class on Egyptian hieroglyphics, or "picture writing."

I. Find a book in your school or public library on Oriental brush painting. Learn to make some of the special brush strokes. Demonstrate them to the class.

TECHNIQUE TIP

Cleaning a Paint Brush

Rinsing a paint brush under running water will not clean it completely. Paint will remain inside the bristles and cause the brush to quickly lose its shape. Use the following procedure to help your brushes last a long time.

1. Rinse the thick paint out of the brush under running water.
2. Gently "paint" the brush over a cake of mild soap, or dip it into a mild liquid detergent.
3. Gently scrub the brush in the palm of your hand to work the soap into the center of the brush. This will remove paint that you did not realize was still in the brush.
4. Rinse the brush under running water while you continue to scrub your palm.
5. Repeat steps 2, 3, and 4.
6. When your brush is thoroughly rinsed, shape it into a point with your fingers.
7. Place the brush in a container with the bristles up so it will retain its shape until dry.

Figure 5.36A   Use soap.

Figure 5.36B   Gently work the paint out of your brush.

Figure 5.36C   Shape your brush carefully.

Line and Value

Value is the art element that refers to darkness or light. Value depends on how much light a surface reflects. A surface has a dark value if it reflects little light. It has a light value if it reflects a lot of light. Because value is closely related to the way every element and principle of art works, it will be mentioned throughout *ArtTalk*.

Every time you make a pencil mark on a piece of white paper, you are creating a line with a certain value. The harder you press, the darker the value. A series of closely placed lines can create areas of dark value. The lines may be parallel or they may cross each other. The technique of using crossed lines for shading is called **crosshatching.** You will learn more about crosshatching in Chapter 6.

The values that line groups create depend on many things: the number of lines, the size of the spaces between the lines, the media, and the tools. A soft pencil (2B, 4B) makes a wide, dark line. A hard pencil (2H, 4H) makes a thin, gray line. A crayon stroked over a rough surface makes a broken line. A crayon stroked over smooth paper makes a dark, solid line.

Look at the Dürer etching in Figure 5-1 on page 60. Use a magnifying glass to study the way Dürer has used a variety of line combinations to create dark and light values. What method did he use in the lightest areas? How did he create the darkest values? How many different kinds of line combinations can you find? How many different uses does Dürer make of line in this one work?

DEVELOPING YOUR SKILLS

17. Fold a small sheet of white drawing paper into sixteen squares. In each square use a different combination of parallel or crosshatched lines (see page 112) to create a different value (Figure 5-37). Try a variety of pencils, from hard 2H to soft 4B lead. Try quill pens, ballpoint pens, and felt-tip pens. Think of some other tools and materials to use.

18. Create a crosshatched value scale using a medium HB pencil on white paper. First, draw a long, thin rectangle using a ruler. Divide the rectangle into seven parts. Leave the far-left section blank. The section on the far right should be as black as you can make it. Crosshatch the middle section so that it is a middle gray. Now crosshatch the other squares so the values move in gradual steps from white to black.

Figure 5.37   Student work. Using lines to create values.

IMAGINE AND CREATE

The activities in this section are different in several ways from the activities you have been doing so far. These in-depth activities will take more of your time. You will also need to be more creative. The projects are designed to help you use the concepts and skills you have learned in the chapter.

You and your teacher will have to decide how many of the projects you will undertake. Time, space, equipment, and supplies should be considered. Your interest and your ability are also important.

The projects are set up so that you can work either on your own or with the class. If you work on your own, read the directions several times to be sure you understand each step before you begin. Use the evaluation checklist as you work to be sure you don't skip an important step.

Yarn Painting

MATERIALS

You will need the following:

Sketching paper

Heavy cardboard or white poster board

White glue in a squeeze bottle

Yarn of various colors and textures

Scissors

Pencil and ruler

Toothpicks or paperclips

Poster board

Damp sponge and towels

OBJECTIVE

Design and create a yarn painting by gluing sets of parallel strands of yarn to cardboard, as in Figures 5-38, 5-39, and 5-40. Use a variety of patterns, colors, and textures. Cover the entire cardboard surface so no cardboard shows. Mount or mat the finished work for display.

DIRECTIONS

Before you start, cover your work space with newspaper and locate a flat surface on which the work can be stored to dry. Collect all of your materials, including the colors and types of yarn you will use for each area.

Use the sketching paper to sketch several ideas for your yarn painting. Your designs or pictures should be simple, with just a few large shapes. Do not plan any small details. Select the best design or picture and draw it on the cardboard.

Spread the glue over one area of the design. Use the nozzle as a spreader. Then press the yarn into the glue with toothpicks or unbent paperclips, as in Figure 5-41. Fill each area with sets of touching parallel strands. Do not leave any space between them.

In your design, run the yarn strands in different directions for different areas. Note the way the strands were placed in the student example. The yarn forms S-curve patterns in the neck and tail and horizontal patterns in the legs of the dragon.

Figure 5.38 (at right)   Student work. A dragon made with yarn strands.

Figure 5.39 (below)   Student work. The student's name is done in Hindi, the language of India.

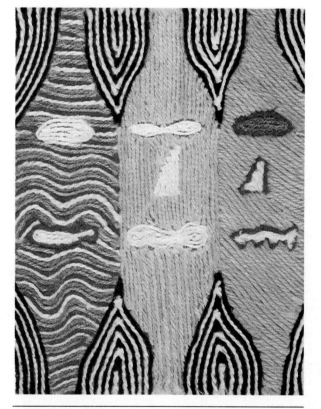

Figure 5.40 (above)   Student work. Abstract patterns in yarn.

Figure 5.41 (at left)   Be sure that the yarn is pressed down into the wet glue. Keep your pressing tool clean so the yarn won't stick to it.

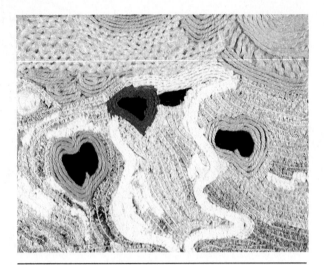

Figure 5.42 Student work. Yarn painting.

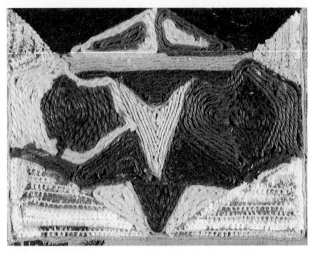

Figure 5.43 Student work. Yarn painting.

Arrange the yarn in ways that fit your design best. Some lines may cross a shape from side to side. Others may cross the shape from top to bottom. Some may start in the center of a shape and spiral outward. Some may start at the outer edge of a shape and move inward, strand by strand.

After the dragon in the example was drawn, dark green yarn was used to outline it. Then strands of yarn were added, working from the outline inward. In the background the spiral swirls in the sky were applied first, and then the white strands, until the entire space was covered.

Whatever method you use, be sure to cover the entire background and fill every space. If your fingers get sticky, use the damp sponge to clean off the glue. Between work sessions, be sure to store the work on a flat surface, uncovered, so nothing sticks to the glue.

Mount or mat the finished work for display.

EVALUATION CHECKLIST

Be sure you did the following:

1. Planned a design with large, simple shapes.
2. Used sets of parallel yarn strands.
3. Used lines running in different directions to fill in the different shapes.
4. Used a variety of yarn colors and textures.
5. Left no cardboard visible between the yarn strands.
6. Attached the yarn firmly to the cardboard.
7. Covered the work area, followed proper cleanup procedures, and stored the work in progress on a flat surface.
8. Prepared the yarn painting for display.

SAFETY NOTE

Do not use rubber cement and airplane glue for your projects. Both contain solvents that are harmful if inhaled or if left on the skin too long.

Contour Wire Sculpture

MATERIALS

You will need the following:

Your contour studies of one object

Needle-nose pliers

Wire clippers

Pliable wire

Optional:

small block of wood

staple gun or staple nail and hammer

string

(At right) Alexander Calder. *Sow.* 1928. Wire sculpture. 19.1 × 43.2 cm (7½ × 17″). Collection, The Museum of Modern Art, New York, New York. Gift of the artist.

OBJECTIVE

Study Calder's wire constructions on this page and the next. Design and create a contour wire sculpture based on your own contour drawings of a single object (page 76). Prepare your finished work for display.

Figure 5.44 (below and on next page)   Notice in Calder's sculptures how simple lines convey humor.

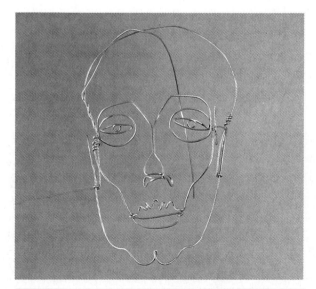

(Above) Alexander Calder. *Portrait of a Man.* 1929–30. Brass-wire sculpture. 22.2 × 32.7 × 34.3 cm (8¾ × 12⅞ × 13½″). Collection, The Museum of Modern Art, New York, New York. Gift of the artist.

(At left) Alexander Calder. *Hostess.* Wire sculpture. 29.2 cm (11½″) high. The Museum of Modern Art, New York, New York.

Alexander Calder. *Cow.* 1929. Wire sculpture. 16.5 × 40.6 cm (6½ × 16″). Collection, The Museum of Modern Art, New York, New York. Gift of Edward M. M. Warburg.

DIRECTIONS

Make a series of contour studies of one object having several parts. Make each drawing from a different point of view. These drawings must be from life, not from photographs. Some objects you might consider are a motorcycle, a car, a houseplant, a reclining chair, a face, a seated person, a rocking chair, or your desk. Do not limit yourself to this list. Think of something that is interesting to you.

Study the photographs of Alexander Calder's wire sculptures. Calder treats his work with a sense of humor. Notice how the wire is used for only a few essential lines. He has carefully joined the pieces so some connections are firm and some look as if the parts could move.

Collect your materials and experiment with some scrap wire. Use the pliers to bend, twist, loop, and cut the wire. The wire clippers can also be used, if needed. Then make a contour wire sculpture based on your drawings.

Prepare your work for display.

You may staple or nail your sculpture to a block of wood so it will stand, you may hang it with string, or you may plan it so the work is free-standing.

SAFETY NOTE

All cutting tools should be used with caution. Scissors, paper cutters, saws, knives, wood and linoleum cutters, metal snips, and wire cutters should be picked up or handed to someone by the handle, not by the blade.

EVALUATION CHECKLIST

Be sure you did the following:

1. Made a series of contour studies of one object.
2. Studied Calder's wire sculptures.
3. Experimented with scrap wire.
4. Made a contour-like wire sculpture based on your own drawings.
5. Cleaned up the work area.
6. Prepared the sculpture for display.

Glue-Line Prints

MATERIALS

You will need the following:

Your contour studies of one object (page 76)

Pencil

One piece of smooth, stiff cardboard, poster board, or illustration board to be used as the printing plate

White glue in a squeeze bottle

Toothpicks

Water-based printing ink

Piece of glass or any hard surface for rolling ink

Soft brayer

Paper for printing (newsprint, colored tissue, ditto paper, or construction paper) that is larger than the cardboard printing plate

Poster board or construction paper for mounting prints

A trash can placed near the printing area

Optional:

Polymer medium and brush

Figure 5.45 Student work. Glue-line print.

OBJECTIVE

Design and create raised glue-line prints (Figures 5-45 and 5-46) on a variety of paper, sign the prints, and mount or mat one.

DIRECTIONS

Make a series of contour drawings of one object.

Collect and organize all of your materials. Prepare two work spaces by covering them with newspaper. Find a flat surface where your work can be left to dry. You will also need a rack for drying the prints. If there is no drying rack, use a line with clothespins or tape the prints on a wall. The prints must be kept separate until dry.

Next, on the cardboard plate, draw a design based on your contour studies, being careful to let the design go all the way to the edges. Do not include small details.

Experiment by squeezing glue lines on scrap paper. Notice that thin lines shrink into dots of glue. Use a toothpick to break the surface tension and pull the glue into a line again. If you want thin lines, try dipping the top of the toothpick into glue and drawing with it. If you make a mistake with the glue, you can scrape it off while it is still wet.

When you have learned to control the glue lines, apply glue to your printing plate. Then let it dry until it looks clear (Figure 5-47).

Figure 5.46 Student work. Glue-line print.

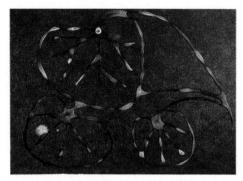

Figure 5.47 Let the glue dry until it looks clear.

Figure 5.48 Inking the printing plate.

If you wish to make more than five prints, brush a coat of polymer medium on the plate to waterproof it. Be sure the polymer is dry before you begin printing.

Place your printing plate on an extra sheet of newspaper that you can use to carry the plate. Squeeze a small amount of ink on the glass. Roll the brayer over the ink so the brayer is completely covered and the ink is sticky. Use strong pressure as you roll the brayer back and forth over the plate. The ink will fill the surface of the plate as well as the raised glue lines, but there will be an uninked area around the lines (Figure 5-48).

Carry the printing plate to your printing area and slide the plate onto new newspaper. Throw the inky carrying paper in the trash. You are now ready to make your print.

With clean hands, place a sheet of printing paper over the plate. Press down on the paper firmly and evenly, all over, using your hands. Begin in the center and work out to the edges. Use your fingers and thumbs as well as the fleshy part of your hands. You want to catch the large areas as well as the raised lines. But don't work too long or the paper will stick to the plate.

Pull the print off of the plate and place it in the drying area.

Try making a second print without re-inking. Experiment with different printing papers to see what different effects you can obtain.

Wash the brayer and inking plate at the end of each work session and throw away all of the inky newspaper.

When your print is dry, trim the edges if necessary, leaving some white space outside the design. Then, in the white space below the lower left corner of the print, write the title of the print in pencil. Sign your name in pencil below the lower right corner of the print.

Mount or mat at least one print for display.

EVALUATION CHECKLIST

Be sure you did the following:

1. Made a series of contour studies of one object.
2. Drew a design that covered the entire printing plate.
3. Experimented with glue lines as directed.
4. Applied glue to the printing plate and let it dry.
5. Followed all directions for inking and printing.
6. Signed the prints properly and prepared at least one for display.
7. Cleaned up the work area.

Foil Relief (Extension of Glue Print)

MATERIALS

You will need the following:

One piece of extra-heavy-duty aluminum foil larger than the printing plate

Ballpoint pen or dull pencil

Black, waterproof ink and brush

Poster board for mounting

OBJECTIVE

Make a foil relief (Figure 5-49) by covering the surface of the glue printing plate with foil. Decorate the flat areas of the foil with line patterns. Mount the finished relief for display.

DIRECTIONS

When you have finished the glue-print activity, place a piece of foil over the glue-print plate while the ink is still damp. The damp ink will act as an adhesive. Use your fingers to stretch and press the foil so the raised lines of the plate show through. When you are finished, fold the foil over the edges of the plate.

Now, by pressing a dull pencil or ballpoint pen into the foil, fill any flat areas with sets of parallel line patterns.

Brush black, waterproof ink over the design so it sinks into the line patterns. When the ink is perfectly dry, rub a flat piece of newspaper over the surface to remove the ink from the raised surfaces. Don't use a crumpled piece of paper. This could cause you to rub the ink out of the impressed lines as well.

Mount the foil relief on poster board for display.

EVALUATION CHECKLIST

Be sure you did the following:

1. Pressed foil on the printing plate while the ink was wet.
2. Rubbed the foil until all of the raised lines showed.
3. Made line patterns between the raised lines.
4. Inked and polished the design to accent the impressed lines.
5. Mounted the foil relief for display.
6. Cleaned up the work area.

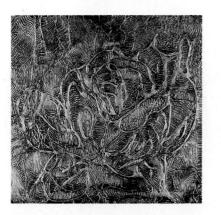

Figure 5.49 Student work. Foil relief.

Figure 5.50   Jacob Lawrence. *Cabinet Maker.* 1957. Casein on paper. 77.4 × 57 cm. (30½ × 22½"). Hirshhorn Museum and Sculpture Garden, Smithsonian Institution, Washington, D.C. Gift of Joseph H. Hirshhorn, 1966.

A R T   C R I T I C I S M

Improving Your Critical-Thinking Skills

Look at the painting, *Cabinet Maker* by Jacob Lawrence, in Figure 5-50. You may want to look back to Chapter 2 to review the art criticism steps before you begin this exercise.

Description: What Do You See?

Remember, the first step in art criticism—description—covers the subject matter of the work. Make a list of all the things you see in this painting. Do not guess—record just the facts. It is not enough, for example, to list *a man*. You must also tell what he is doing, what he is wearing, and everything else you notice about him. After you have described the man, list the other things you recognize. Write down every fact you observe.

Analysis: How Is the Work Organized?

Describe the way Lawrence has used line and value to give meaning to this painting.

Do you see any lines where the edge of one shape meets the edge of another?

Do you see outlines?

Do you see any implied lines?

What line variations does Lawrence use?

Can you find vertical, horizontal, diagonal, curved, or zigzag lines? Indicate where you find any directional lines.

Which line direction seems to dominate the painting? What sort of feeling does the dominant line give the painting?

Can you find any lines that look like contour or gesture lines? Do you see any calligraphic, flowing lines?

Does Lawrence use value contrasts? Where are the lightest values? The darkest?

Interpretation: What Is Happening? What Is the Artist Trying to Say?

Based on the facts you have collected, how would you interpret this work? Remember that just telling a story about the subject matter is not enough. You must discover the theme (meaning) or mood of the painting. Look at the clues you collected during analysis to help you find meaning. Remember, your ideas about what is happening and what the artist is trying to say will depend on your own experiences. Be prepared to defend those ideas.

Write a paragraph explaining your interpretation. Then write a new title for the painting. Your title should sum up your interpretation of the work.

Judgment: What Do You Think of the Work?

Now that you have completed description, analysis, and interpretation, you should be thoroughly familiar with *Cabinet Maker*. You are ready to make a sound judgment. Decide now whether you like the work or not. Give reasons for your judgment. You may use one or more of the theories of art to defend your opinion. To review the theories, look back to Chapter 2.

SOMETHING EXTRA

What kind of music do you think the man in *Cabinet Maker* would listen to? Name a specific piece of pop, rock, country, jazz, or classical music. Now, using the music you have chosen, plan and perform a pantomime (a play without words) or dance to illustrate this painting.

ABOUT THE ARTIST

Jacob Lawrence

Figure 5.51   Jacob Lawrence, American, 1917—

Jacob Lawrence's life is an American success story. He was born in Atlantic City, New Jersey, in 1917. When he was seven, the family moved to Philadelphia. They moved again in 1929 to New York City, just in time for the Great Depression, which brought hard times to all Americans. Because Lawrence was black, he also had to deal with racial prejudice.

During the Depression, the government established a program, called the *Federal Arts Project*, to help artists. The program created jobs for artists so they could support themselves and their families. Many famous American artists survived the Depression through government support. For instance, some of our best artists were employed as teachers in community art centers.

Jacob Lawrence was lucky to live near the Harlem Community Art Center, and he had many excellent teachers, including Charles Alston. Alston noticed that Lawrence had unusual talents, and he tutored him until Lawrence won a scholarship to the American Artists School. While Lawrence attended the school, he created a number of paintings featuring outstanding black people, such as Toussaint L'Ouverture, Frederick Douglass, and Harriet Tubman. For Jacob Lawrence, single pictures were not enough to express all he wanted to say. So he made paintings in series. His series about Frederick Douglass, for example, turned out to be thirty-three pictures.

Lawrence had his first one-man show in 1939 at the Harlem YWCA. His work became well known in 1941, when he exhibited in a show called "American Negro Art: Nineteenth and Twentieth Centuries." At the same time, *Fortune Magazine* published twenty-six of his paintings from a series called *The Migration of the Negro*.

As with many other Americans, Jacob Lawrence's life and career were interrupted by World War II. He served in the U.S. Coast Guard and painted a series of works about his experiences. The paintings were displayed at the Museum of Modern Art in 1944.

Lawrence painted *Cabinet Maker* in 1957. It is from a series called *The Builders*. The series centers around the tools that people have developed over the centuries. Lawrence feels that the forms of tools are both beautiful and exciting.

Gouache, the medium Lawrence used most often, is an opaque watercolor. He used *casein* paint, which contains a binder derived from milk, to make *Cabinet Maker*. Both gouache and casein resemble school temperas or poster paints.

Chapter 5 Review: Talking about Art

USING THE LANGUAGE OF ART

For each new art term below, choose a work of art from this chapter. Then write a sentence about that work using the new term correctly in the sentence.

contour lines   implied lines
crosshatching   line
dimension   static
calligraphy   value
gesture

LEARNING THE ART ELEMENTS AND PRINCIPLES

1. Name the five main kinds of lines. Tell which three do not change direction, which kind changes direction gradually, and which changes direction suddenly.
2. Name five major ways in which lines can vary.
3. What kind of line has often been connected with religious feelings? Why is this?
4. Which type of line—gesture or contour—is most often used to represent the interior of an object?
5. What type of line is often made with brush strokes that change from thin to thick in one stroke?
6. What are four factors that affect the value of groups of lines?

INCREASING YOUR ART AWARENESS

1. Choose one of the photographs in Figure 5-2. Name the kinds of lines you see and the ways in which those lines vary.
2. Choose an artwork from this chapter that you feel shows the widest variety of lines. What kinds of lines do you see?
3. From the artworks shown in Chapters 1 through 5, give five examples of lines made with different tools or materials.
4. What photograph of architecture in Chapter 3 shows how vertical lines have been used to express a religious feeling?

5. Name a painting in this chapter that expresses calmness and one that expresses excitement. How were these different effects created?

UNDERSTANDING ART CULTURE AND HERITAGE

1. Name three works of art shown in this chapter that were created by American artists.
2. Name one artwork shown in this chapter that was created in the fifteenth century.
3. Name one work of art shown in this chapter for each of the following centuries: 16th, 17th, and 18th. Which one is a non-Western work?
4. What artist whose work you studied in this chapter is also known for creating mobiles?
5. Find the work in this chapter done by an artist who focused on the beauty and abundance of America (see Chapter 3). List another work by this artist from Chapter 3.

JUDGING THE QUALITY OF ART

Imagine that you are a German art critic in the year 1495. Albrecht Dürer has just presented his new drawing, *An Oriental Ruler Seated on His Throne* (Figure 5-1). Write a review of this drawing using the four steps of art criticism. Use the questions from the analysis of the *Cabinet Maker* (page 90) to help you analyze the lines during step two. In the fourth step you must decide whether this work is worth seeing or purchasing.

LEARNING MORE ABOUT ART

Find some books at the library about Chinese, Japanese, or Persian art before the twentieth century. Study the reproductions in the books and then prepare a report for your class describing the use of line in the art from that country. Use visual aids to help make your report as interesting and creative as possible.

Figure 6.1 Leonardo da Vinci completed very few paintings. *Ginevra de Benci* is his only work permanently exhibited in the United States. It is one of three portraits of women, the most famous being the *Mona Lisa,* that he painted.

Leonardo da Vinci. *Ginevra de'Benci.* c. 1474. Paint on wood. 38.8 × 36.7 cm (15¼ × 14½″). National Gallery of Art, Washington, D.C. Ailsa Mellon Bruce Fund.

Shape, Form, and Space

After reading this chapter and doing the exercises, you will be able to

- ☐ explain the difference between shapes and forms.
- ☐ create two- and three-dimensional works of art.
- ☐ observe more carefully the shapes and forms in the space around you.
- ☐ understand point of view and perspective.
- ☐ use point of view and perspective to create drawings and paintings.
- ☐ understand the expressive qualities, or meanings, of shapes, forms, and spaces in a work of art.

WORDS TO LEARN

In this chapter you will learn the meanings of the words listed below.

assemblage	shape
chiaroscuro	silhouette
form	space
free-form shapes	
geometric shapes	
perspective	

You live in space, in a world full of objects. Each object—whether it be a car, an apple, this book, or you—has a shape or form. Often it is by their shapes or forms that you recognize objects. You identify a stop sign in the distance by its shape long before you can read the word "Stop" on it. You identify a friend in the distance long before you see a face.

Shape, form, and space are all closely related to one another. They are elements of art, and artists use their knowledge of how these elements work together to speak the language of art. In this chapter you will learn how to "read" the meaning of these elements and how to use them to express your own ideas and feelings.

DEVELOPING YOUR SKILLS

1. Look out a window. Take the time to become fully aware of the scene outside the window. Then, without naming any objects, list and describe the shapes, forms, and spaces that you see. Read this description in class. Can your classmates guess what you are describing?
2. Look around the space in which you are sitting. Describe three shapes in this space without naming the objects. Can your classmates guess the objects when you read your description?

Figure 6.2   Shadow is the shape of darkness.

Photography by Robert Nix.

Figure 6.3   Geometric shapes.

Shapes

A **shape** is a two-dimensional area that is defined in some way. A shape may have an outline or boundary around it, or you may recognize it by its area, such as in Figure 6-2. For instance, if you draw the outline of a square on a sheet of paper, you have created a shape. You could also create the same shape without an outline by painting the area of the square red.

You see many two-dimensional shapes every day. They are found in most designs, which in turn can be seen on many flat surfaces. Look for them on such things as floor coverings, fabrics, and wallpapers. Floors and walls are two-dimensional shapes. Table tops, book pages, posters, and billboards are others.

One type of shape is the **silhouette,** which originally meant a profile portrait that looked like a solid shadow. Now it is used to describe any two-dimensional, shadow-like shape (Figure 6-4).

All shapes can be classified as either *geometric* or *free-form*. **Geometric shapes** are precise shapes

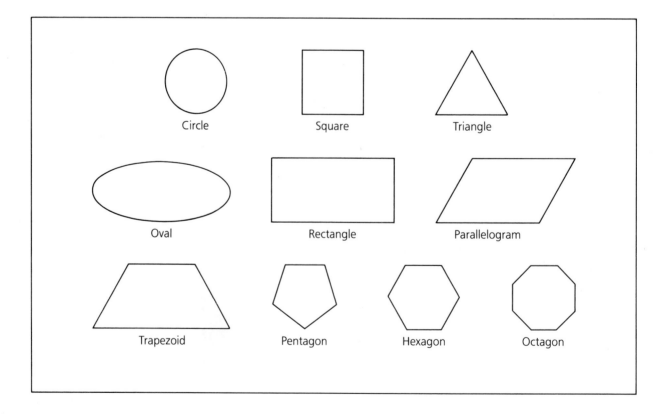

Figure 6.4 This weather vane, representing the Angel Gabriel blowing his trumpet, was silhouetted against the New England sky. It symbolized the strong religious feelings in New England during the mid-nineteenth century.

Gabriel weathervane. Index of American Design. National Gallery of Art, Washington, D.C.

that can be described using mathematical formulas (Figure 6-3). The basic geometric shapes are the circle, the square, and the triangle. All other geometric shapes are either variations or combinations of these basic shapes. Some of the variations include the oval, rectangle, parallelogram, trapezoid, pentagon, pentagram, hexagon, and octagon.

Geometric shapes are used for decoration, uniformity, and organization. Road signs, for example, must be uniform. The same kind of sign must always have the same shape. Do you know the shape of a stop sign? Which shape is used for "Yield?" Which shape is used for TV screens? Why do you think ceiling tiles and window panes have geometric shapes?

Free-form shapes are irregular and uneven shapes (Figure 6-5). Their outlines may be curved, angular, or a combination of both. They often occur in nature. Free-form shapes may be silhouettes of living things, such as animals, people, or trees.

Figure 6.5 Free-form shapes.

DEVELOPING YOUR SKILLS

3. Search your pockets or purse for objects small enough to fit on an overhead projector. Place the objects, one at a time, on the projector. Project the silhouette of the object on a screen or blank wall. Then draw only the outline of each object on a piece of white paper. After you have drawn several shapes, cut them out carefully. Arrange and glue them on a dark background.

4. Using the printed areas of a newspaper, make two cut-paper designs. Make one design by measuring and cutting precise geometric shapes. Make the second design by tearing free-form shapes. Arrange the shapes and glue them on a sheet of black construction paper. Use a white crayon to print the words "free form" and "geometric" on the appropriate design. Try to make the letters for "geometric" look geometric, and the letters for "free-form" look free-form.

SOMETHING EXTRA

A. Ask your science teacher for permission to look at a drop of water through a microscope. Draw the free-form shapes you see. Discuss this activity with your science teacher, who may make other suggestions for sources of free-form shapes.

B. Look up the mathematical formulas for some geometric shapes. Make some charts to report your findings to the class.

Figure 6.6 Do you see the relationship between two-dimensional shapes and three-dimensional forms?

Forms

Although the words *shape* and *form* are often used interchangeably in everyday language, they have different meanings in the language of art. **Forms** are objects having three dimensions. Like shapes they have both length and width. But forms also have depth. *You* are a three-dimensional form. So is a tree or a table.

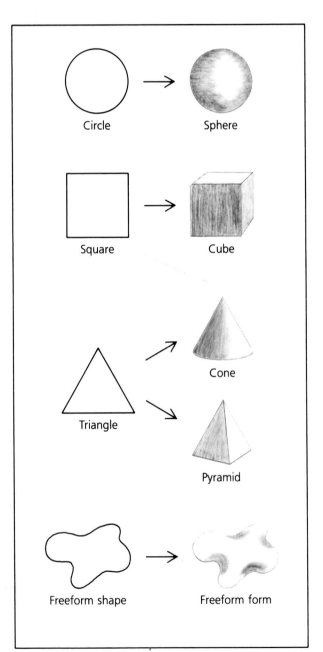

Circle → Sphere

Square → Cube

Triangle → Cone

Triangle → Pyramid

Freeform shape → Freeform form

Figure 6.7 Cézanne painted solid, massive-looking forms by omitting details and reducing objects to basic geometric forms. The houses in this painting are solid looking, and the rocks look heavy.

Paul Cézanne. *Houses in Provence.* c. 1880. Oil on canvas. 65 × 81.3 cm (25⅝ × 32″). National Gallery of Art, Washington, D.C. Collection of Mr. and Mrs. Paul Mellon.

Two-dimensional shapes and three-dimensional forms are related. The end of a cylinder is a circle. One side of a cube is a square (Figure 6-6). A triangle can "grow" into a cone or a pyramid.

Like shapes, forms may be either geometric or free-form. Geometric forms are used in construction, for organization, and as parts in machines. Look around you. What forms were used to build your school, your church, your home? Are they like those in Figure 6-7? Look under the hood of a car. What forms were used to build the motor? Did you know that common table salt is made of a series of interlocking cubes? You can see these cubes when you look at salt through a microscope.

Free-form objects include such things as stones, puddles, and clouds. Your own body and the bodies of animals and plants are free-forms.

DEVELOPING YOUR SKILLS

5. Make a flat sheet of construction paper into a three-dimensional paper sculpture by using cutting and scoring techniques (see below). Give your sculpture a minimum of five different surfaces. Do not cut the paper into separate pieces. Use only slots and tabs if you wish to join any parts. Experiment with scrap paper before you make your final paper sculpture.

6. Choose either of two materials to make three-dimensional forms. Model a cube, a cylinder or sphere, and a cone or pyramid from clay, or construct them with paper.

7. Find a three-dimensional geometric object. Use a water-based felt-tip pen to draw its contours. Next, find a three-dimensional free-form object. Using brush and ink, draw it with flowing, calligraphic contour lines.

SOMETHING EXTRA

C. Draw a building or a motor using a pencil and mechanical drawing tools, such as a ruler, a compass, and a protractor. Make a diagram of the main geometric forms you see. Draw every line with a tool. Do not draw small details.

TECHNIQUE TIP

Scoring Paper

Neat, sharp folds can be made in a variety of papers if you score them first.

To score a straight fold, place a ruler on the paper where you want the fold. Run the sharp point of a knife or a pair of scissors along the ruler's edge, without cutting through the paper. This will weaken the paper, causing it to fold precisely along the score.

You can also score curved lines, but you must do this with gradually bending curves or wide arcs. If you try to make a tight curve, such as a semicircle, the paper will not give. For a tight curve you will have to make cuts to relieve the tension.

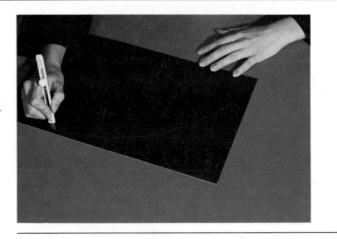

Figure 6.8 Scoring a curve.

Figure 6.9 Bending a curve.

Space and Its Relationship to Shape and Form

Shapes and forms exist in **space,** which is the emptiness or area between, around, above, below, or within objects. All objects take up space. *You*, for example, are a living, breathing form moving through space.

Shapes and forms are defined by the space around and within them. They depend on space for their existence. This is why it is important to understand the relationship of space to shapes and forms.

Positive and Negative Spaces

In both two- and three-dimensional art, the shapes or forms are called the *positive area*, or the *figure*. The empty spaces between the shapes or forms are called *negative spaces* or *ground* (Figure 6-10). In a portrait, for example, the image of the person is the positive space; the negative space is the area surrounding the person (Figure 6-11).

The shape and size of negative spaces affect the way you interpret the positive spaces. Large negative spaces around positive spaces may say "lonely" or "free" (Figure 6-12 on the next page). When the positive spaces are crowded together, you may feel "tension" or "togetherness." The full meaning of

Figure 6.10 Drawings like this have been used for years to explain the relationship of positive and negative spaces. If you think of the white area as the positive space, you see a white vase against a dark background. But if you concentrate on the dark shapes as the positive areas, you see two profiles.

Figure 6.11 In this portrait of a young princess, it is easy to tell the positive space—the young girl—from the negative space—the dark background.

Lucas Cranach, the Elder. *A Princess of Saxony.* c. 1517. Paint on wood. 43.6 × 34.3 cm (17⅛ × 13½"). National Gallery of Art, Washington, D.C. Ralph and Mary Booth Collection.

Figure 6.12 The young men in this painting are playing a game, but it seems joyless. The artist has used the negative spaces between the young men to express a sense of loneliness.

Ben Shahn. *Handball.* 1939. Tempera on paper over composition board. 57.8 × 79.4 cm (22¾ × 31¼"). Collection, The Museum of Modern Art, New York, New York. Abby Aldrich Rockerfeller Fund.

the work depends on the way these elements work together.

It is not always easy to tell which are the positive and which are the negative spaces in two-dimensional art. Sometimes it is hard to find any negative space. This is because some artists give equal emphasis to both the figure and the ground.

Some artists even try to confuse the viewer. They create positive and negative spaces that reverse themselves while you are looking at them. These visual puzzles fascinate some viewers (Figure 6-13).

DEVELOPING YOUR SKILLS

8. Cut a large geometric shape from a sheet of black paper. Then cut the shape into nine or more separate pieces. Re-form the pieces into the original shape on a large sheet of white paper. Expand the shape by gradually sliding the pieces apart. Experiment with different amounts of space between the pieces; then glue down the best arrangement. You may not add or subtract any pieces from the original number, and the original shape must be recognizable.

9. Select a group of objects to draw. Make an arrangement with a variety of negative spaces between the shapes. Draw the arrangement lightly with pencil or chalk. Finish the work by (a) coloring only the negative spaces with crayons or paint, or (b) filling the negative

Figure 6.13 Escher is a master of optical illusion. Follow one flight of steps and see what you discover. Notice how walls become floors, and floors turn into walls.

M. C. Escher. *Relativity.* 1953. Lithograph. The National Gallery of Art, Washington, D.C. Cornelius Van S. Roosevelt Collection.

spaces with closely drawn sets of parallel lines. Leave the positive spaces empty. What shapes did the negative spaces take?

10. Use a viewing frame (see the next page) to help you study the negative spaces in and around an ordinary chair. Hold the frame so the edges of the chair touch the edges of the frame. Draw the shapes of the negative spaces in and around the chair. Color the negative spaces or fill them with similar patterns. Leave the positive spaces empty.

Viewing Frame

A viewing frame helps you focus in on an area or object that you intend to draw.

To make the viewing frame, cut a small rectangle approximately 1″ × 2″ in the center of a sheet of paper. Hold the frame at arm's length and look through it at your subject.

Imagine that the opening represents your drawing paper. You can decide how much of the subject you want to include in your drawing by moving the frame up, down, or sideways. You can also move it closer or farther away.

Figure 6.14 Use a viewing frame to concentrate on an area for a drawing.

Space in Three-Dimensional Art

"Over," "under," "through," "behind," and "around" are words that describe three-dimensional space. Architecture, sculpture, weaving, ceramics, and jewelry are three-dimensional art forms. They all take up real space. You can walk around, look through, peek behind, peer over, and reach into three-dimensional art.

Architects shape space. They design structures that enclose a variety of spaces for people. They create large spaces for group activities, such as you

see in Figure 6-15. They also create small spaces for privacy. Landscape architects and city planners are also involved in planning spaces for people to use.

Negative areas in three-dimensional art are very real. Most three-dimensional works are meant to be *freestanding*, which means that they are surrounded by negative areas (Figure 6-16). The viewer must move through these negative areas to see all of the different views of a three-dimensional work.

Relief sculpture is not intended to be freestanding. It projects out from a flat surface into negative

Figure 6.15 The architect designed this auditorium to seat representatives from every country in the world. It was designed to look as if it could hold all of the world's people.

Wallace Kirkman Harrison. United Nations Buildings. 1949. New York, New York. Assembly Building, Main Auditorium. Photography by Sandak, Inc., Stamford, Connecticut.

Figure 6.16 The negative shapes that pierce the shell of this form are as important to the structure as the solid bronze. They create the feeling of a person. The small, curved opening at the top defines an area that could be a face surrounded by hair or a hood. Use your imagination to help you find other human qualities in the work.

Dame Barbara Hepworth. *Figure for Landscape.* 1960. Bronze sculpture. 269.2 × 128.3 × 67.3 cm. (106 × 50½ × 26½"). Hirshhorn Museum and Sculpture Garden, Smithsonian Institution, Washington, D.C. Gift from Joseph H. Hirshhorn, 1966.

Figure 6.17   This ancient relief of a lion is not carved. It was constructed of molded and glazed bricks. The lion was one of sixty pairs that lined an important street in the ancient city of Babylon.

Mesopotamian, Babylonian. Panel: walking lions in relief (one of a pair). 605–562 B.C. Bricks; tin-enameled earthenware, molded and glazed in colors. 97.2 × 227.3 cm (3′2¼ × 7′5½″). Present thickness 7.6 cm (3″). The Metropolitan Museum of Art, New York, New York. Fletcher Fund, 1931.

space, as seen in Figure 6-17. You can find relief sculpture on ceramic pots and plaster ceilings. When the positive areas project slightly from the flat surface, the work is called *bas-relief*, or *low relief*. When the positive areas project far out, the work is called *high relief*.

Most jewelry is planned as relief sculpture to decorate human surfaces. The inside of a ring or the back of a pendant is smooth. It is not meant to be seen; it simply rests on the person's surface.

Printmakers make relief prints. Relief designs can also be molded in handmade paper.

Today many artists are experimenting and changing traditional art forms. Printmakers are creating relief prints. Some are molding relief designs in handmade paper. Painters are adding a third dimension to the painted surface. Some are cutting or tearing real negative spaces in two-dimensional surfaces.

Weaving also has gone in new directions. It started as a practical craft, with weavers making two-dimensional fabrics for clothing. Today hand weavers are creating relief hangings and three-dimensional woven sculptures. An art form has evolved from a practical craft.

Photographers are creating *holograms* (images in three dimensions created with a laser beam). Sculptors are making kinetic, or moving, sculpture. Some artists are beginning to team up with engineers to create art with computers.

DEVELOPING YOUR SKILLS

11. For one week list the different enclosed spaces you use. Arrange the list in order of size. Think about large spaces that you share with many people and small private spaces that you use alone.

12. Make a freestanding, three-dimensional design that projects into negative space on all sides. Using pieces of cardboard tubing and small boxes, join the design pieces with glue and tape. Paint the finished work in one color so the form is emphasized. Set up a spotlight and turn your sculpture in different ways so its shadow changes.

13. Make a cardboard relief design by gluing layers of flat cardboard shapes onto a flat piece of cardboard. Cover the finished design with foil or paint it.

How You Perceive Shape, Form, and Space

Look up from this book to an object across the room to see if you can feel the movement of your eye muscles. If you didn't feel anything, try again until you are aware of your eyes working to refocus.

You have just taken a trip through visual space. Your brain measured the amount of space between you and the object and sent a message to your eye muscles to adjust. The muscles then refocused your eyes so that you could clearly see the object you were looking at.

Perceiving Depth

Your eyes and brain work together to enable you to see in three dimensions—*length*, *width*, and *depth*. Each eye sees an object from a slightly different angle. The brain merges these two separate and slightly different views into one, creating a three-dimensional image.

Have you ever looked through a hand-held slide viewer? If so, you have seen depth created artificially. The viewer is made so that each of your eyes receives a separate image. Your brain merges the two images into one, and, as a result, that image appears to have three dimensions.

The same principle is used for 3-D movies. You must watch these movies through special glasses that cause the eyes to see two different images. Because the brain is then "tricked" into thinking it sees depth, it merges the two images into one.

DEVELOPING YOUR SKILLS

14. Try this experiment by following each step carefully.
    - Cover your right eye. Point with your finger to a specific spot in the room. Note the position of the spot now.
    - Without moving your pointing finger, cover your left eye. Note how the spot looks now.

- Again, without moving your pointing finger, uncover both eyes and focus on the tip of your finger.
- Describe exactly what you saw in each step of this experiment. Based on your experience, what can you conclude about someone who is blind in one eye? Can this person function as well as someone with two good eyes? Can he or she drive a car? Explain your conclusions.

Point of View

The shapes and forms you see depend on your *point of view*. Your point of view is the angle from which you see an object. Another person, at another location, will see the same shape or form differently. For example, a person looking down on a circle drawn on the sidewalk sees a round shape. If that person lies on the ground beside the circle and looks at it, the circle will appear to have an oblong shape. A person looking at the front end of a car will see a form different from the form a person looking at the side of that same car sees. Figure 6-18 (on the next page) shows three different views of a sculpture.

You can learn about points of view by doing the following experiments. Place your hand flat on the desk and spread your fingers apart. The shape and form you see are the shape and form you would probably draw. They are part of the mental image you have of the object "hand." Now lift your hand and let your fingers relax. Notice how the shape and form of your hand change. Turn your hand and watch what happens. Your hand is still the same hand. Only its shape and form are different.

Next, look at a rectangular table. What shape does the top have when you are sitting at the table? Look at the top through a rectangular viewing frame. Are the edges of the table parallel to the edges of the frame? You know the top is a rectangle, but does it really look rectangular now? What shape does the top seem to take if you are sitting across the room from it? What would the shape look like from the top of a tall ladder? Do you think the shape you see will change if you lie on the floor directly under the table?

Figure 6.18 (above)   Notice how the feeling expressed by this ceramic sculpture changes as your point of view changes. You must view sculpture from all angles to truly understand it.

Bob Owens. *Warrior with Carnivorous Helmet*. Ceramic sculpture. Private collection.

Figure 6.19   Notice the shape the artist has used to represent the top of this table. What does that shape tell you about the artist's point of view?

Henri de Toulouse-Lautrec. *Monsieur Boileau at the Cafe*. 1893. Gouache on cardboard. 80 × 64.8 cm (31½ × 25½"). The Cleveland Museum of Art, Cleveland, Ohio. Hinman B. Hurlbut Collection.

When you looked at your hand, your eyes stayed in the same place, but your hand moved. When you studied the table, it remained in one place, but you moved. In both cases, what you saw changed because your relationship to the object changed. Your point of view depends on where you are and where the object is.

DEVELOPING YOUR SKILLS

15. Study the three photographs of a baseball glove in Figure 6-20. Each picture looks different because the relationship between the camera and the glove changes. Using a pencil, make a contour drawing of each view of the glove. Go over the outline of each glove with a crayon or watercolor marker to emphasize shape changes.

16. Look through magazines for three or more different views of one type of object. Look for TV sets, sofas, spoons, toasters, cars, or shoes. Cut out the objects and mount each one on a sheet of typing paper. Emphasize the changes in shape by drawing around each outline with crayon or marker.

SOMETHING EXTRA

D. Photograph one of your favorite possessions from many different points of view. For each photo try to change the outline of the object by moving the camera or the object. Mount the photos on white poster board for display. Give your work a creative title.

Figure 6.20 How does your perception of the glove change in each view?

Photography by Robert Nix.

Figure 6.21   Matisse cut the shapes for this work directly from sheets of paper that he had colored with paint. He did not use anything to draw the shapes before he cut. Some of the shapes to look for are fish, sea animals, sea plants, and coral.

Henri Matisse. *Beasts of the Sea*. 1950. Paper on canvas (collage) 295.5 × 154.0 cm (116⅜ × 60⅝"). National Gallery of Art, Washington, D.C. Ailsa Mellon Bruce Fund.

How Artists Create Shapes and Forms in Space

Shapes and forms can be classified as *natural* or *manufactured*. Natural shapes and forms have been made by the forces of nature. For instance, animals and plants are natural forms. Manufactured forms are those made by people, whether mass-produced by the thousands in factories or made by hand. Many handmade things are unique, one of a kind.

Artists use many materials and techniques to make shapes. They concentrate on both outline and area. Some artists outline shapes in drawings and paintings. Others may paint shapes by placing brush strokes together without using even a beginning outline. They pour shapes and print shapes as well (Figure 6-21).

Like shapes, forms can be made in many ways. Artists model clay forms, mold metal forms, and carve forms from wood or stone. They use glass, plastics, bricks, and cement to make forms, as well as shapes.

The Illusion of Form

Artists can create the illusion of three-dimensional form on a two-dimensional surface. They can give the impression of depth and solidity by using changes in value. Figure 6-22 is an example.

The arrangement of light and shadow is called *chiaroscuro* (kī-är-ah-skyoó-rō). In Italian, *chiaro* means "bright," and *oscuro* means "dark." Chiaroscuro was introduced by Italian artists during the Renaissance. Figure 6-1 is an example. Later it was used for dramatic lighting effects by Baroque artists (Figure 12-5). Through careful observation, artists have learned how light is reflected from three-dimensional forms. They have learned the behavior of shadows. Today, chiaroscuro is often called *modeling* or *shading*.

Look, for instance, at an object with angular surfaces, such as a cube. You will see a large jump in value from one surface of the cube to the next. One surface may be very light in value and the next very dark. Now look at an object such as a baseball.

Figure 6.22 Giotto was the first artist to break away from the flat look of Byzantine painting. He studied the human form and used gestures and expressions that showed human qualities. Giotto's figures are so solid that they seem to be carved from rock.

Giotto. *Madonna and Child.* c. 1320/1330. Paint on wood. 85.5 × 62 cm (33⅝ × 24⅜"). National Gallery of Art, Washington, D.C. Samuel H. Kress Collection.

The curved surfaces of spheres and cylinders show gradual changes in value.

The area of a curved surface that reflects the most light is, of course, the lightest in a drawing. It is the area that the light rays hit most directly. *Highlights*, small areas of white, are used to show the very brightest spots. Starting at the highlights, the value changes gradually from light values of gray to dark gray. The darkest values are used to show areas that receive the least light. An area that is turned completely away from a light source is almost black. Look at Figure 6-24 to see the different ways an artist has created the illusion of form.

DEVELOPING YOUR SKILLS

17. Experiment with materials and techniques for shading curved and flat surfaces (see below). Use as many media as you can with each technique. Note those you like best.
18. Set up an arrangement of geometric forms. Use boxes and books, balls, and cylindrical containers. Study the way light reflects from the surfaces of the objects. Draw the arrangement. Give the shapes in your drawing the illusion of three dimensions by using the medium and shading technique of your choice. Use values that range from black to white, and employ many value steps between.
19. Using yourself as the model, make a shaded drawing of a face (Figure 6-25). Sit so you can look into a mirror. Set up a lamp to light your face from one side. Study the lights and shadows. Notice that there appears to be no edge to the side of your nose. It is a form with a rounded surface. Then, using the medium and shading technique that you prefer, model shadows and highlights. Avoid drawing contour lines. This drawing does not have to look like you.

TECHNIQUE TIP

Shading Techniques

The following techniques help create shading values.

Hatching: Shading with a series of fine parallel lines.

Crosshatching: Shading with two or more intersecting sets of parallel lines.

Blending: Shading through the smooth, gradual application of dark value. For example, pencil lines may be blended with a finger.

Stippling: Shading with dots.

To be effective in forming the shaded areas, your lines and strokes must follow the form of the object. Use lines to show the surface of a flat surface. Let the lines run parallel to one edge of the surface. To show a curved surface, draw a series of parallel curved lines to give the illusion of roundness. The lines should follow the curve of the object.

Lines or dots placed close together create dark values. Lines or dots spaced far apart create lighter values. In order to show a gradual change from light to dark, begin with lines or dots far apart and, bit by bit, bring them closer together.

Figure 6.23 Shading Techniques.

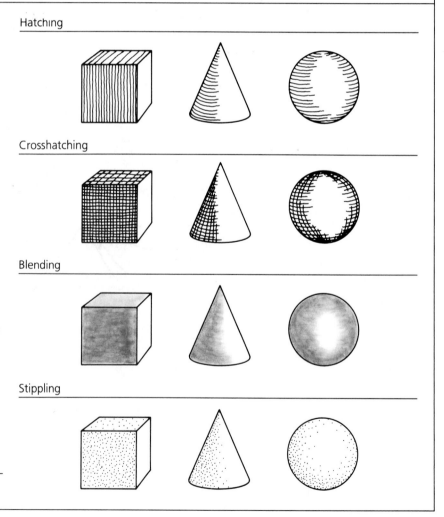

Hatching

Crosshatching

Blending

Stippling

Figure 6.24 This work is full of realistic details. Notice the different ways value is used. You can find the three jumps in value on the flat planes of the books. There are six books in this painting, and no two have been painted in the same way. Notice the very light book on the right: the front cover is slightly darker than the white spine. Notice how he changes value on the sheet of music to indicate bent corners. Now look for the curved surfaces: the blue ceramic pitcher, the pewter lamp, the ink well, the pipe, and the piccolo. Which object shows bright highlights? Identify and describe other ways Harnett has used value to create the illusion of form in this painting.

William M. Harnett. *My Gems.* 1888. Paint on wood. 45.7 × 35.5 cm (18 × 14″). National Gallery of Art, Washington, D.C. Gift of the Avalon Foundation.

Figure 6.25 Student work. A self-portrait.

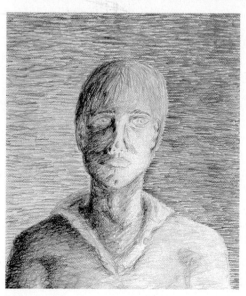

E. Choose a manufactured object, such as a telephone. Research the history of its form. Make a chart showing how and when the form changed over the years. Why do you think these changes occurred? Other items you might choose are ships, TV sets, sewing machines, shoes, eyeglasses, and cars.

F. Look around your environment for shapes and forms that have been made by people. Look for both mass-produced and handmade objects. List at least ten forms you notice and describe how you think they were made.

The Illusion of Depth

In their paintings artists often create the illusion of depth. When you look at these paintings, you see objects and shapes—some of which seem closer to you than others. You seem to be looking through a window into a real place (Figure 6-26).

This idea—that a painting should be like a window to the real world—has dominated traditional Western art since the early Renaissance.

The method for creating the illusion of depth on a two-dimensional surface is called **perspective.** In the following pages you will learn techniques artists use to give their paintings and drawings perspective.

Figure 6.26 Everything is carefully placed within the frame of this scene. In the foreground, figures dressed in bright robes kneel before the Christ Child. Beyond the human activity there is a background of calm, rolling green hills. Notice how the artist tries to focus your attention upon the Child. After reading about *perspective,* see if you find examples of each of the six devices used for creating perspective in this painting.

Botticelli. *The Adoration of the Magi.* Early 1480s. Paint on wood. 70.2 × 104.2 cm (27⅝ × 41″). National Gallery of Art, Washington, D.C. Andrew W. Mellon Collection.

There are several terms that will help you as you talk about and use perspective. The surface of a painting or drawing is sometimes called the *picture plane*. The part of the picture plane that appears nearest to you is the *foreground*. The part that appears farthest away is the *background*. The area in between is called the *middle ground*.

Overlapping

When one object covers part of a second object, the first seems to be closer to the viewer, as in Figure 6-27. However, this illusion works only when the objects are opaque. If they are made to look transparent, the viewer cannot tell which shape is in front and which is behind.

Size

Large objects appear to be closer to the viewer than small objects, as in Figure 6-28. The farther an object is from you, the smaller it appears. Cars far down the road seem to be much smaller than the ones nearer to you. If you stand at the end of a long hallway and raise your hand, you can block your view of a whole crowd of people. You know that each person is about your size, but at a distance the crowd appears to be smaller than your hand.

Placement

Objects that are placed either low or high on the picture plane seem to be closer to the viewer than objects placed closer to eye level. The most distant shapes are those that seem to be exactly at eye level (Figure 6-29).

Look at your feet and then look away along the floor. The farther away you look, the higher you raise your eyes. In looking up, you reverse the process. Ceiling tiles closest to you are high over your head. As you look farther away, you will feel your eyes lowering.

Detail

Objects with clear, sharp edges and visible details seem to be close to you (Figure 6-30). Objects that lack detail and have hazy outlines seem to be farther away. Look closely at your own hand. You can see very tiny lines clearly. Now look at the hand of someone across the room. You will have trouble seeing the lines between the fingers. All the details will seem to melt together.

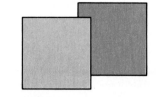
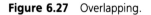

Figure 6.27 Overlapping.

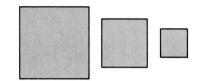

Figure 6.28 Size.

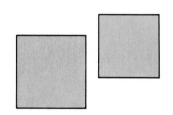

Figure 6.29 Placement.

Figure 6.30 Detail.

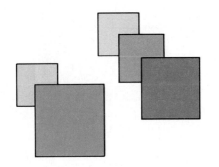

Figure 6.31   Color.

Color

Brightly colored objects seem closer to you, and objects with dull, light colors seem to be farther away (Figure 6-31). This is called *atmospheric perspective*. The air around us is not empty. It is full of moisture and dust that create a haze. The more air between you and an object, the more the object seems to fade. Have you ever noticed that trees close to you seem to be a much brighter green than trees farther down the road? You have probably been coloring mountains gray since first grade, but of course they aren't really gray.

Converging Lines

Linear perspective is one way of using lines to show distance and depth. As parallel lines move away from you, they seem to move closer together. When you look ahead on a highway, the sides of the road appear to be moving together. You don't worry, though, because you know this is an illusion. You know that the sides of the road ahead of you will be just as far apart as they are in your present position.

Sometimes lines appear to meet at a point on the horizon, called the *vanishing point* (Figure 6-32). In one-point linear perspective, all receding lines meet at a single point. In two-point linear perspective, different sets of parallel lines meet at different points (Figure 6-33). Because two-point perspective creates more diagonal lines in a painting, it seems more active. Renaissance artists used strict mathematical rules to calculate perspective. Most of today's artists rely on visual perception rather than mathematical rules (Figure 6-34).

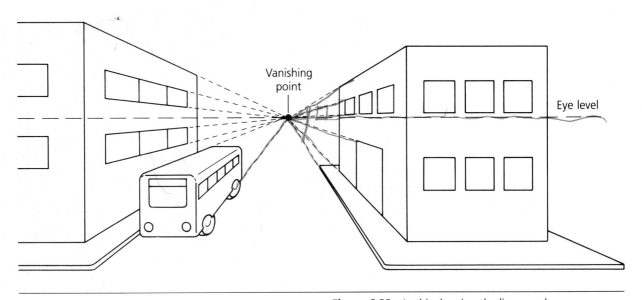

Figure 6.32   In this drawing the lines gradually come together and meet at one point in the distance. This is a one-point linear perspective.

Figure 6.33 In this drawing the lines come together and meet at *two* points. This is a two-point linear perspective.

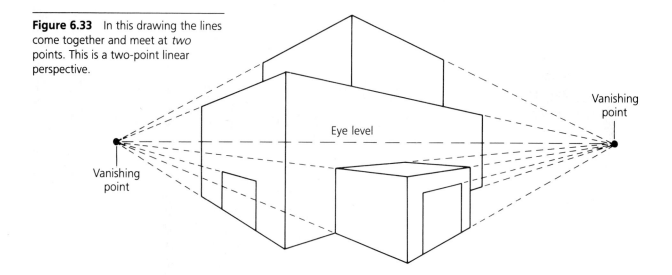

Vanishing point

Eye level

Vanishing point

Figure 6.34 Can you find the six perspective techniques in this scene?

Doris Lee. *Thanksgiving*. 1935. Oil on canvas. 71.4 × 101.6 cm (28.1 × 40"). The Art Institute of Chicago, Chicago, Illinois and Mr. and Mrs. Frank G. Logan. Purchase Prize, 1935.313 © 1987 The Art Institute of Chicago. All rights reserved.

DEVELOPING YOUR SKILLS

20. Create three different designs on three separate sheets of paper. Each design should contain five forms or shapes. Use the same five forms or shapes in each of the designs as follows:
    - Draw all of the items as close to the foreground as possible.
    - Draw one item close to the foreground and make the others look as if they are slightly farther back.
    - Draw one item close to the foreground, one far into the background, and the other three in the middle ground.

21. Cut out seven magazine photos of objects that are all related to each other, such as animals. Others might be plates of food, cars, shoes, furniture, and people. Each object should be a different size. Use overlapping, differing sizes, placement, varying detail, and color to create the illusion of depth. Arrange the cutouts on a dark sheet of paper and glue the pictures down. (Helpful hint: You can blur details and lighten colors in a magazine photograph by rubbing it lightly with an eraser.)

22. Find a newspaper or magazine photograph of rectangular solids, such as buildings or furniture (Figure 6-35). Use tracing paper and trace the main shapes. Mount the tracing paper on a large sheet of white paper. Use ruler and pencil to extend any parallel lines that recede (go back) into the distance (Figure 6-36). Determine the vanishing point(s) and the horizon line.

Figure 6.35 Cathedral interior.

Figure 6.36 A diagram showing linear perspective in the cathedral from Figure 6.35.

What Different Spaces, Shapes, and Forms Express

Shapes, forms, and spaces in art communicate certain feelings. This is possible because you associate them with similar shapes, forms, and spaces in real life. When you see a certain shape or form in a work of art, you may think of an object from real life. Any feelings you have about that object will affect your feelings about the artistic work. Artists use this relationship between art and your environment to communicate with you.

Outline and Surface

The outline of a shape and the surface of a form carry messages. Artists often use free-form shapes and forms to symbolize living things. When they want to please and soothe viewers, they use shapes and forms with smooth, curved outlines and surfaces (Figure 6-37). Forms that remind us of well-worn river rocks or curled-up kittens tempt us to touch them. These forms are comfortable. They appeal to us through our memories of pleasant touching experiences.

Angular shapes with zigzag outlines and forms with pointed projections remind us of sharp, jagged things (Figure 6-38 on the next page). We remember the pain caused by broken glass and sharp knives. We would never carelessly grab a pointed, angular form. If we were to touch it at all, we would do so very carefully.

Geometric shapes suggest mechanical perfection. It is impossible to draw a circle freehand with any degree of accuracy. The special appeal of geometric shapes and forms has been felt throughout the ages. Their lines, contours, and surfaces are clean and crisp. This appeals to people's idealism. Perfect or pure shapes and forms often express a spiritual ideal (Figure 6-39 on page 121).

As used by modern artists, geometric shapes and forms express less feeling than other types. They are unemotional. In fact, they may express a total lack of feeling. Geometric paintings appeal to viewers' minds rather than to their emotions. See Figure 10-27 for an example.

Figure 6.37 "William," this round, roly-poly hippo, has such an appealing shape that he has become the unofficial mascot of the Metropolitan Museum of Art in New York City.

Egyptian. Figure of hippopotamus. ¾ left. XII dynasty (1991–1786 B.C.). Ceramics-Faience. Meir, Tomb of Senbi. 11 × 20 cm (4.3 × 7.9"). The Metropolitan Museum of Art, New York, New York. Gift of Edward S. Harkness, 1917. 17.9.1

Figure 6.38 Sutherland painted four versions of this subject while he was working on a painting of the Crucifixion for a church. He had been studying the forms of real thorns for the crown of thorns in his painting. But the shapes of the thorns themselves began to take on a meaning all their own. He was fascinated with this unsettling view of nature. The sharp points and zigzag lines are reminders of thorns and other jagged, sharp things.

Graham Sutherland. *Thorn Trees,* 1945. Oil on cardboard. 108.6 × 101 cm (42¾ × 39¾"). Albright-Knox Art Gallery, Buffalo, New York. Room of Contemporary Art Fund, 1946.

Figure 6.39 This religious image for a household altar is largely geometric. The skirt is a solid cone. The figure was carved from wood, covered with a thick, white substance, and then painted. It is the result of a mixture of the Spanish and American Indian cultures.

Bultos. Southwest United States. Index of American Design, National Gallery of Art, Washington, D.C.

Density

The *density* of an object refers to how compact it is. Dense materials are solid and heavy. Granite and lead, for example, are very dense. They are so solid and firm that you cannot make a dent on their surfaces when you press on them (Figure 6-40).

Dense forms seem unyielding. They resist impact. For this reason, you may associate them with the idea of protection.

In two-dimensional art, shapes with clearly defined outlines are called *hard-edge.* They look dense and sometimes forbidding.

Soft, fluffy forms are less dense. When you press on them, you can make a dent. These forms

have air inside them, and they are more comfortable than denser forms. You would not hesitate to sink down on a fat, fluffy sofa.

In two-dimensional art, soft shapes are suggested by means of vague, fuzzy edges. The outlines of these soft shapes are difficult to trace (Figure 7-34). For this reason, the shapes seem to fade into the background. While dense, hard shapes and forms seem durable and heavy, soft shapes and forms look light, inviting, and even fragile.

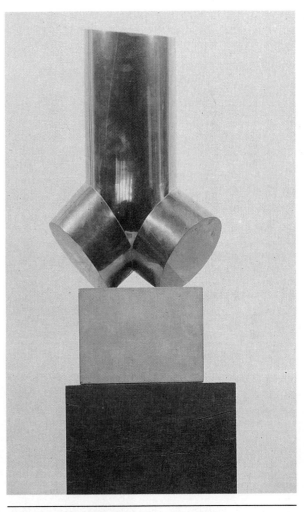

Figure 6.40 The artist has transformed the free-form, soft human torso into a metallic, dense, geometric abstraction.

Constantin Brancusi. *Torso of a Young Man.* 1924. Polished bronze on stone and wood base. 45.7 × 27.9 × 17.8 cm (18 × 11 × 7″). Hirshhorn Museum and Sculpture Garden, Smithsonian Institution, Washington, D.C. Gift of Joseph H. Hirshhorn, 1966.

Figures 6.41 and 6.42 (below) The openness of the transparent glass walls of this house invite you to look inside. But when you are inside, the transparent walls invite you to look out at the beauty of the natural surroundings.

Phillip Johnson. Johnson House. 1949. New Canaan, Connecticut. View: exterior (above) and interior (below) of glass house. Photography by Sandak, Inc., Stamford, Connecticut.

Openness

An open shape or form appears inviting. It seems to say, "Come in." You can see into or through it. An armchair is an open form that invites you to sit. An open door invites you to enter. A cup invites you to fill it. Because you can see through transparent objects, such as a glass wall, they invite you to look inside (Figures 6-41 and 6-42). The form of your outstretched hand when you invite someone to join you is an open form.

Open spaces in sculpture invite your eyes to wander through. Weavers leave openings in fabrics and hangings to let you see through them. Rings, bracelets, and necklaces are open pieces of jewelry. Because of their form, they invite you to decorate your body. If you remove an oak table from a room and replace it with a glass table, the room will seem less crowded. Architects use glass walls to open small spaces. Windows open a building and bring in the outdoors.

Closed shapes and forms look solid and self-contained. Windowless buildings look forbidding. Closed doors keep people out; closed drapes and shades keep light out. When you make a tight fist, your hand is a closed form that seems to say, "Keep away." Your arms, folded tightly to your body, close you off from others. Open arms invite people to come closer to you.

Figure 6.43 In what ways does this work seem to be alive?

David Smith. *Cubi XXVI.* 1965. Steel 303.4 × 383.4 × 65.6 cm (9'11½" × 12'7" × 25⅞"). National Gallery of Art, Washington, D.C. Ailsa Mellon Bruce Fund, 1978.

Activity and Stability

You have already learned about active and static lines. Shapes and forms, too, can look as if they are about to move or as if they are fixed in one place.

Active shapes and forms seem to defy gravity. They slant diagonally, as if they are falling or running. Although David Smith's *Cubi XXVI* (Figure 6-43) is composed entirely of geometric metal forms, it reminds the viewer of the movement of a living creature. The diagonal forms create an unstable feeling. Even the cube in the lower right has been turned on its edge. How long do you suppose it could stay in that position without support?

Static shapes and forms are motionless, or stable. Their direction is usually horizontal (Figure 6-44 on the next page). However, if two diagonal shapes or forms are balanced against one another, a static shape results. For instance, if an equilateral triangle rests on a horizontal base, the two diagonal edges balance each other.

Because static shapes and forms are firmly fixed in position, they look quiet and calm. For instance, in landscape paintings the land forms are horizontal and the trees are vertical. They look very peaceful. This is probably why so many landscape paintings are chosen for people's homes.

Figure 6.44   This figure looks very stable because of its long, horizontal base and because it is composed of two very stable triangular forms. One is a right triangle and the second is almost an isosceles triangle. Can you find these forms?

Henry Moore. *Draped Reclining Figure.* 1952–53. Cast 1956. Bronze sculpture. 100.5 × 169.0 × 86.5 cm (39⅗ × 66½ × 34⅛″). Hirshhorn Museum and Sculpture Garden, Smithsonian Institution, Washington, D.C. Gift of Joseph H. Hirshhorn, 1966.

DEVELOPING YOUR SKILLS

23. Cut photographs of geometrically-shaped objects from magazines. Look for cans, boxes, tires, gears, etc., and arrange the shapes to create a mechanical creature. Glue the design onto paper. Draw or paint a mechanical, geometric environment for the creature.

24. Cut out pictures of free-form objects from magazines. Arrange them to create a living fantasy creature (Figure 6-45). Use parts of people if you wish, but include other shapes as well. Glue your creature to paper. Draw or paint an environment full of free-form shapes for this creature.

25. Make a simple design with geometric shapes. Lightly draw it with pencil on a small sheet of watercolor paper. Repeat the same design on another sheet of watercolor paper of the same size. Next, paint the first design precisely (Figure 6-46A). Use a pointed brush to assure that all of the edges are clearly defined. Wet the second sheet of paper by sponging it with water. Using exactly the same colors, paint the second design while the paper is wet so the edges of the shapes run and look soft (Figure 6-46B). Mount the two designs, side by side, on a sheet of black paper. Label the first "hard-edged," and the second "soft-edged."

26. Cut out a set of rectangles and a set of triangles from black construction paper. Be sure that the shapes vary in size. On a sheet of white paper, arrange and glue the rectangles to create a static feeling. Using a ruler, add static black lines to the design. Now, on a second sheet of white paper, arrange and glue the triangles to

Figure 6.45 Student work. A living fantasy creature.

Figure 6.46A Student work. Hard edges.

Figure 6.46B Student work. Soft edges.

create an active feeling. Use a ruler to add active black lines. Label the designs either static or active.

27. Design and use your own "shape/word" survey. Make a set of ten or more cards. Place a different type of shape on each card. Use geometric, free-form, open, closed, smooth, jagged, hard, soft, static, and active shapes. Number the cards. Now show the cards to different people. Tell each person, "Don't name the shape. Say the first word that the shape brings to your mind." Keep a record of the words mentioned for each card and then share the list with your class. Do you see any similarities? Can you draw any conclusions from your survey?

SOMETHING EXTRA

G. Make a report on body language. Relate your findings to open and closed shapes and forms. Enlist friends to help you create a dramatic presentation of your findings, or make charts to illustrate your report.

H. Do you know sign language, or do you have a friend who does? Learn some of the signs for words that might express feelings about shape and form, such as "mechanical," "hard," "fuzzy," "dense," and "jagged." Study the body gesture as the word is formed, or "signed." Make drawings of the gestures for each word. Do you see any similarity between the body positions and the meaning of the word? Only word gestures should be considered. Spelling a word with the hand alphabet is not expressive. Prepare a demonstration for the class.

I M A G I N E   A N D   C R E A T E

Drawing an Outdoor Scene

MATERIALS

You will need the following:

Large sheet of white drawing paper

Drawing board and tape

Pencils and erasers

Viewing frame

Poster board for mounting or matting the finished drawing

Figure 6.47 Student work. Outdoor scene.

Make a pencil drawing of an outdoor scene (Figure 6-47). Create the illusion of three-dimensional forms in this scene by using a variety of shading techniques. Use values that range from black to white. Create the illusion of deep, three-dimensional space by using perspective techniques. Mount or mat the finished work for display.

DIRECTIONS

Find an outdoor scene that interests you by looking around your neighborhood or out your window. Perhaps you will want to try a shopping center, a farm scene, or a view of boats in the harbor. Do not use a photograph or another drawing.

Use a viewing frame to help select the exact view. Be sure to include a large shape in the foreground. All of this large shape does not have to fit into the picture. Take enough time to study the relationship of each shape and form to the frame. Each shape and form will have the same relationship to the edges of the paper as it does to the viewing frame. Look for overlapping, placement, sizes, detail, values, and receding parallel lines.

Tape your paper to the drawing board.

Lightly draw in the shapes.

Shade the shapes using a value scale that includes white and black. The strongest values will be in the foreground. Distant shapes will be in the middle-gray range. Create flat and round surfaces with shading.

Mount or mat your finished drawing with poster board for display.

EVALUATION CHECKLIST

Be sure you did the following:

1. Took the time to select a good scene.
2. Used the viewing frame.
3. Studied the scene for several minutes before starting to draw.
4. Lightly drew in the shapes and used several perspective techniques.
5. Used a wide range of values.
6. Shaded flat surfaces to look flat.
7. Made round shapes look round.
8. Mounted the drawing for display.

Plaster Sculpture

MATERIALS

You will need the following:

Plastic bowl or bucket and spoon

Trash can lined with newspaper

Plaster powder and water

Plastic storage bag and twist-tie

Assorted carving tools, such as knives, rasps, files, can openers, nut picks, sandpaper, broken scissors, and more

A base, such as a piece of scrap wood, a section of a tree trunk or driftwood

Optional:

Slightly diluted white glue and staining material

Figure 6.48 Notice the smooth, flowing, free-form quality of this sculpture.

Jean Arp. *Torso Fruit.* 1960. Marble sculpture. 74.9 × 30.5 × 29.2 cm (29½ × 12 × 11½"). Hirshhorn Museum and Sculpture Garden, Smithsonian Institution, Washington, D.C. Gift of Joseph H. Hirshhorn, 1966.

SAFETY NOTE

If you are asthmatic or have any breathing difficulties, dry dusts such as plaster, dry clay, chalks, and wheat paste may be harmful to your health. Stay away from mixing areas or wear a dust mask. Always inform your instructor if you think a material will be harmful to you.

OBJECTIVE

Mold plaster in a plastic bag to create a freestanding, lifelike form that looks interesting from every point of view. Refine the surface of the molded form by carving and sanding. Mount the finished work for display.

DIRECTIONS

Study the sculptures in Figures 6-44 and 6-48. Notice the smooth surfaces and negative areas in and around the positive areas.

Collect your materials and arrange your storage area.

Cover your work space.

Measure enough water to fill the plastic bag half way. Pour the water into the mixing container and add the plaster powder to the water (see the Technique Tip on the next page).

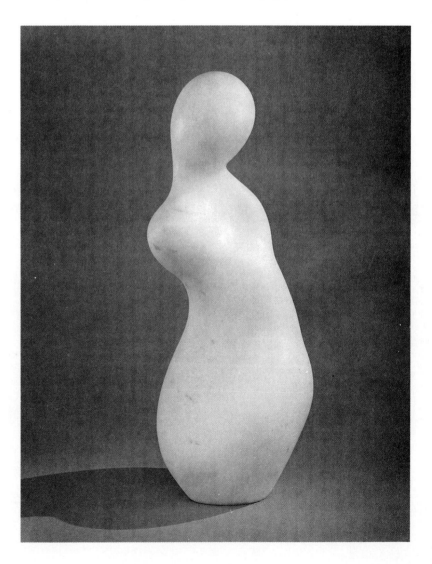

With a partner, mix the plaster. Stir it about one hundred times, until it begins to set. Then pour it into the plastic bag. Close the bag and form the plaster in the bag while it continues to set. By bending and twisting the bag, squeeze out forms, push in hollow spaces, and make openings. Work to mold the plaster into a smooth, flowing, rounded form. Keep turning the bag so you can study it from every side.

As soon as the plaster begins to resist, or if it starts to crack, stop working immediately. Do not move it or touch it more than necessary. Open the bag to let the moisture evaporate. Notice how hot the plaster gets as it hardens.

When the plaster is hard, remove the plastic bag carefully. You may have to cut the bag. Study the form you have made. Where do you need to carve? Use the carving tools to accent the form, make hollows deeper, smooth some surfaces, and add texture to others.

When the plaster is thoroughly dry, seal it with a coat of diluted white glue. Then, if you wish, stain it with wood stain, oil paint diluted with turpentine, or shoe polish.

Mount your sculpture on a base for display.

EVALUATION CHECKLIST

Be sure you did the following:

1. Studied the sculptures in Figures 6-44 and 6-48.
2. Followed directions for mixing the plaster.
3. Molded a free-form object according to directions.
4. Kept turning the work to study it from every side.
5. Finished forming the plaster with carving tools.

TECHNIQUE TIP

Mixing Plaster

Mixing plaster is a very messy process, so cover your work space carefully. If you are asthmatic or have breathing difficulties, wear a dust mask.

Use a plastic bowl or bucket for mixing, and a stick for stirring. The plaster must be fine, like sifted flour, not grainy.

Pour cold water into the bowl. Sift plaster into the water until islands of plaster form on the surface and cracks form in the island. Stir the mixture slowly. The moment the whole mixture begins to thicken, pour it into the mold you have chosen.

Warning: Don't add more plaster or water to a mixture that is beginning to set. Don't pour plaster down the drain. Unused plaster should be left to dry in the mixing bowl. To remove it, twist the bowl and crack the plaster loose into a trash container.

Figure 6.49 Islands of plaster forming above the surface of the water.

6. Used tools for smoothing, for creating textures, and for finishing the surface.
7. Mounted the sculpture for display.
8. Cleaned up the work area.

Soft Sculpture

MATERIALS

You will need the following:

Pencil and paper

Scissors, pins, needles, and thread

Assorted fabrics

Material for stuffing, such as fiberfill

Yarns and other trims

A bag or box for storage

Optional:
sewing machine

OBJECTIVE

Create a humorous soft sculpture of an object that you use every day, such as the one shown in Figure 6-50.

DIRECTIONS

Choose a three-dimensional object as a model for your sculpture. Following are some suggestions to start you thinking. Consider a stove, a bottle of aspirin, a radio, a car, a houseplant, a roller skate, or a calculator. For your first try, avoid objects with many projecting parts. Study and sketch the model from every point of view, and note how each part fits into the whole. Plan how you will sew and stuff the sculpture.

Figure 6.50 Although this sculpture is made with canvas filled with kapok to create a soft quality, it is a fairly accurate map of Manhattan's postal zones. Oldenburg painted it with gray and terra-cotta because he wanted it to have the feeling of a very old map. Oldenburg is famous for taking ordinary objects, such as fans and hamburgers, and turning them into soft sculptures.

Claes Oldenburg. *Soft Manhattan #1 (Postal Zones).* 1966. Canvas filled with kapok. 194.3 × 71.1 × 20.3 cm (76½ × 28 × 8″). Albright-Knox Art Gallery, Buffalo, New York. Gift of Seymour H. Knox, 1966.

Select fabrics. Trace the pattern onto the fabric. Cut around the tracing, adding about one-half inch (1.27 cm) for seams.

Pin the pieces of cut fabric, right side together, making sure that the seams match. Sew the pieces together by machine or by hand. Leave enough of an opening in one seam to turn the piece right side out. Turn the sculpture right side out and stuff it. Sew the opening by hand.

Add details by sewing or gluing on yarns, fabric shapes, or other trims.

EVALUATION CHECKLIST

Be sure you did the following:

1. Selected an ordinary object without too many projecting parts.
2. Studied the subject and made several sketches of it from different points of view.
3. Made an accurate paper pattern for every part.
4. Planned each step ahead of time.
5. Selected fabrics carefully for the best effect.
6. Traced the patterns and cut the fabric correctly.
7. Sewed the seams carefully.
8. Stuffed the object so it was round and smooth, not lumpy.
9. Added details using different materials.
10. Kept all fabric pieces in the storage container.
11. Cleaned up the work area.

Photogram

MATERIALS

You will need the following:

Blueprint paper

Heavy cardboard

A variety of found objects such as leaves, oddly shaped pebbles, onion skins, coins, costume jewelry, lace, keys, and scrap paper

Ammonia (sudsy household-type)

Sponge

Tray with glass cover

Piece of screen to cover tray

Poster board

OBJECTIVE

Make a photogram (Figures 6-51 and 6-52) with found objects and prepare the finished work for display.

DIRECTIONS

Because light affects blueprint paper, store blueprint paper in its package until you are ready to use it. When you cut a piece from a larger sheet, return the unused portion to the package.

Place the sponge soaked in ammonia on the tray. Place the wire screen over the sponge. The screen will prevent the paper from touching the liquid ammonia. Only the fumes will develop the print.

Organize the found objects you plan to use on a piece of ordinary paper the same size as the piece of blueprint paper you will use. Plan and arrange your composition.

Cut your blueprint paper to size and place it on a stiff piece of cardboard.

Figure 6.51 Student work. Photogram.

Place the found materials on the blueprint paper.

Expose the paper with the objects on it to sunlight, or a sunlamp, for about one minute. The color of the paper will change. Do not overexpose the paper.

Remove the objects and place the exposed paper on the screen atop the tray. Be careful not to inhale the ammonia fumes. Put the glass cover over the tray.

Development only takes a few seconds.

Mount or mat one finished print for display.

Figure 6.52 Student work. Photogram.

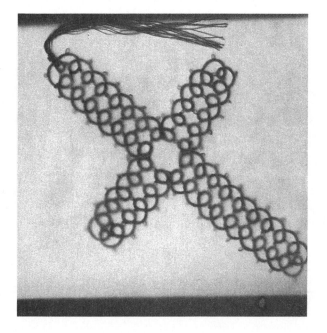

EVALUATION CHECKLIST

Be sure you did the following:

1. Collected all of the materials and organized the workplace.
2. Soaked the sponge in ammonia and placed it on the tray. Covered the sponge with the screen and the glass.
3. Collected objects to place on the blueprint paper, and rearranged the objects to achieve the desired composition. Were careful not to overexpose.
4. Exposed the blueprint paper to the light.
5. Placed the exposed paper in the tray while being very careful not to inhale the fumes.
6. Developed the blueprint paper properly.
7. Mounted or matted one finished print for display.
8. Cleaned up the workplace.

Drawing with a Computer

MATERIALS

You will need the following:

A computer with high-resolution graphic capabilities

An input device, such as a touch-sensitive pad, a mouse, or light pen

Appropriate software

OBJECTIVE

Using a computer with high-resolution graphic capabilities and appropriate software, create a black, white, and gray drawing illustrating distance. The subject of your work may be a landscape, a cityscape, or an arrangement of abstract shapes (Figures 6-53 and 6-54).

Figure 6.53 Student work. Computer drawing.

Figure 6.54 Student work. Computer drawing.

DIRECTIONS

If you are not familiar with drawing on the computer, be sure to allow yourself enough time to practice different techniques.

Work directly on the computer screen. Planning your drawing on paper will not save time. Save your work in memory as you try different ideas on the screen. First draw the lines and then shade the forms, following the directions for the software you are using.

Either make a printout of your drawing or take a photograph of the screen.

EVALUATION CHECKLIST

Be sure you did the following:

1. Planned time to practice drawing and shading on the computer.
2. Created a line drawing to illustrate distance.
3. Created different values to shade in the drawing.
4. Either made a printout or photographed the work.

Figure 6.55 Louise Nevelson. *Dawn.* 1962. Wood painted gold. 240 × 191.8 × 19.7 cm (94½ × 75½ × 7¾"). Collection Pace Editions, Inc. The Pace Gallery, New York, New York.

A R T   C R I T I C I S M

Improving Your Critical-Thinking Skills

Look at the photograph of the sculpture, *Dawn*, in Figure 6-55. You may wonder how to respond to a work that does not represent something you can recognize, such as people or a landscape. You will find, however, that there is much to discover.

Description: What Do You See?

This work is called an **assemblage**, which is a composition consisting of many pieces assembled together. An assemblage is a three-dimensional *collage* (see page 181).

What material is *Dawn* made from? This information is given in the credit line. How big is the work? How does its height compare with your own? How much wall space would its 75½-inch (191.8-cm) width take? Would it fit in the room where you are now? What does the depth tell you? What kind of a sculpture is it? Is it free-standing or relief?

Write down every fact you observe. Look over the small parts to see if you can recognize any objects. List and describe the forms or shapes you recognize.

Analysis: How Is the Work Organized?

Before you study the shapes and forms of this work, look at its lines. Refer back to Chapter 5 if you have questions about line and value.

Is the work two- or three-dimensional? Do you see any silhouettes? Are there any changes in value? If so, describe them.

Consider the feelings the forms suggest. Study the surfaces and outlines. Do you find geometric forms? Do you find free or lifelike forms? If so, describe them. Which type of form seems to dominate this structure?

Do the forms look dense or soft? Do the individual forms look open or closed? Does the whole work create an open or closed feeling?

Do the individual forms look static or active? Does the total arrangement look static or active?

How has the artist used space? Is it real or an illusion?

How has the artist used positive and negative spaces? Describe the arrangement of forms within forms. Do you see similarities? Where are the differences?

Is there an attempt to create the illusion of distance?

Interpretation: What Is Happening? What Is the Artist Trying to Say?

This work does not tell a story. You must go to the clues you found during analysis to make meaning out of it.

What kind of a statement is the artist making about your world with this sculpture? The forms will suggest different things to each person.

Write a paragraph explaining your interpretation. Then create a new title for the work. Your title should sum up your interpretation of *Dawn*.

Judgment: What Do You Think of the Work?

You have now had a visual "conversation" with a work of art that does not tell an obvious story. Do you feel more confident about abstract art?

Do you like Nevelson's technique for organizing shapes and forms? Why or why not?

Does the sculpture make you think? Does it start your imagination working?

Would you like to touch it? Why or why not?

Do you like this work? Why or why not? Use at least one of the three art theories (see Chapter 2) to defend your choice.

A B O U T   T H E   A R T I S T

Louise Nevelson

Figure 6.56 Louise Nevelson; born Kiev, Russia, American citizen; 1899—

Lynn Gilbert. *Portrait of Louise Nevelson.* Photograph. Courtesy of The Pace Gallery, New York, New York.

Louise Nevelson is the glamorous, fascinating person that everyone always imagines an artist should be. Over 80 years old, she is noted for the exotic clothing she wears. She has said that she wants people to enjoy looking at something besides an old hag! So she dangles huge earrings from her ears, wraps her head in brightly colored turbans, wears flowing robes, and glues three sets of false lashes on her eyelids.

Art has always been her life. She claims that by the time she was seven she knew she would be a sculptor.

Nevelson was born in Kiev, Russia, in 1899. At the age of five she and her family moved to Rockland, Maine, where her father built a successful lumber business. She enjoyed playing in her father's lumberyard. She loved to carve and assemble pieces of wood.

Nevelson's independent thinking was nourished by a mother who was a free thinker and a father who believed in equal rights for women. She was always an outsider in her small town.

In 1920 she married Charles Nevelson, and they moved to New York. Her only child, Myron, was born in 1922. But she resented the responsibilities of marriage and motherhood because they took her away from art. Finally, after eleven years, she separated from her husband. Nevelson took her son to stay with her parents in Maine, and she went to Europe to study.

When she returned to New York, she sold her jewelry for money to live on and devoted every moment to her work. In 1941 she had her first show. The reviews were good. But one insulting reviewer said that the sculpture might have been great if only the artist had not been a woman.

During the forties she experimented with all art media. Some discarded wood scraps from an old building inspired her first three-dimensional assemblage.

In the fifties she began to paint each assemblage a solid color so that color would not interfere with the viewer's perceptions of the forms. In the seventies she experimented with new materials such as Cor-ten steel, lucite, and aluminum. These new materials enabled her to produce gigantic outdoor pieces. She created an entire chapel of white-painted wood inside a skyscraper in Manhattan.

Today there is a square in New York City named for Louise Nevelson. It contains seven mammoth steel sculptures that are about 90 feet (30 meters) high. These sculptures are a tribute to her dedication to her art.

Chapter 6 Review: Talking about Art

USING THE LANGUAGE OF ART

For each new art term below, choose a work of art from this chapter. Then write a sentence about that work using the new term correctly in the sentence.

assemblage	perspective
chiaroscuro	shape
form	silhouette
free-form shapes	space
geometric shapes	

LEARNING THE ART ELEMENTS AND PRINCIPLES

1. Name the two main types of shapes and tell which is more often used in decoration.
2. What is the difference between shape and form?
3. By what are shapes and forms defined?
4. Name the two kinds of space found in art.
5. Name the six devices for creating perspective.
6. Name two types of perspective.

INCREASING YOUR ART AWARENESS

1. Pretend that you are to take photos for this chapter to show different shapes in nature. What would you photograph?
2. Describe a common, manufactured object used in the home so that someone else could guess what the object is without your naming it. Refer to the elements of line, shape, form, and space in your description.
3. Compare the artists' use of positive and negative space in Figures 5-21 and 6-12. What feelings are expressed in each?
4. Study Figures 6-16, 6-40, and 6-48. Which work contains negative space within positive space? Is this negative space free-form or geometric? What does each work express?
5. Look at Figures 3-14 and 6-21. Which appears to have more form and depth? How has the artist achieved this?
6. Compare the lines, forms, and spaces that you see in Figures 5-25 and 6-42.

UNDERSTANDING ART CULTURE AND HERITAGE

1. One of the works in this chapter was done by an artist whose work was used as an example of Post-Impressionism. Name the artist and the title of his work that appears in this chapter.
2. Two works of art in this chapter were created before the birth of Christ. Give the subject matters and the cultures of these two works.
3. Explain why Figures 6-1 and 6-26 are good examples of Italian Renaissance art (see Chapter 3). What similarities do you see between these works and Figure 1-1?
4. What artwork in this chapter (clue: read the captions) represents a break from the style of art in Figure 3-6? How do these works differ?
5. What artistic styles are shown in Figures 3-11 and 6-7? Compare the treatment of forms and shapes in each (see Chapter 3).

JUDGING THE QUALITY OF ART

Leonardo da Vinci is considered one of the greatest artists of all time. Study Figure 6-1, *Ginevra de Benci,* and use the four steps of art criticism to write about this work. Since da Vinci was one of the artists who perfected the science of perspective, be sure to note the perspective techniques he used to create the illusion of depth.

LEARNING MORE ABOUT ART

1. Find out which geometric forms were used by ancient cultures to build tombs and religious structures. Then, based on your knowledge of the culture, its geographic location, and its natural resources, explain why you think specific shapes were chosen by each culture.
2. Laser beams and computers are modern-day inventions that the ancients would not have dreamed possible. Artists are now using these devices to create three-dimensional illusions. Research and report on how holograms or computerized special effects in films are created.

Figure 7.1 Tchelitchew was a surrealist who made colors sing. If you were standing in front of this painting, you would think it had a light behind it. The yellows are so intense they seem to glow.

Pavel Tchelitchew. *Hide-and-Seek (Cache-cache)*. 1940–42. Oil on canvas. 199.3 × 215.3 cm (78½ × 84¾"). Museum of Modern Art, New York, New York. Mrs. Simon Guggenheim Fund.

Color

LEARNING OBJECTIVES

After reading this chapter and doing the exercises, you will be able to

- □ understand how your eyes see color.
- □ name the properties of color and the colors of the spectrum.
- □ identify different color schemes.
- □ mix your own paints using different pigments and vehicles.
- □ use color as the expressive element in creating two- and three-dimensional art works.
- □ recognize the expressive qualities of color that artists use to create meaning.

WORDS TO LEARN

In this chapter you will learn the meanings of the words listed below.

analogous colors	shade
color	tint
color spectrum	vehicle
color wheel	
complementary colors	
hue	
intensity	
monochrome	
pigments	

Color is exciting! Human beings are so sensitive to color that it appeals directly to our emotions. Few people ever think about a favorite type of line or shape, but almost everyone has a favorite color. Color is the most expressive element of art, but it is also the most difficult to talk about. Try to imagine how you would tell a blind person the difference between red and orange. It is almost impossible to describe color without also talking about other colors.

Colors stand for ideas and feelings. You use color symbolically when you say, "I feel blue," "She's green with envy," or "He's a yellow coward."

You may remember a time when you mixed some beautiful bright colors into a dull gray, muddy mess. Color can be very frustrating. Sometimes it acts like a wild thing, but it *can* be tamed. In this chapter you will learn how to speak with color in the language of art.

DEVELOPING YOUR SKILLS

1. Survey ten people your own age and ten adults to discover their favorite color. Does age affect color preference? Report your findings to the class.
2. Think of a "colorful" phrase, such as "tickled pink." Illustrate the phrase with a humorous drawing, including the words of the phrase somewhere in your design.

Figure 7.2 Can you imagine how dull and drab our world would be without color?

Photography by Nick Pavloff.

Figure 7.3 These colors glow as daylight shines through the stained-glass window.

Bronislaw M. Bak. *Holocaust.* 1969. Stained glass windows. 3 × 9.1 m (10′ × 30′). Temple Emanu-El, Chicago, Illinois.

How We See Color

Color is an element of art that is derived from reflected light (Figure 7-3). You see color because light waves are reflected from objects to your eyes. White light from the sun is really a combination of all colors.

When light passes through a wedge-shaped glass called a *prism*, the beam of white light is bent and separated into all the colors, called the **color spectrum.** The colors of the spectrum always appear in the same order: red, orange, yellow, green, blue, and violet.

A natural example of a spectrum in your world is a rainbow. You can find rainbows in the sky, in the spray from a garden hose, or floating on an oil puddle in a parking lot. Rainbows occur when sunlight is bent by water, oil, or a prism-type glass.

Objects absorb some waves of light and reflect others. A red apple looks red because it reflects red waves and absorbs the rest (Figure 7-4). Your mind reads the light as being a certain color because human eyes have special color receivers.

Light enters your eye and travels to a membrane of nerve tissue (the retina) at the back of your eyeball. There, two types of cells react to the light. One type receives impressions of light and dark. The other type receives color.

Our eyes have trouble seeing colors in dim light. It does not matter whether the source of light is the sun or an electric bulb. Colors don't really change, but our ability to distinguish between them does.

Some people are color-blind. There are many different types of color-blindness. Some people cannot tell the difference between red and green,

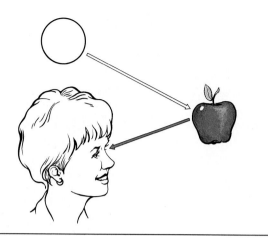

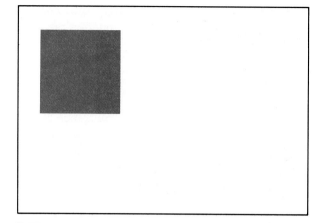

Figure 7.4 The red apple absorbs all of the other colors and reflects the red waves. This is why we see the apple as red.

Figure 7.5 What color do you see when you shift your gaze from the red to the white area? Your eyes can fool you about color.

and others see only black, white, and gray. Many animals have limited color vision. Others—birds and bees, for example—see light waves that are invisible to humans.

Your eyes can fool you about color. For instance, stare at the bright red shape in Figure 7-5 for thirty seconds; then look quickly away to the white area next to it. Did you see a green shape on the white surface? This is called an *afterimage*.

Afterimages are opposites. Green is the opposite of red. The afterimage of black is white, and the afterimage of blue is orange. Don't expect an afterimage to be a strong color—it is only the ghost of a color. The afterimage is created by your brain as a reaction to the color you stared at originally. Some artists make use of the way your eyes work when they create optical illusions of color and movement (Figure 7-6).

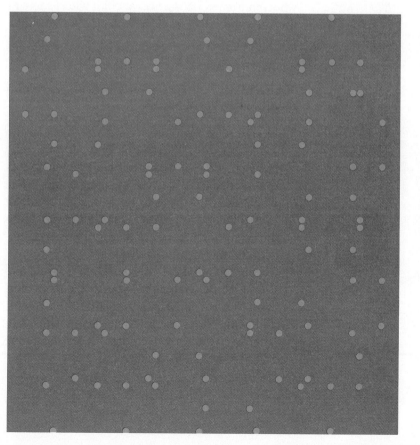

Figure 7.6 This painting is named for the soft drink that has an unnatural, man-made color, similar to the orange of this painting. It may seem that the blue-green dots have no order, but they were carefully planned. The dots are meant to suggest musical notes. As you stare at this work, the after-image of the dots creates the feeling of dance-like movements. Try to make the dots remain still!

Larry Poons. *Orange Crush*. 1963. Acrylic on canvas. 203.2 × 203.2 cm (80 × 80″). Albright-Knox Art Gallery, Buffalo, New York. Gift of Seymour H. Knox, 1964.

Understanding the three properties of color will help you work with color. The properties are *hue*, *value*, and *intensity*.

Hue

Hue is the name of a spectral color, such as red, blue, or yellow. Red, yellow, and blue are the primary hues. You cannot make primary hues by mixing other hues together. However, by using only the three primaries and black and white, you can produce almost every other color.

Each secondary hue is made by mixing two primaries (Figure 7-7). Red and yellow make orange; red and blue make violet; and blue and yellow make green. Orange, violet, and green are the secondary hues.

The six intermediate colors are made by mixing a primary color with its adjacent secondary color. For example, red and orange make red-orange, red and violet make red-violet, blue and violet make

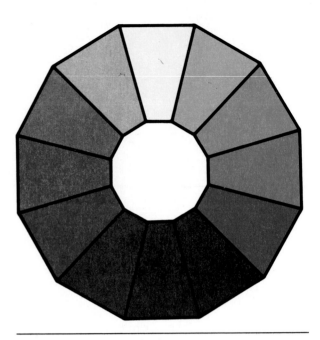

Figure 7.8   The color wheel.

blue-violet, and so on. You can, of course, make many additional variations using the newly created intermediate colors.

A **color wheel** is the spectrum bent into a circle. It is a useful tool for organizing colors. The color wheel in Figure 7-8 is a twelve-color wheel showing the three primary, three secondary, and six intermediate hues.

DEVELOPING YOUR SKILLS

3. Design your own unique color wheel (Figure 7-9A and 7-9B). Show the correct color relationships. Use only primary paint colors to mix the secondary and intermediate colors. The wheel does not have to be perfectly round, or even a circle. Be creative. Plan some way to indicate the differences among primary, secondary, and intermediate colors.
4. Make a color-wheel collage. Draw a circle and divide it into twelve equal parts. Collect colors from construction paper, magazine photographs, and fabric scraps and fill each section with a collection of the proper colors. Cover the entire area. Do not let the background show.

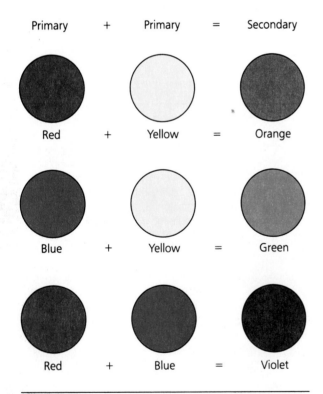

Primary	+	Primary	=	Secondary
Red	+	Yellow	=	Orange
Blue	+	Yellow	=	Green
Red	+	Blue	=	Violet

Figure 7.7   Primary and secondary hues.

Figure 7.9A Student work. Creative color wheel.

Figure 7.9B Student work. Creative color wheel.

Figure 7.10 Neutral colors: black, white, and gray.

SOMETHING EXTRA

A. Do some research on color-blindness. If you have a color-blind friend, ask about the special problems your friend has. How does your friend cope with these problems?
B. Contact the lighting director of a local theater group. How are colors used in stage lighting?

Value

As you have already learned, value is the art element that refers to darkness or light. Color value is related to the amount of light a color reflects. Not all hues of the spectrum have the same value. Yellow is the lightest hue, and violet is the darkest.

Black, white, and gray are neutral colors (Figure 7-10). A white object does not absorb color waves. When white light shines on a white object, all of the color waves are reflected. You see the color of the light—you see white.

SAFETY NOTE

When paints are called for, use watercolors, liquid tempera, or school acrylics if possible. If you must use powdered tempera, wear a dust mask and work away from other class members.

Remember to check your paints for safety labels. All materials used in the classroom should be properly labeled. You should know the following safety labels:

AP–Approved Product
CP–Certified Product
HL–Health Label

AP and CP labels assure you that the product contains no materials in sufficient amounts to be dangerous or toxic. The CP label further assures you that the art materials meet certain quality standards. An HL label can indicate that the art materials contain toxic ingredients.

Tints   Shades

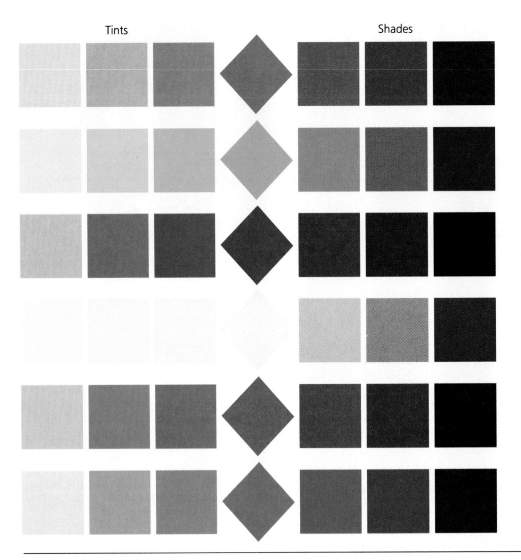

Figure 7.11 Color value scales.

A black object absorbs all of the color waves. Black reflects no light; black is the absence of light. Gray is impure white—it reflects all color waves equally, but only partially. The more light that gray reflects, the lighter it looks; and the more it absorbs, the darker it looks.

You can change the value of any hue by adding black or white (Figure 7-11). A light value of a hue is called a **tint,** and a dark value of a hue is called a **shade.** The term shade is often used incorrectly to refer to both tints and shades.

When artists want to show a bright, sunny day, they use tints (Figure 7-12). Paintings having many tints are referred to as *high-key paintings. Low-key paintings* have dark values. Dark values are used

when the artist wants to represent dark, gloomy days, nighttime, and dusk (Figure 7-13). Dark values add a feeling of mystery to a work.

If the change in value is gradual, the design produces a calm feeling. If the values take large jumps up and down the scale, from almost white to almost black, the effect is active, even nervous.

Figure 7.12 (facing page)   Twachtman has used tints of violet and yellow along with bright white. What kind of mood does this scene convey?

John Henry Twachtman. *The Waterfall.* 1890s. Oil on canvas. 55.8 × 76.7 cm (22 × 30¼″). Hirshhorn Museum and Sculpture Garden, Smithsonian Institution, Washington, D.C. Gift of Joseph H. Hirshhorn, 1966.

TECHNIQUE TIP

Mixing Paint to Change Value

If you are using opaque paint, such as tempera, to mix a light value, add only a small amount of hue to white. You can always make the color stronger by adding more hue. To mix a dark value, add small amounts of black to the hue—never add hue to black.

If you are using transparent watercolor paint to make a light value, thin the paint with water to allow more white paper to show through. Make a hue darker by adding a small amount of black.

Figure 7.11A The colors used to produce this landscape were thinned with water to create light values. Notice how the sky has been left almost pure white to indicate a bright, sunny day.

Figure 7.13 At the time this picture was painted, public boxing was illegal. Fights were staged at "private" clubs, such as Sharkey's, where both spectators and fighters were members. Of course, the fighters were members for the night of the fight only. Bellows used low-key colors to exaggerate the mood of this work.

George Wesley Bellows. *Both Members of This Club.* 1909. Oil on canvas. 115 × 160.5 cm (45¼ × 63⅛″). National Gallery of Art, Washington, D.C. Chester Dale Collection.

5. Make a seven-step value scale for each hue. (See Figure 7-11.) For each hue, draw a row of seven equal shapes, one for each step. Make the first step almost white; make the fourth step the pure hue; and make the seventh step almost black. The second step should be a very light tint, and the third step should be a little darker. The fifth step needs a small amount of black; the sixth, a little more.

Intensity

Intensity is the brightness or dullness of a hue (Figure 7-14). If a surface reflects only yellow light waves, for example, you see an intensely bright yellow. A pure hue is called a *high-intensity color.* Dulled hues are called *low-intensity colors.*

Complementary colors are the colors opposite one another on the color wheel. The complement of a hue absorbs all of the light waves that the hue reflects (Figure 7-15). Red and green are complements. Red absorbs blue and yellow waves and reflects red waves. Green absorbs red waves and reflects blue and yellow waves.

Mixing a hue with its complement dulls it, or lowers its intensity. The more complement you add to a hue, the duller the hue looks. Finally, the hue will lose its own color quality and appear gray.

The hue used in the greatest amount in a mixture becomes dominant. For this reason, a mixture might look like a dull orange or a dull blue, depending on the amount of color used. Orange and blue mixtures usually yield brownish results.

Hue, value, and intensity do not operate independently. When you observe colors, you will see dull tints and bright tints; you will find dull shades and bright shades. Look around you. When you can classify types of colors, you will understand color.

DEVELOPING YOUR SKILLS

6. Create nine-step intensity scales for the three primary colors. The first step should be painted with the pure primary. Dull the second step with a very small amount of the complement. Add

Figure 7.14 Intensity scale. The green on the left is a pure hue. A small amount of red (the complement of green) has been added in the second box, lowering the green's intensity. More and more red has been added to each box. At the right end of the scale the green is so dull, it has almost lost its greenness.

Figure 7.15 Sets of complements make exciting designs.

more of the complement to the third step, even more to the fourth, and so on until the ninth step, which should be a neutral, grayish color.

7. Contrary to what you may have thought, tree trunks are not really brown. They are a variety of light and dark low-intensity grays. Draw seven or more bare trees on a large sheet of white paper (Figure 7-16). Draw from real trees, if possible; if not, find photographs. Use one primary color, its complement, white, and black to create a number of different, low-intensity light- and dark-valued colors. Then use these colors to paint each tree a different color from the others.

8. Choose one hue. Look through magazines and cut out examples of all the variations of that hue that you can find. Classify the colors into five groups: (1) pure hue, (2) dull tint, (3) dull shade, (4) bright tint, and (5) bright shade. Glue them to a small sheet of white paper and label each group.

SOMETHING EXTRA

C. Collect color-sample charts from local paint stores and art stores. Try to classify the commercial colors and the artists' paints according to hue, value, and intensity. For example, *yellow ochre* is a yellow hue of light-middle value and low intensity.

Figure 7.16 Student work. Notice the range of intensity.

Color Schemes

Single colors are like musical instruments. Each instrument has its own special sound. When you hear an instrument as part of an orchestra, the sound you hear is affected by the sounds of the other instruments. When the musicians tune up before a performance, you hear confusing noises. When they play together in an organized way, they can make beautiful sounds. Unplanned colors can be as confusing to your eyes as unplanned sound is to your ears. Color without organization can look like a visual argument.

When two colors come into direct contact, their differences increase. A yellow-green surrounded by green looks yellower. A yellow-green surrounded by yellow seems greener. Grayish green will brighten upon a gray background (Figure 7-17).

Color schemes are plans for organizing colors. Someone may have told you that certain colors "belong" together. Or you may hear someone refer to colors that "clash." These are merely statements of personal likes and dislikes. Some years ago it was considered poor taste to use blue and green together. Today color combinations are used more freely. The following are some of the most frequently used color plans. Color plans are called *color schemes*.

Monochromatic Colors

Monochrome means "one color." A monochromatic color scheme, or **monochrome,** is a color scheme that uses only one hue and all the values of that hue. It uses all of the tints and shades of that hue. Because this is such a limited scheme, it has a strong, unifying effect on a design. It is very easy to organize furniture or clothing using monochromatic colors. The major problem with a monochromatic color scheme is that it can be boring. See Figure 7-18.

Figure 7.17 Your perception of any color is affected by the colors that surround it. This effect is called *simultaneous contrast*.

Figure 7.18 (below)   Hartley was fascinated with the mysterious solitude of "Dogtown." To capture this feeling, he eliminated details, painted with bold brush strokes, and limited his colors to a monochrome of reds. The wide range of values prevents monotony.

Marsden Hartley. *Blueberry Highway, Dogtown.* 1931. Oil on composition board. 44.5 × 59.7 cm (17½ × 23½ "). High Museum of Art, Atlanta, Georgia.

Analogous Colors

Analogous colors are colors that sit side by side on the color wheel and have a common hue (Figure 7-19). Violet, red-violet, red, red-orange, and orange have red in common. A more closely related scheme would be limited to only three hues, such as violet, red-violet, and red.

Analogous colors blend together to create a design that ties one shape to the next by means of a common color (Figure 7-21). Because of the common hue, these colors are easy to organize.

Complementary Colors

The strongest contrast of a hue is produced by complementary colors. When a pair of high-intensity complements are placed side by side, they seem to vibrate. It is difficult to focus on the edge where the complements touch. Some artists use

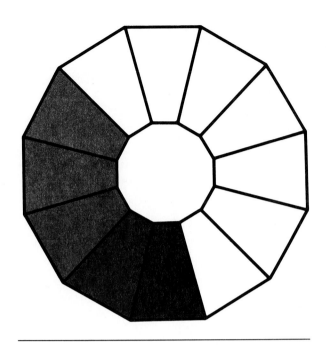

Figure 7.19   Analogous colors are related.

Figure 7.20 (at left)   This painting is an experiment with the effects of full-intensity, complementary colors. The well-defined squares have been created by precise lines, evenly placed. Notice how the red ground changes color according to the density of the alternating blue and green lines. Stare at this painting. Do the afterimages affect your perception?

Richard Anuszkiewicz. *Iridescence.* 1965. Acrylic on canvas. 152.4 × 152.4 cm (60 × 60"). Albright-Knox Art Gallery, Buffalo, New York. Gift of Seymour H. Knox, 1966.

Figure 7.21 (facing page)   Rothko limited the colors in this painting to an analogous scheme of yellow and orange. His style is based on soft edges and colors that blend so there seem to be no borders or edges. The yellow and orange float against a ground that glows mysteriously. Standing in front of this work, which is almost eight feet high, the viewer can have an intense visual experience.

Mark Rothko. *Orange and Yellow.* 1956. Oil on canvas. 91 × 71" (231.1 × 180.3 cm.). Albright-Knox Art Gallery, Buffalo, New York. Gift of Seymour H. Knox, 1956.

this visual vibration to create special effects. They make designs that sparkle, snap, and sizzle, as if they were charged with electricity. See Figure 7-20.

Complementary color schemes are exciting. They are loud, and they demand to be noticed. They are frequently used to catch the viewer's attention. How many ways do people use the red-and-green color scheme? What time of year does the yellow-and-violet color scheme symbolize?

Not all color schemes based on complements are loud and demanding. If the hues are of low in-

tensity, the contrast is not so harsh. Changing the values of the hues will also soften the effect.

Color Triads

A color triad is composed of three colors spaced an equal distance apart on the color wheel. The contrast between triad colors is not as strong as that between complements. The primary triad is composed of red, yellow, and blue. The secondary triad contains orange, green, and violet (Figure 7-23).

Figure 7.22 Even though this painting is based on the primary triad, it is very comfortable to view. What has the artist done with the colors to make this painting easy to look at?

Fritz Glarner. *Relational Painting #93*. 1962. Oil on canvas. 169.9 × 111.8 cm (66⅞ × 44″). Albright-Knox Art Gallery, Buffalo, New York. Gift of The Seymour H. Knox Foundation, Inc., 1966.

Figure 7.23 Color triads.

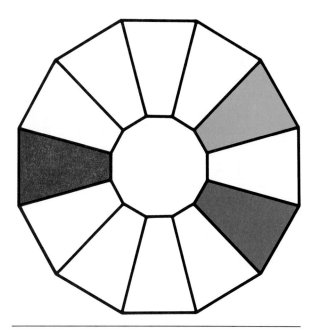

Figure 7.24 Split complement.

A high-intensity primary triad is very difficult to work with. The contrast between the three hues is so strong that they make many people uncomfortable. However, a triad can be made more comfortable to the viewer by changing the intensity or values (Figure 7-22). A triad of secondary colors is less disturbing.

Split Complements

A split complement is the combination of one hue plus the hues on each side of its complement (Figure 7-24). This is easier to work with than a straight complementary scheme. It offers more variety.

For example, start with red-orange. Check the color wheel to find its complement, blue-green. The two hues next to blue-green are blue and green. Red-orange, blue, and green form a split complementary color scheme.

Warm and Cool Colors

Sometimes the colors are divided into two groups called *warm* and *cool* (Figure 7-25). Warm colors are red, orange, and yellow. They are usually associated with warm things, such as sunshine or fire. Cool colors are blue, green, and violet. They are

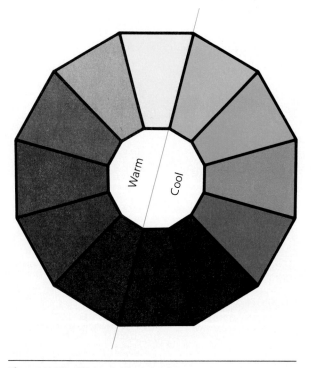

Figure 7.25 Warm and cool colors.

usually associated with cool things, such as ice, snow, water, or grass (Figures 7-26 and 7-27). Warm colors seem to move toward the viewer and cool colors seem to recede, or move away.

The sensation of warmth and coolness of colors has been scientifically tested. Warm and cool colors really have different temperatures. Blind people have been able to recognize color from the temperature of color patches.

Figures 7.26 (below) **and 7.27** (facing page) The paintings in Figures 7.26 and 7.27 have different subjects. Notice how each artist has used a color scheme to enhance the mood of the work. Compare the actions and color schemes of the two works. Look for similarities and differences.

The amount of warmth or coolness depends upon a color's surroundings. Violet on a red background appears much cooler than the violet alone. However, the very same violet on a blue background seems much warmer than the violet alone.

DEVELOPING YOUR SKILLS

9. Make a chart to demonstrate the effects of colors on one another. Select a sheet of construction paper of a primary hue. Cut the paper into sixteen equal rectangles. Mount each of the small rectangles on a different-colored background. Use a variety of materials for the backgrounds. Try colored photos, painted areas, fabric samples, construction paper, and tissue

Figure 7.26   Reginald Marsh. *George C. Tilyou's Steeplechase Park.* 1936. Egg tempera on fiberboard. 91.4 × 121.9 cm (36 × 48"). Hirshhorn Museum and Sculpture Garden, Smithsonian Institution, Washington, D.C. Gift of Joseph H. Hirshhorn, 1966.

paper. Group the color pairs according to color scheme or degree of contrast. Can you think of another way to group them?

10. Arrange your initials or the letters of your name into a design on a square piece of paper (Figures 7-28A and 7-28B on the next page). The letters must touch the four edges of the square. Play with the letters—turn them upside down or twist them out of shape. Try making them fat or overlap them. Consider the letters as shapes. They do not have to be readable.

When you find a design you like, reproduce it on four squares of white paper. Now paint each design using one of the following color schemes:
- Monochromatic
- Analogous
- Complementary
- Triad
- Split-complementary
- Warm
- Cool

How do the color arrangements affect the design?

SOMETHING EXTRA

D. Do you have access to a computer with high-resolution, color-graphic capabilities? If you personally do not have such a computer, perhaps your school or the public library can make one available. Once you obtain access, do skill 10 again—this time with the computer. Print your final designs to share them with the class.

Figure 7.27 Frederick Frieseke. *La Chaise Longue.* 1919. Oil on canvas. 100.8 × 153.7 cm (39⅝ × 60½"). Hirshhorn Museum and Sculpture Garden, Smithsonian Institution, Washington, D.C. Gift of Joseph H. Hirshhorn Foundation, 1972.

Figure 7.28A Student work. Designing the letters of a name.

Figure 7.28B Student work. Designing the letters of a name.

Color in Pigments

Artists' **pigments** are finely ground, colored powders that, when mixed with a liquid, form paint. Pigment colors cannot match the purity and intensity of the colors of light.

Artists' paints are sometimes named according to the mineral the pigment powder is made from. For example, cadmium yellow is made with the mineral cadmium sulphide. Sometimes the place where the pigment was first discovered is part of the name. Burnt sienna, for instance, is made with clay found in the soil in Siena, Italy.

Before you buy paint, look at the manufacturer's color chart to find out what the color looks like. You will see that ultramarine blue, cobalt blue, cerulean blue, and thalo blue all look different.

Paint Vehicles

Whether an artist draws with wax crayons or paints with oil paints, he or she is using pigment. The liquid that pigments are mixed with is called the **vehicle.** The vehicle carries the pigment and makes it possible for the paint to adhere to surfaces, such as canvas. When pigments are mixed with wax, wax crayons are produced. To make oil paint, pigments must be ground in linseed oil.

Paint pigments do not dissolve—they remain suspended in the vehicle. When applied to a surface, the pigments stay on top of the surface. Pigments that dissolve in liquid are called *dyes*. Dyes do not remain on surfaces as paints do; dyes sink into the material and color by staining.

The pigment, the vehicle, and the surface to which the paint is applied all affect the color you see. Wet colors look brighter and darker than dry ones. Tempera and watercolor paints always look lighter and duller after they dry. Oil paints glow even when dry because of their oil vehicle. If diluted with turpentine, oil paints dry to a dull finish.

The density and color of the surface receiving the paint affects the way in which the light waves are reflected back to your eyes. Have your ever applied wax crayon over colored paper? The crayon lets some light through to the paper, and the colored paper absorbs some of these light waves. Only

Figure 7.29 This is a prehistoric cave painting. Notice how many subtle variations of color the prehistoric artist was able to create from the earth pigments.

Deer. c. 15,000 B.C. Altamira Caves, Spain. SCALA New York/Florence. Art Resource, New York, New York.

white paper reflects all of the light—only white allows the true color of the crayon to show.

Have you ever tried to match colors on two different surfaces? A brown, fluffy sweater can never truly match a brown leather bag. A shiny green, polyester shirt looks brighter than green knit pants even though the same dye is used. Shiny, dense surfaces always look brighter because they reflect more light.

Sources of Pigment

In the past, pigments came from animals, vegetables, and minerals. A kind of beetle and the root of a certain plant were both sources for reds. Another plant produced a deep, transparent blue. Ultramarine blue was made by grinding a semiprecious stone. The color ochre is natural clay colored by iron rust. Prehistoric people made paint from natural minerals. They ground the different earth colors into animal fat (Figure 7-29).

Figure 7.30   Student work. Earth pigments were used to create this painting. What difference would result if the student painted the same scene with synthetic paints?

Today, synthetic (artificially made) pigments have been developed by scientists. The synthetics are brighter and more permanent than natural pigments. But some artists still prefer to use natural colors. Many weavers color their yarns with natural dyes. Andrew Wyeth is a modern artist who uses only natural earth pigments.

DEVELOPING YOUR SKILLS

11. Collect and grind three of your own earth pigments (see below). Mix them with a vehicle and experiment with them. Try using a variety of brushes and surfaces. Finally, paint a design that shows all of the colors you can obtain from the pigments. See Figure 7-30.
12. Experiment by applying a variety of paint media to many different surfaces. Collect as many paints and surfaces as possible and cut the surfaces into regular, matching shapes. Try every paint on every surface. What conclusions can you make about paints, vehicles, and surfaces?

TECHNIQUE TIPS

Making Natural Earth Pigments

Anywhere there is dirt, clay, and sand, you can find natural earth pigments. Collect as many different kinds of earth colors as you can find (Figure 7-31).

Grind them as finely as possible. If you can, borrow a mortar and pestle from the science lab (Figure 7-32). Regardless of the method you use, your finished product will still be a little gritty. It will not have the smooth texture of commercial pigment.

For the vehicle, use one part white glue to one part water. Put a few spoons of powder into a small container and add the vehicle. Experiment with different proportions of powder and vehicle. When you have found the best proportion, apply the mixture to paper with a variety of brushes. The brushes you use should not be allowed to dry before you wash them because

the glue will solidify. Keep stirring your paint as you work to keep the earth grains from settling.

The powder will keep indefinitely. However, the mixed paint is difficult to store for more than a few days.

Figure 7.31   How many colors can you see in this clay?

Figure 7.32   Grinding earth pigments.

How Artists Use Color

You have studied the facts of color. Now you need to look at how artists use color in the language of art.

Optical Color

Sometimes artists reproduce colors as they see them. Until the late nineteenth century, this was the way all Western artists painted.

For example, in an automobile dealer's showroom, the color of a blue car is affected by light and other factors surrounding it. The car may sparkle as it reflects the showroom lights. Shadows on the car may look dark blue, or blue-violet. The red from the next car may cause a red-violet reflection on the blue surface.

A painter who is trying to show the car in its setting will use all of the colors involved. He or she will make use of *optical color*, the color that results

when a true color is affected by the atmosphere or unusual lighting. Optical color is the color that people actually perceive. Compare Figures 7-34 and 7-35 on the next page to see how the time of day affects color.

The Impressionists were deeply involved with optical color. They tried to express the sensation of light and atmosphere with their unique style of painting. They applied dots and dabs of spectral colors and did not mix black with any colors. They made gray, low-intensity colors by placing complements together. These low-intensity grays, such as

Figure 7.33 Gauguin thought about color as a musician thinks about music. His paintings were based on real-looking shapes, but he organized colors into abstract patterns that did not necessarily match the patterns in the objects being painted.

Paul Gauguin. *Fatata te Miti (By the Sea)*. 1892. Oil on canvas. 67.9 × 91.5 cm (26¾ × 36″). National Gallery of Art, Washington, D.C. Chester Dale Collection.

Figures 7.34 (at right) **and 7.35** (facing page)   Monet was one of the first artists to take his paints and canvases outside to view the subject directly. Before his time, artists made sketches outside. Then, working from their sketches, they created finished landscapes in the comfort of the studio. Monet quickly realized that the colors changed as the day progressed. To better understand the effect of light on color, he decided to paint the same subject at different times of the day, as the light changed. He created over thirty paintings of this cathedral. Notice how the shadows in these paintings are not black. Their colors are just not as bright as the colors lit by the sun.

Figure 7.34   Claude Monet. *Rouen Cathedral, West Facade, Sunlight.* 1894. Oil on canvas. 100.2 × 66 cm (39½ × 26″). National Gallery of Art, Washington, D.C. Chester Dale Collection.

dull blue and dull green are much richer and look more natural in landscapes than do grays made by mixing black and white.

Arbitrary Color

When artists use color to express feelings, they usually ignore the optical colors of objects. They choose the colors *arbitrarily*, which means they make their choices on the basis of personal prefer-ence. They choose arbitrary colors rather than op-tical colors because they want to use color to express meaning (Figure 7-33 on the preceding page). In abstract art, color teams up with the other elements to become the subject as well as the meaning of the work (Figures 7-20 on page 150 and 7-36 on page 162).

Bright colors are loud. Light, bright colors can create happy, upbeat moods. Cool, dark colors are often mysterious or depressing. Warm, low-intensity

Figure 7.35 Claude Monet. *Rouen Cathedral, West Facade.* 1894. Oil on canvas. 100.4 × 66 cm (39½ × 26″). National Gallery of Art, Washington, D.C. Chester Dale Collection.

earth tones are very comfortable and friendly and are often used to decorate rooms where people get together. A unique light value of red-orange has been used to calm people, and has even been successful in calming violent prisoners. Bright yellow is stimulating; blue soothes; and red excites.

Artists today have put their knowledge of color psychology to work to develop unusual methods for using color. Many of their choices are personal—they make color say what they wish to express.

Space

The placement of warm and cool colors can create illusions of depth. Warm colors expand toward the viewer and cool colors seem to contract and pull away. The French artist, Paul Cézanne, was the first to use warm and cool colors to create depth. He painted a cool, blue outline around the shape of a warm, round orange. The fruit seemed to be pushed forward by the surrounding blue.

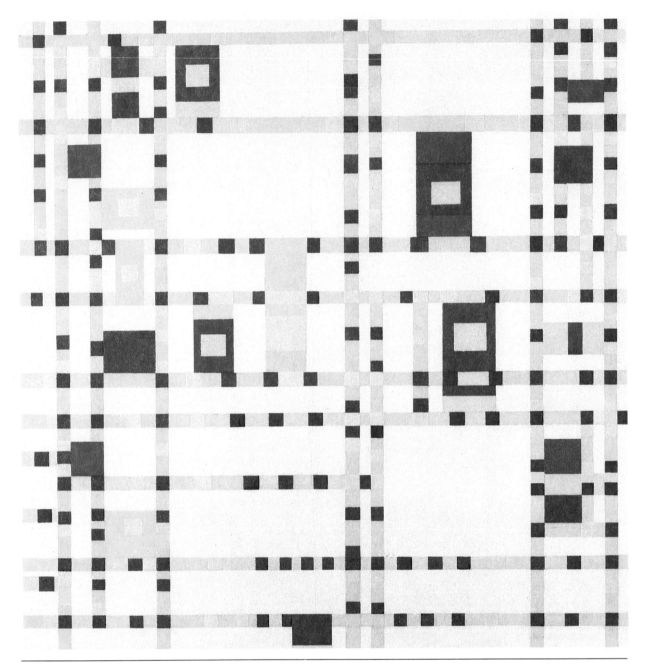

Figure 7.36   In this painting the value jumps are caused
by differences in the pure hues, as well as changes in value.
This painting was created in New York City during World
War II when the big bands played *boogie-woogie.*
Mondrian has captured the beat of the frantic dance by
his arrangement of very dark blue, medium dark red, light
yellow, and even lighter gray and white.

Piet Mondrian. *Broadway Boogie Woogie.* 1942–43. Oil on canvas.
127 × 127 cm (50 × 50″). Collection, Museum of Modern Art,
New York, New York. Given anonymously.

Movement

Color can create a sense of movement. When the values in a work jump quickly from very high-key to very low-key, a feeling of excitement and movement is created (Figure 7-36). When all of the values are close together, the work seems much calmer. Today's artists use color to create movement and depth in abstract art.

When you work with color to create movement, remember to use values of pure hues as well as those of tints and shades. You will need to remember, for instance, that the pure hue yellow is much lighter than red or blue.

Tonality

Sometimes an artist lets one color, such as blue, dominate the work. In such a case, the work is said to have a blue *tonality*. See Figure 7-37. The painting does not have to be a monochrome—there may be other colors present. However, the overall effect of the work is an impression of blueness. Tonality has a unifying effect.

DEVELOPING YOUR SKILLS

13. Make five small sketches of trees with leaves. Use a simple color medium, such as crayon. Paint each sketch to illustrate one of the following:
    - True color
    - Optical color
    - Color that expresses personal feelings
    - Depth through the use of warm and cool colors
    - Movement through value
    - Tonality

SOMETHING EXTRA

E. Research the symbolic meanings people have given to various colors. Have colors had different meanings in different cultures throughout history? Ask your English teacher if poets and writers have talked about color in different ways.

Figure 7.37 Picasso did not paint this work using a monochromatic color scheme. Look closely and you will find a little red and some yellow. The dominance of blue creates a tonality. Do you think blue conveys tragedy?

Pablo Picasso. *The Tragedy.* 1903. Oil paint on wood. 105.4 × 69 cm (41½ × 27⅛"). National Gallery of Art, Washington, D.C. Chester Dale Collection.

I M A G I N E   A N D   C R E A T E

Through the Looking Circle

MATERIALS

You will need the following:

Sheet of construction paper

Scissors, pencils, and tape

A round shape, approximately 6 inches (15.2 cm) in diameter, to trace around

Sheet of drawing paper, 12 × 18 inches (30.5 × 45.7 cm)

Large sheet of paper for painting, 18 × 24 inches (45.7 × 61 cm)

Drawing board

Another round shape, approximately 12 to 15 inches (30.5 to 38.1 cm) in diameter, to trace around

Variety of brushes and water

Opaque paints (tempera or school acrylics) in two primary colors and white and black

Palette on which to mix colors

Poster board

OBJECTIVE

Make a round viewing frame. Then, using the frame, make sketches of grasses and weeds. Next, create a round painting using an analogous color scheme. Mount the painting on a square piece of poster board for display. See Figure 7-38.

DIRECTIONS

Using the smaller round shape, trace a small circle in the middle of the construction paper and cut it out. You now have a round hole in the paper, which becomes your viewing frame (Figure 7-40). Trace the same shape onto your smaller sheet of drawing paper. Tape the

Figure 7.38   Student work. Using analogous colors.

Figure 7.39 Enlarge your original drawing.

Figure 7.40 Using the viewing frame.

drawing paper to your drawing board. Find an area where you can sit to observe growing things, such as grass and weeds, close up. Study the different shapes of grass and leaves through your viewing frame. Now, within the circle on your drawing paper, draw what you see. Using the larger round shape, trace a circle on the large paper and freely enlarge your first drawing to fill the circle (Figure 7-39). Then, using your creativity, add imaginary or real creatures and things to this new world.

Prepare a drying area and cover your work area. For paint, use only two primary colors and the secondary color they make when mixed together. Then add black and white, as needed, to create a variety of values from very pale tints to very dark shades. For example, if you choose blue and red, you will need to use different amounts of white to create the lighter values of violet, because violet is dark. You may also change the values of the two primaries.

When the painting is dry, cut it out and mount it on a square piece of poster board for display.

EVALUATION CHECKLIST

Be sure you did the following:

1. Drew a small sketch, following directions.
2. Enlarged the drawing freely without measuring.
3. Added imaginary creatures.
4. Used an analogous color scheme.
5. Mounted the round painting on a poster board for display.

Three-dimensional Amusement Park Ride

MATERIALS

You will need the following:

Sketching paper and pencils

Construction paper in the six colors of the spectrum

Cardboard and found materials, such as cardboard tubes, wire, yarn, paper plates, and paper cups

Scissors, white glue, tape, and pins

Storage container

OBJECTIVE

Design and build a model for a ride at the "Rainbow Amusement Park" (Figure 7-41). Use construction paper, cardboard, and found materials or materials used basically in their natural state. The ride must be decorated with hues from the spectrum in proper order.

Figure 7.41 Student work. A spectral ride.

DIRECTIONS

Plan your ride and make rough sketches of your plan.

Collect the necessary materials, place them in your storage container, and protect the work space.

Build your model carefully, using pins to hold the cardboard joints in place until the glue dries.

Decorate the ride with colors, using them in the same sequence as they appear in the spectrum.

Display the finished project.

EVALUATION CHECKLIST

Be sure you did the following:

1. Made rough sketches.
2. Collected the necessary materials.
3. Built a model using cardboard and found materials.

4. Joined the sections neatly.
5. Decorated the model with colors in their proper order (same order as in the spectrum).

Painting with Expressive Colors

MATERIALS

You will need the following:

Sketching paper and pencils

Heavy white paper

Yellow chalk

Painting medium and tools (your choice)

Poster board

Figure 7.42 Student work. Expressive colors.

OBJECTIVE

Make a painting of any subject, real or fantastic, using expressive colors (Figure 7-42). Let the colors help create the meaning. Mount or mat the finished work for display.

DIRECTIONS

Choose a subject for your painting, either a fantasy or real scene. Do rough pencil sketches and choose the best. Make the final drawing on the white paper using yellow chalk. Choose a color scheme to create the effect you wish. Do not be objective; paint with colors that express your feelings. Use the medium of your choice.

Protect your work space, plan a drying area, and clean up properly. Mount or mat the finished work for display.

EVALUATION CHECKLIST

Be sure you did the following:

1. Chose an interesting subject.
2. Made rough pencil sketches first.
3. Drew the subject on the white paper with yellow chalk.
4. Used a color scheme that expressed your feelings.
5. Were successful in creating the mood.
6. Took proper care of the materials and work space and planned for storage.
7. Prepared the finished work for display.

Painting—One Scene in Two Moods

MATERIALS

You will need the following:

Sketching paper and pencils

Two sheets of heavy white paper

Paints—limited to the three primaries and black and white

A palette or tray for mixing paint

Brushes and water

Large sheet of poster board

OBJECTIVE

Create two paintings from the same drawing of one building or a group of buildings. For the first painting create a bright, happy mood. For the second painting create a dreary, gloomy look (Figures 7-43 and 7-44).

DIRECTIONS

Study Monet's paintings of *Rouen Cathedral*, Figures 7-34 and 7-35, to see how he has used color to create different moods of the same subject matter.

Locate an interesting building—it can be a private home, a store, city hall, a barn, or even part of a large stadium.

Make a series of pencil sketches of the building.

Lightly sketch the building on the two sheets of white paper. Draw freely, without a ruler.

Collect your materials; plan a drying area; and protect your work space.

Using only the three primaries and black and white, mix your colors. Give one painting a dreary, gloomy look by using cool, low-intensity colors. Give the second a bright happy look by using warm, high-intensity colors.

Mount both scenes on one sheet of poster board for display.

EVALUATION CHECKLIST

Be sure you did the following:

1. Studied Monet's paintings of *Rouen Cathedral*.
2. Made a series of sketches of a building or a group of buildings.
3. Sketched the building or group of buildings freely on both sheets of paper without using a ruler.

4. Mixed all of the colors from the three primaries and black and white.
5. Used an opaque painting medium.
6. Took proper care of the materials and work space, and planned for storage.
7. Mounted the finished work as directed.

Figure 7.43   Student work. Bright and happy.

Figure 7.44   Student work. Dark and sad.

Figure 7.45 Henri Matisse. *The Red Studio*. 1911. Oil on canvas. 181 × 219.1 cm (71¼ × 86¼"). Collection. The Museum of Modern Art, New York, New York. Mrs. Simon Guggenheim Fund.

A R T C R I T I C I S M

Improving Your Critical-Thinking Skills

Description: What Do You See?

Read the credit line of *The Red Studio* by Henri Matisse to discover its size. Visualize it on the wall in your room. How much wall space would it fill?

Now list everything you see in the studio. Divide your list into objects that have been painted the same red as the studio and objects that have been painted in optical colors.

Write down every fact that you observe.

Analysis: How Is the Work Organized?

Although color has been the main topic of this chapter, you also need to look at the lines, shapes, forms, spaces, and their values, in the painting. In the language of art, all of the elements work together and can seldom be considered alone.

Notice Matisse's unusual use of line. Describe the pale yellow lines in this work. Where do you find them? What do they do?

What kinds of shapes stand out?

Does he use value to create the illusion of three-dimensional form? Is there any use of perspective to create the illusion of depth?

Can you find negative spaces?

What hues do you see?

Does any hue dominate this work?

Can you find primary, secondary, and intermediate colors in this work?

How does value affect this painting?

Do you see any tints or shades?

Do you see any neutral colors?

Are the colors high-key, low-key, or neither one?

Do you see colors of high or low intensity? Which ones dominate?

Is the effect of color contrasts at work here?

Has Matisse used a specific color scheme? If so, which one and for what reason?

Has Matisse used color objectively or to communicate feeling? Explain your answer.

Does he use warm and cool colors to create depth in this painting?

Do color values change gradually or rapidly? How does this affect the painting?

Is there color tonality?

Which element of art has the strongest effect on this painting? Explain your answer.

Interpretation: What Is Happening? What Is the Artist Trying to Say?

Based on the clues you have collected and your own ideas, what do you think the artist is trying to say about this studio? At the time he painted this, how do you think he felt about being an artist? What message is he sending to the viewer?

Write a paragraph explaining your interpretation of the work.

Judgment: What Do You Think of the Work?

Do you like this work? Do you like the way Matisse has organized the painting? Does the painting stir your emotions?

Use one or more of the three theories of art to defend the way you feel about this painting.

SOMETHING EXTRA

Think about your own room at home. What color would you use to represent your room? Using a piece of construction paper of that color and some wax crayons, make a drawing showing the important objects in your room.

A B O U T   T H E   A R T I S T

Henri Matisse

Figure 7.46   Henri Matisse, French, 1869–1954.

Photograph of Henri Matisse. Courtesy of The Bettmann Archive, Inc.

Nothing in the early life of Henri Matisse indicated the fame he was to achieve in the world of modern art. Matisse was born in 1869 in a small town in northern France. He showed no interest in art while attending high school. When he graduated, his father sent him to law school in Paris, where he received a degree.

Matisse might have spent the rest of his life as a lawyer if he had not had an attack of appendicitis at the age of twenty-one. He had to stay in bed for a long time, and Matisse soon became bored. His mother, who liked to paint and thought that painting might help him pass the time, bought him a paint box. This was the turning point in his life.

Matisse suddenly felt free. He knew what he wanted to do with the rest of his life. As soon as he was well enough, he persuaded his father to let him study art.

Paris in the 1890s was the most exciting place in the world for an artist. The Impressionists had made the world aware of color. Van Gogh and Cézanne were experimenting with new techniques, and a young artist named Picasso had just arrived from Spain.

Matisse experimented with different styles. By 1905 he had found a style of his own. He wanted to create works using flat shapes and simple colors, and he wanted to flatten out Renaissance space. He was not comfortable with shading and perspective. He was interested in organizing the visual qualities of objects, rather than representing the objects themselves.

At the age of 73, Matisse became bedridden. Instead of feeling defeated, he used the time to develop a new form of art. He hired some helpers and had them paint huge sheets of paper with the brightest colors. While they painted, he made many, many drawings. Then, when he was ready, Matisse cut all kinds of shapes—animals, acrobats, dancers, clowns—out of the colored papers. He then asked his assistants to pin the shapes to the wall. He had them arrange and rearrange the shapes.

Matisse called this new way of working "drawing with scissors." He spent the last fifteen years of his life in bed creating fantasies with cut paper. He covered the walls, the ceiling, the bed, and the floor with his shapes. Soon he was surrounded with a universe of his own creation.

To many people Matisse's work looks childlike. But this kind of simplicity is extremely difficult to accomplish. It is the result of his ability to look at a complex subject and reduce it to its simplest elements using line, shape, and color.

Chapter 7 Review: Talking about Art

USING THE LANGUAGE OF ART

For each new art term below, choose a work of art from this chapter. Then write a sentence about that work using the new term correctly in the sentence.

analogous colors
color
color spectrum
color wheel
complementary colors
hue

intensity
monochrome
pigments
shade
tint
vehicle

LEARNING THE ART ELEMENTS AND PRINCIPLES

1. Explain how the eye sees color.
2. What are the properties of color?
3. What are the colors of the spectrum?
4. Name seven color schemes.
5. What kind of surface would allow the true color of paint to show? Why? What kind of surface always looks the brightest? Why?
6. Name five ways in which artists use color to achieve different effects.

INCREASING YOUR ART AWARENESS

1. Why do you think the artist used mainly warm colors in Figure 7-26?
2. Look around your school at the colors of the walls. Which kinds of colors are they? What would you do, using color, to improve the visual quality of the school? Explain why you would make the changes and how you think the changes would affect the teachers and students.
3. Study Figures 3-1 and 7-27. Compare the ways each artist used color to achieve different effects.
4. Study Figures 7-13 and 7-37. Compare the ways the artists have used line, shape, form, space, and color to express different moods or feelings.
5. Study Figures 3-19 and 7-12. Compare the artists' use of shape, color, and value. Which work seems calmer?

UNDERSTANDING ART CULTURE AND HERITAGE

1. What is the oldest work of art shown in this chapter? What are some reasons this painting may have been created (see Chapter 3)?
2. List the artworks shown in this chapter that were created in the late nineteenth century. How are they alike? How are they different?
3. Which work of art in this chapter was painted by a man who was described as an outstanding Post-Impressionist in Chapter 3? What is the meaning of this work?
4. What work of art shown in this chapter is an example of Color Field Painting (see Chapter 3)?
5. Why would Figure 7-6 be considered an example of Op Art (see Chapter 3)?

JUDGING THE QUALITY OF ART

Look back at Tchelitchew's *Hide-and-Seek* (Figure 7-1). Use the four steps of art criticism to get to know this work. This is a very complex painting, so take your time hunting for the visual information.

As you describe the work, look very carefully at its dark center shape and the surrounding negative spaces. During analysis note how value alters your perception of which areas are positive and which are negative. (Look at the color questions on page 171 to help you study the effect that color has on this work.) Use all of this information when you interpret the painting—subject matter alone will not reveal the real meaning of the work. In your judgment of the painting, defend it with one of the three art theories.

LEARNING MORE ABOUT ART

How did artists make paint in the days before paints were commercially manufactured? When did the manufacture of commercial paints begin?

Figure 8.1 Today Vermeer is considered one of the greatest painters who ever lived. He painted ordinary, everyday things with extraordinary techniques. Notice in the painting below how he used light to make colors and textures look real.

Jan Vermeer. *Woman Holding a Balance.* c. 1664. Oil on canvas. 42.5 × 38 cm (16¾ × 15″). National Gallery of Art, Washington, D.C. Widener Collection.

Texture

LEARNING OBJECTIVES

After reading this chapter and doing the exercises, you will be able to

☐ understand how we perceive texture.

☐ describe various textures.

☐ reproduce textures by changing values.

☐ use texture as the expressive element in creating two- and three-dimensional works of art.

☐ understand how artists communicate by means of textures.

WORDS TO LEARN

In this chapter you will learn the meanings of the words listed below.

collages

decalcomania

frottage

grattage

matte surface

texture

visual texture

Every surface has a **texture.** Texture is the element of art that refers to how things feel, or how they *look* as if they might feel on the surface. No one needs to teach you about texture—you know what is rough and what is smooth. There are certain textures you enjoy touching, and there are surfaces you avoid because you do not like the way they feel.

Textures play an active part in many of the clothing decisions you make. Think how many times fabric textures have influenced your choices. Would you buy skintight pants made from rough burlap? Clothing manufacturers consider textures when they decide what fabrics to use. Why do they put silky linings inside winter coats and jackets? Which are more comfortable—prewashed jeans or stiff, scratchy new jeans?

The textures of foods influence what you eat. Think about the smoothness of ice cream, and consider how different it is from the angular roughness of potato chips. Would grilled steak taste the same if it were whirled around in a blender?

DEVELOPING YOUR SKILLS

1. Look around the room. List and describe the different kinds of textured surfaces.
2. Make a list of as many rough surfaces as you can think of. Make another list of smooth surfaces. Compare your lists in class.

Figure 8.2 What textures are represented in these photographs?

Photographs by Robert Nix.

How We Perceive Texture

We perceive texture with two of our senses: touch and vision. As infants we learned about things by touching them and by putting them into our mouths. Toddlers cannot keep their hands off anything—all breakable objects have to be placed out of reach. In a way we are still using our sense of touch when we look at surfaces. Our eyes tell us what something would feel like if we were to touch it.

When you actually touch something to determine its texture, you experience real texture. When you look at a photograph of velvet, leather, cement, or ice, you see surface patterns of light and dark that bring back memories of how those things really feel. When this happens, you are experiencing **visual texture,** which is the illusion of a three-dimensional surface. If you touch visual textures, you do not feel what your eyes told you to expect.

There are two kinds of visual texture: *simulated* and *invented*. Simulated textures imitate real textures. Plastic table tops are made to look like wood. Vinyl flooring is supposed to look like ceramic tile or stone. Manufactured fabrics imitate natural leather and fur. Figure 8-3 is an example of simulated texture in a painting.

Figure 8.3 There is not a brush stroke showing on this painting. The artist was an excellent draftsman, and before he began to paint he made many careful drawings of his subject. How many textured surfaces are shown in this painting? Notice the difference between the satin of the woman's dress and the white fabric of the two armchairs. At first glance you might think that the fabric on the blue mantelpiece is the same as the shawl on one of the chairs. Look again.

Jean-Auguste-Dominique Ingres. *Comtesse d'Haussanville*. 1845. Oil on canvas. 171.8 × 92 cm (51⅞ × 36¼"). The Frick Collection, New York, New York.

Figure 8.4 In this print the artist has invented textures by attaching textured materials to the printing plate. Looking closely you can see areas that appear to be wrinkled fabrics and papers. But if you look at the work as a whole, the textures remind you of rocks and layers of earth.

Hedi Bak. *Grand Canyon #2*. 1980. Collograph print, 76.2 × 111.8 cm (30 × 44″). Photo by Steve Elwood.

Invented textures are two-dimensional patterns created by the repetition of lines or shapes. These textures do not represent any real surface qualities, but somehow the patterns of light and dark in invented textures stimulate your memories of real textures. The purpose of invented texture is to create decorated surfaces that stimulate unusual textural memories (Figure 8-4).

DEVELOPING YOUR SKILLS

3. Think about how much you depend upon your sense of touch. Make a list of ten normal daily activities that involve your sense of touch. Then describe how the touching sensation affects your activity.

   For example, food has already been mentioned. Can you think of a food you like or dislike because of its texture? Think about walking. Your sense of touch works every time you put your foot down on the ground. You don't have to look down; you feel the ground with your foot, and without thinking, you allow that foot to support all of your weight.

4. Make a collection of texture rubbings (Figure 8-6). Cut the textured areas into interesting shapes. Arrange them on a dark sheet of construction paper and glue them down (Figure 8-7).

5. Choose two of your most interesting texture rubbings. Make a realistic pencil drawing on white paper of the textures. Examine the rubbings closely, paying special attention to the lines, dots, shapes, and values.

TECHNIQUE TIP

Rubbing

To make a rubbing, place a sheet of thin paper against an object or surface to be rubbed. See Figure 8-5. Hold the paper in place with one hand. Use the flat side of an unwrapped crayon or the side of a pencil point to rub over the paper. Always rub away from the hand holding the paper. Never rub back and forth because the paper or the object may slip. When you need to change hands, do so. You can make rubbings with either hand.

Figure 8.5 Rub the surface carefully.

Figure 8.6 Student work. A page full of texture rubbings.

Figure 8.7 Student work. Texture rubbings cut out and rearranged into a design.

Figure 8.8 Student work. Can you recognize the original textures in this composition?

6. Make a small dream landscape by cutting shapes of visual textures from magazines and arranging them on a background sheet of paper. Look for textures from different objects. Turn your imagination loose. Concentrate more on the textures than on the shapes. Look at a large photograph of chocolate cake; look at the texture of dog food. What can you do with the texture of hair? Of a rug (Figure 8-8)?

Texture and Value

What a surface looks like depends on the manner in which it reflects light. Every surface is an arrangement of light and dark values.

Rough and Smooth Textures

The roughness or smoothness of a texture can be recognized by means of the shadows. A rough surface reflects light unevenly (Figure 8-9). Rough textures show irregular patterns of light and shadow. Look at a shag run, an orange, tree bark, or a patch of bare ground. Notice how the high places catch the light, creating shadows of different sizes and shapes.

A smooth texture reflects light evenly (Figure 8-10). Look at a sheet of paper, an apple, or a new, unmarked desk top. Your eyes glide across these objects, uninterrupted by shadows, just as your fingers would glide across them, uninterrupted by bumps and dents.

Figure 8.9 Even though you can't touch the real texture, your eyes recognize the irregular patterns of light and dark. As a result, you can guess what this surface would feel like.

Figure 8.10 These apples reflect light evenly. The shadows you see on these apples are due to their round forms.

Figure 8.11 The soft, white, downy fiber of the cotton plant has been lit with bright light, but you see no highlights. Even though the fibers are not smoothly arranged, they reflect light evenly. The cotton has a matte surface.

Matte and Shiny Textures

A **matte surface** is a surface that reflects a soft, dull light. It absorbs some light and reflects the rest. Matte surfaces, such as paper, grocery bags, denim, unfinished wood, and your skin, have a soft, dull look (Figure 8-11).

A shiny surface is the opposite of a matte surface. A shiny surface reflects so much light so brightly that it seems to glow (Figure 8-12). Shiny surfaces also have highlights. Some surfaces glare in bright sunlight with such intensity that you have to squint your eyes. Window glass is shiny; so is a new car, a polished brass lamp, and the surface of a pool of water.

Matte and shiny surfaces can be rough or smooth. Sandpaper is matte rough, and a freshly ironed pillowcase is matte smooth. Aluminum foil is shiny and smooth until it gets wrinkled; then it becomes shiny and rough.

DEVELOPING YOUR SKILLS

7. Collect three examples of each of the four types of textures. Cut out a small shape from each and organize the shapes into the four groups. Glue the shapes on a small sheet of paper and label each group properly.

8. A **collage** is an artistic composition made by pasting various two-dimensional materials onto a surface. Use the rest of your collection from the preceding skill activity to make a texture collage on a small piece of heavy paper or cardboard (Figure 8-13). Cover all of the background with the materials. Place contrasting textures next to each other to make the design interesting. Consider color and shape as you work.

9. Draw the texture collage from the preceding activity with pencil or pen. First, sketch your shapes; then copy the texture of each shape using dots, lines, and value blending. Concentrate on the shadows, lights, and highlights of each different texture.

10. Make a series of small drawings and paintings of objects having different textures. Try to reproduce both smooth and rough textures (Figure 8-14). You may use a different medium for each study. Study the lights and shadows on each object before you choose each medium. For example, you might choose a hairbrush, an old work shoe, weathered wood, a wig, a fuzzy slipper, or a satin slip.

Figure 8.12 This rock is far from smooth. The irregular pattern of dark and light tells you that. But those white highlights tell you that this surface is also shiny. Those streaks are the highlights that indicate shiny surfaces.

Figure 8.13 (at right)   Student work. A texture collage.

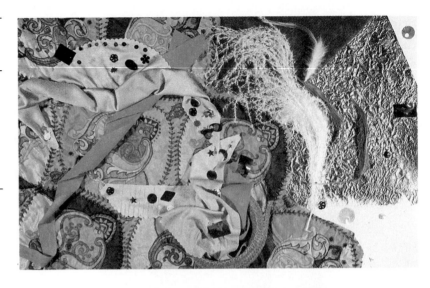

Figure 8.14 (below)   Looking for textures in this painting is like going on a treasure hunt. How many shiny surfaces can you find? Notice that each one has a different kind of highlight. Don't overlook the matte surfaces. They are just not as flashy.

Janet I. Fish. *Raspberries and Goldfish*. 1981. Oil on canvas. 182.9 × 162.6 cm (72 × 64"). The Metropolitan Museum of Art, New York, New York. Purchase. The Cape Branch Foundation and Lila Acheson Wallace gifts, 1983. 1983.171.

How Artists Use Texture

The texture of surfaces is important to every form of visual art. Our minds are full of texture memories. Artists use both visual and real textures to make you remember those texture experiences.

The artist Pierre Auguste Renoir painted young people with healthy, glowing complexions (Figure 8-15). Another artist, Ivan Albright, was concerned with the wrinkles of old age (Figure 8-16). In their works, both of these artists have imitated human skin. In one the skin is appealing; in the other it is repulsive because of the excessive attention to de-tail. Both artists try to control your reactions to the people in the paintings through the use of visual texture.

In the past, many painters reproduced the color and value patterns of textures. Look, for instance, at a painting by Jan Vermeer (Figure 8-1) or Rembrandt van Rijn (Figure 3-9). These artists were experts at suggesting textures such as soft velvet, shiny satin, delicate laces, and fluffy feathers. When you look closely at their paintings, you discover that they do not paint every texture in photographic de-tail. They use a few brush strokes to suggest the texture from a certain distance.

The *trompe-l'oeil* (French for "fool the eye") painters were masters of visual texture. See Figure

Figure 8.15 Renoir started his career as an artist in a porcelain factory. His job was to copy famous paintings of beautiful women onto the procelain plates. Renoir spent the rest of his life painting beautiful people. Even in his later years, when his fingers were crippled with painful arthritis, Renoir painted beautiful scenes full of happy people.

Auguste Renoir. *Young Woman Braiding Her Hair.* 1876. Oil on canvas. 55.6 × 46.4 cm (21⅞ × 18¼"). National Gallery of Art, Washington, D.C. Ailsa Mellon Bruce Collection.

6-24. All of the objects were shown in sharp focus with great care. Every color and value pattern of every surface was copied exactly. In these works the appearance of the objects is so realistic that, for a moment, you think you can touch what you see.

Many painters have added real textures to their paintings. Vincent van Gogh used such thick paint on his canvas that the swirling brush strokes created a rough surface (Figure 8-17 on the next page). The surface ridges of this thick paint actually make the paint look brighter. The ridges catch more light and reflect brighter color back to the viewer.

Figure 8.16 (below) Albright's painting is full of so many details that he reveals much more than would ever be noted in a casual glance. In this painting, Ida is a pathetic sight. Her face reveals the unhappiness of a woman who can do nothing to restore her lost youth.

Ivan Albright. *Into the World There Came a Soul Called Ida (The Lord in His Heaven and I in My Room Below).* 1929–30. Oil on canvas. 142.9 × 119.2 cm (56¼ × 47″). Courtesy of The Art Institute of Chicago, Chicago, Illinois. Gift of Ivan Albright. ©1987 The Art Institute of Chicago. All rights reserved.

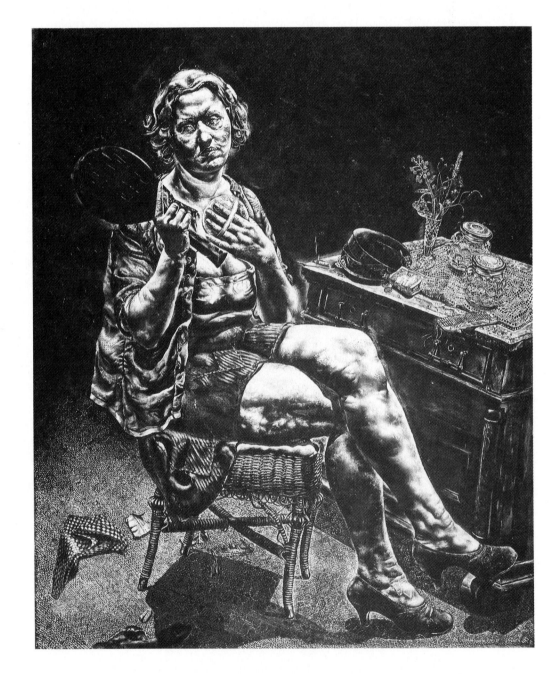

Figure 8.17   At times van Gogh became so impatient that he squeezed the paint from the tube directly onto the canvas. Then he used anything that was handy, including his fingers, to move the paint around.

Vincent van Gogh. *Cypresses.* c. 1889. Oil on canvas. 93.3 × 74 cm (36¾ × 29⅛"). The Metropolitan Museum of Art, New York, New York. Rogers Fund, 1949.

Figure 8.18   Picasso took many first steps that other artists followed. He was the first to create a mixed media painting by pasting on paper and adding pencil marks.

Pablo Picasso. *Glass, Guitar and Bottle*. 1913 spring. Oil, pasted paper, gesso, and pencil on canvas. 65.4 × 53.6 cm (25¾ × 21⅛"). Gift to The Museum of Modern Art, New York, New York. The Sidney and Harriet Janis Collection.

Some painters have added real textures to their work by attaching various materials to the work's surface. Some artists have added sand and other materials to the paint. In some cases, bits and pieces of textured paper and fabric have been pasted into paintings to create collages. Folk artists have used this technique for centuries. Picasso added bits of newspaper, tickets, and stamps to his paintings to enrich the surfaces (Figure 8-18). Today, artists use all kinds of materials to make collages and assemblages.

Architects use a variety of materials to create interesting surfaces on buildings. You can find stucco, brick, wood, stone, cement, metal, and glass in modern buildings (Figure 8-19). Interior designers select textures for rugs, drapes, furniture, pottery, and sculpture that complement different wall textures (Figure 8-20).

Sculptors must be aware of texture as they work because the texture of each surface must fit the whole. Some sculptors imitate the real texture of skin, hair, and cloth, and some create new textures to fit new forms (Figure 8-21 on the next page).

Weavers control texture through the use of fibers and weaving techniques (Figure 8-22). Potters

Figure 8.19   I. M. Pei designed this building, which is the East Building for the National Gallery of Art. Pei used the texture of pink Tennessee marble to link the new building with the old. Some of the works of art reproduced in this book are on exhibit in this building.

I. M. Pei. East Building: Exterior, National Gallery. 1978. Courtesy of the National Gallery of Art, Washington, D.C.

Figure 8.20   Pei also used pink marble in the interior of the East Building of the National Gallery.

I. M. Pei. East Building: Interior View, National Gallery. 1978. Courtesy of the National Gallery of Art, Washington, D.C.

Figure 8.21 What an unusual combination of textures! The figure of the young dancer is cast in bronze. Even the vest and the ballet shoes she wears are bronze. To that Degas added a skirt made of gauze-like fabric and a satin hair ribbon. Why do you think he added real textures to the metal figure?

Hilaire Germain Edgar Degas. *Little Fourteen-Year-Old Dancer.* Executed c. 1880, cast c. 1922. Bronze, tulle skirt and satin hair ribbon. 99.1 cm (39″) high. The Metropolitan Museum of Art, New York, New York. The H. O. Havemeyer Collection. Bequest of Mrs. H. O. Havemeyer, 1929.

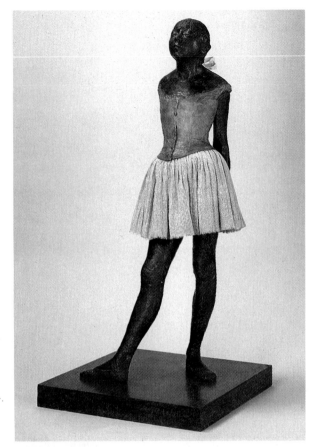

Figure 8.22 (below)   This wall hanging combines manufactured yarns with natural grasses.

Dorothy Gordon. *Wall Hanging.* 1978. Yarns and natural grasses. 40.6 × 15.2 cm (16 × 6″). Private collection.

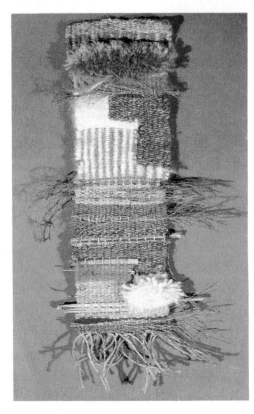

change textures by pressing different objects into wet clay. They can also change surfaces with glazes. Some glazes are shiny, and some have matte finishes (Figure 8-23). Feathers, river rocks, sea shells, seeds, bones, and teeth have been used to make jewelry (Figure 8-24).

Today, the true textures of paint, stone, and fibers are more important to artists. A sculptor leaves marks on his work that can be recognized as tool marks (Figure 8-25). There is no attempt to hide the record of the tool that shaped the work. A painter brushes on paint and does not try to smooth away the brush strokes (Figure 8-26).

Painters and printmakers invent textures to enrich their works. Max Ernst (Figure 8-27, page 191) used three unusual techniques—*frottage, grattage,* and *decalcomania*—to create his fantasies. To create **frottage** Ernst placed freshly painted canvas right-side-up over a raised texture and scraped across the surface of the paint. The paint that remained created a pattern that was an image of the texture below. To create **grattage** effects, Ernst scratched into wet paint with a variety of tools, such as forks,

Figure 8.23 (at left)   The contrasts on this pot are created entirely by surface textures. The pot is made with black clay from the Southwest. The shiny areas were polished with a smooth river stone before the pot was fired. The matte areas are the clay's natural surface.

Artist Unknown. *Black on Black Clay Pot.* Clay. 20.3 cm (8″) tall. Private collection.

Figure 8.24 (above)   The forest Indians of Ecuador use brilliant tropical bird feathers to create ornaments. These ornaments were created to decorate ears and hair.

South American Indian. *Featherwork Ornaments.* Collected 1938 by E. Erskine. Museum of American Indian, Heye Foundation, New York, New York.

Figure 8.25 (at left)   The artist made no attempt to hide the way these flowing forms were welded and forged to create these giant symbols of celebration. This Menorah (candle holder used in Jewish worship) seems to dance like the flames of the candles.

Gunther Aron. *Menorah for Synagogue.* c. 1970. Welded and forged steel. 198.1 cm (78″) high. Photograph by Charles Reynolds. Private collection.

Figure 8.26 The crowded confusion of brush strokes explodes into a wild expression of modern life. The subject of the painting, as well as its visual quality, is the thickly textured paint and the brush strokes themselves.

Willem deKooning. *Untitled V.* 1977. Oil on canvas. 201.9 × 175.9 cm (79½ × 69¼″). Albright-Knox Art Gallery, Buffalo, New York. Gift of Seymour H. Knox, 1977.

razors, and combs. Finally, Ernst squeezed wet blobs of paint between two canvas surfaces and then pulled the canvases apart. This technique is called **decalcomania.** The paint was forced into random textured patterns. With this as a basis, Ernst elaborated on the design. The patterns inspired him to create fantasy landscapes.

DEVELOPING YOUR SKILLS

11. Use fingerpaint or acrylic paint on strong paper or fabric. Then experiment with frottage, grattage, and decalcomania.
12. On a small piece of white paper, draw nine shapes of different sizes with pencil or felt-tip pen. Have some shapes touching the edges of the paper. Fill each shape with sketches of a

different texture. The textures should be invented. For instance, you could use lines of writing placed closely together in one shape, or you could try repeating small shapes in another. Try line patterns, stippling, or smooth shadow.

Figure 8.27 Ernst was a surrealist who invented new methods of creating textures. Can you identify different textures in the fantasy landscape above?

Max Ernst. *Eye of Silence.* 1943–44. Oil on canvas. 108 × 141 cm (42½ × 55½"). Washington University Gallery of Art, St. Louis, Missouri. Kende Sale Fund. WU 3786.

SOMETHING EXTRA

A. Imagine that you have just become best friends with someone who has been blind since birth. You want to share your visual world with this person. To do so you must talk about how things feel, their textures, to describe how they look. How could you describe clouds, blue sky, the first light of dawn, or the glow of sunset? Think of five other things you might describe.

I M A G I N E   A N D   C R E A T E

Textured Fantasy Landscape

MATERIALS

You will need the following:

Paint: school acrylics or tempera

Two sheets of heavy paper or two canvases

Scratching and rubbing tools, such as combs and rulers

Brushes, palette, and jars of water

Magazine photographs

Scissors and white glue

Poster board for mounting finished work

OBJECTIVE

Create a fantasy landscape with paint using Max Ernst's techniques for textured areas. Add details such as people, animals, and plants using paint or collage. See Figure 8-29.

DIRECTIONS

Study the painting by Max Ernst (Figure 8-27). Analyze the techniques he used to create the textured areas.

Collect all of the materials you will need, plan for storage and drying areas, and protect your work space.

Apply blobs of color to the surface of your painting. Place a second painting surface over the painting and use pressure to push the paints around. Then pull the two surfaces apart quickly (Figure 8-28). Rub or scratch the surfaces if you wish to enhance the textured areas, and then let the paint dry.

Study the textured shapes you have made and let the shapes give you ideas for your fantasy picture. Do you see land or animal forms

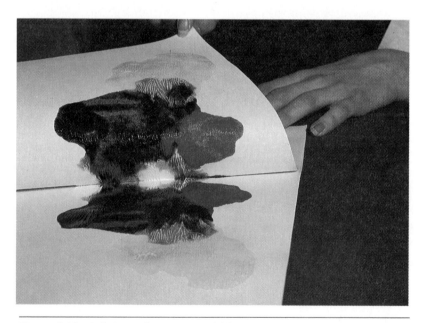

Figure 8.28 Pull the surfaces apart quickly.

Figure 8.29 Student work. Fantasy landscape.

among the shapes and textures? Do you feel you need to paint out some parts, or do you need to add more textured areas?

Turn you imagination loose and add details using paint and/or collage.

Mount or mat your fantasy landscape for display.

EVALUATION CHECKLIST

Be sure you did the following:

1. Studied the painting by Ernst.
2. Used a variety of media.
3. Used a variety of techniques to invent textures.
4. Studied the textures to determine what things to add.
5. Made additions and/or subtractions to the original textures.
6. Planned for storage and drying areas.
7. Protected the work space.
8. Cleaned up properly.
9. Mounted the work for display.

Textured-Clay Wind Chimes

MATERIALS

You will need the following:

Paper, pencils, and scissors

Wet ceramic clay, ready to use

Jar of water

Cloth-covered board

Cutting tool—paring knife, nail, or open paperclip

Texturing objects—bolts, sea shells, gears, wire mesh, burlap, tree bark, comb, weeds and twigs, rope, gears, etc.

Rolling pin

Scrap fabric

Hole-cutting tool or drinking straw

Piece of bamboo, dowel, or tree branch

Thin, strong yarn or string

OBJECTIVE

Design and make a set of five or more wind chimes from textured ceramic clay (Figure 8-30). Create real textures by pressing found objects onto the surfaces of the chimes while they are still wet. Hang the chimes.
Note: This project requires a kiln to fire the clay.

DIRECTIONS

Design an interesting shape or set of shapes for your wind chimes. Then draw and cut out paper patterns for them.

Plan for storage of your materials and make sure your work space is protected.

First, experiment with some textures. Flatten out some of the clay on the cloth-covered board. Next, place the scrap fabric over the clay and use the rolling pin to roll the clay flat and thin (Figure 8-31). Press the different texture-making objects into it. Decide which textures will best suit your chimes by trying various effects. Repeat the same impression in the clay, over and over.

Figure 8.30 Student work. Hanging textured wind chimes.

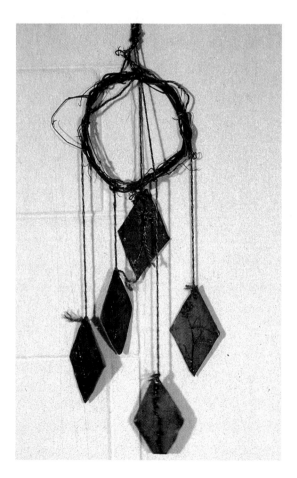

Figure 8.31 Roll the clay flat.

Figure 8.32 Trace the pattern onto the clay.

SAFETY NOTE

Like other powders, clay dust may be harmful to people who are asthmatic or who have breathing difficulties. If you are such a person, wear a face mask. Even if you are working with wet clay, a certain amount of dust will be released into the air.

If the clay dries too quickly, add some water and knead the clay until it feels as it did when you began to work.

Now roll out the clay for your first workpiece. Trace around the paper patterns on the clay and cut out the shapes (Figure 8-32).

Add texture to one surface of each chime by using the texture-making objects you found most effective. Smooth the edges and the back of each chime (Figure 8-33). You may find it easier to work with wet fingers at this point. Be careful not to use too much water.

Next, cut a hole in each chime with a straw so that you can tie a string to it later. The hole must be made while the clay is still wet (Figure 8-34).

Let the chimes dry slowly. Cover them lightly with plastic, and turn them over after a few hours so that they do not warp.

When the chimes are bone dry, they are ready to fire in the kiln.

After the chimes are fired, cut different lengths of string and tie the chimes to the piece of bamboo. However, you don't want the lengths so different that the chimes fail to touch at all. Be sure the chimes are close enough to each other that they will touch and clink in the wind.

Tie a string to both ends of the bamboo and make a loop for hanging.

Figure 8.33 Smooth the edges.

Figure 8.34 Cut a hole with the straw.

EVALUATION CHECKLIST

Be sure you did the following:

1. Made paper patterns.
2. Experimented with a variety of textures, using different objects.
3. Rolled out a thin slab of clay on the cloth-covered board.
4. Traced the paper patterns onto the clay and cut out the chimes.
5. Textured one surface of the chimes.
6. Smoothed the edges and the backs of the chimes.
7. Cut a hole in each chime for hanging.
8. Turned the chimes while they dried so that they would not warp.
9. Organized and tied the chimes so that they would bump and make sounds.
10. Planned for storage and drying areas.
11. Cleaned up the work space.

Texture Stitchery *

MATERIALS

You will need the following:

A 12-inch (30.5-cm) square of open-weave fabric, such as burlap or monk's cloth

Fabric scraps

Variety of fibers—thick and thin yarns, embroidery threads, sewing thread, crochet thread, etc.

Variety of needles—tapestry and crewel

Scissors

Sketch paper, pencil, and white wax crayon

Tape

Whatever you need to complete a hanging or box, etc.

Storage container

Optional:

embroidery hoop

OBJECTIVE

Cover a small square of fabric with a variety of stitches and fibers, but limit the colors so that texture is the outstanding element. Use the finished textured fabric to make a wall hanging, a cover for a box lid, one side of a pillow, or something else you would like (Figure 8-35).

DIRECTIONS

Study Figure 8-37 on page 199. Notice how the artist has used a variety of stitches to create different surface textures.

Hem or tape the edges of your fabric square so that the threads don't unravel.

Use the sketch paper and pencil to plan a design. The design should fill an area 10 inches (25.4 cm) square, leaving a margin on each side. Use any kind of shapes you wish as long as they vary in size.

Gather together all of the materials you will use. Remember to limit the colors but vary fiber size and type. Keep all of your project materials in the storage container.

Copy your design onto the fabric with the white crayon.

Study the stitches in Figure 8-36 and practice them on scrap fabrics.

Fill each shape in your design with different stitches. Be sure to use the right needle for each fiber. Use different types of yarn to help vary textures (Figure 8-35).

When you finish, the entire surface of the fabric should be covered with stitches.

Decide how you will use the finished stitchery. For use as a wall hanging, hem both sides and sew the top and bottom around a thin rod. To decorate a box, glue the hemmed fabric to the lid. If you wish to use it for a pillow, you may sew it to one side of a purchased pillow.

Figure 8.35 Student work. Embroidery stitches.

*This is NOT a "girls only" activity! Even famous football players do stitchery to relax.

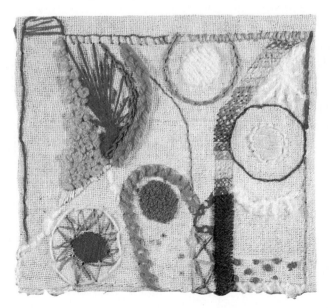

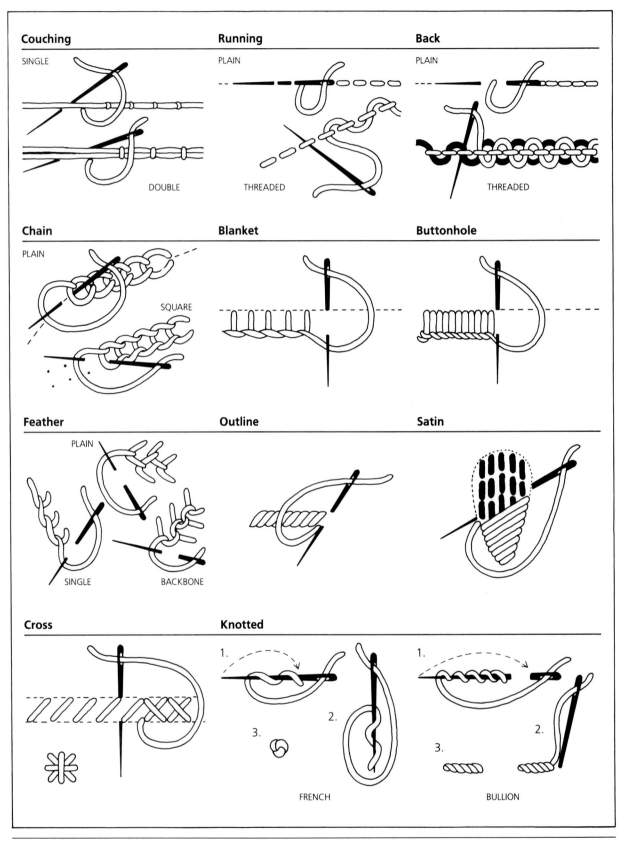

Figure 8.36 Basic stitches.

Figure 8.37 How many different embroidery stitches can you find? Use the stitch chart (Figure 8-36 on the opposite page) to help you identify different stitches.

Marguerite Zorach. *The Circus, 1929.* Colored wool on unbleached linen. 52.1 × 57.2 cm (20½ × 22½"). The Metropolitan Museum of Art, New York, New York. Gift of Irwin Untermyer, 1964. 64.101.1404.

EVALUATION CHECKLIST

Be sure you did the following:

1. Studied Marguerite Zorach's stitchery in Figure 8-37.
2. Bound the edges of the fabric to prevent unraveling.
3. Planned a design and drew it on the fabric.
4. Kept all materials in a storage container.
5. Chose a limited color scheme.
6. Studied and practiced stitches.
7. Filled shapes with different stitches made with different fibers.
8. Covered the entire design surface.
9. Turned the stitchery into a finished product.

Weaving

MATERIALS

You will need the following:

Large rectangle of heavy cardboard no smaller than 9 × 12 inches (22.9 × 30.5 cm) and no larger than 12 × 18 inches (30.5 × 45.7 cm)

Scissors, ruler, pencil, and tape

Strong, thin fiber for the warp, such as crochet thread or plain string

Variety of yarns, strings, and found materials for the weft

Tapestry needles and a comb

Dowel rod or tree branch

Figures 8.38A and **8.38B**   Student works. Finished weavings.

OBJECTIVE

Create a piece of fabric for a wall hanging using a cardboard loom and a variety of fibers and found materials (Figures 8-38 A and B). Limit the color scheme and emphasize texture by varying the fibers and materials. Sew or tie the finished fabric to a rod for hanging.

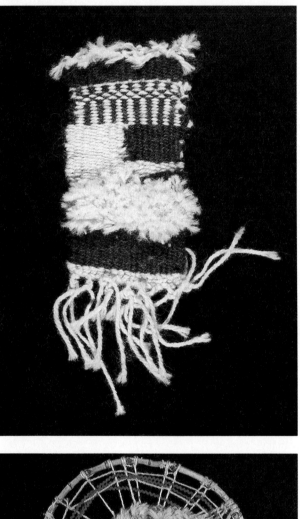

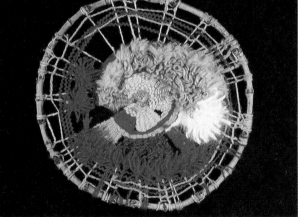

DIRECTIONS

Make your cardboard loom. Use a ruler to mark every 1/4 inch (0.6 cm) across the top and bottom of the cardboard rectangle (Figure 8-39). Make a cut about 1/2 inch (1.3 cm) deep at each mark.

Tape the warp thread to the back of the loom. (The warp thread is the vertical yarn held stationary by the loom.) Bring it to the front through the top left notch. Pull it down to the bottom of the loom and pass it through the bottom left notch to the back (Figure 8-40). Now move one notch to the right and continue until you reach the last notch. Then tape the end of the warp thread to the back.

Collect the various yarns and fibers that you will use to weave. Include fat, fluffy yarns; thin, smooth yarns; and strips of fabric. Look for other fiber-like materials to add texture, such as long grasses and weeds, vines, paper strips, shoelaces, and ribbons. Remember to limit the colors so that texture will be noticed.

Start to weave at the bottom of your loom using a thin yarn (Figure 8-41). The weft yarns are the horizontal yarns that intersect the warp to make fabric. The easiest way is to pull your weft yarn through the warp threads using an over-one-under-one motion. Leave a few inches of weft hanging when you start; it can be woven in later. At the end of the first row, you reverse. If you wove over the last thread,

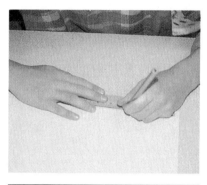

Figure 8.39 Measure carefully.

Figure 8.40 Warping a loom.

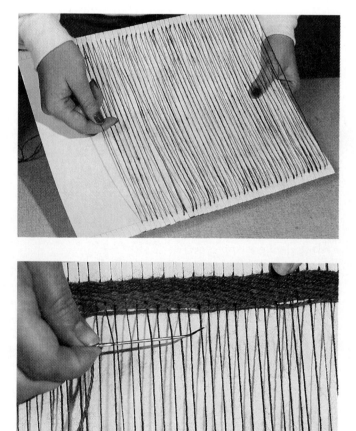

Figure 8.41 Weave over and under.

you must weave under it when you start the next row (Figure 8-42). Do not pull the weft too tight. You may use the tapestry needle to help you.

After you have woven a few rows of weft, you can pack the threads together with the comb (Figure 8-43). The tighter the weave, the stronger it will be.

After you have about one inch (2.5 cm) of thin, tight weave, you can experiment with different fibers and different weaving techniques (Figure 8-44). Be sure to end at the top with another inch (2.5 cm) of thin, tight weave.

Before you remove the fabric from the loom, weave in the loose ends. Cut the warp threads from the loom carefully, and tie two at a time with simple knots so they will not unravel.

Tie or sew the finished fabric to a dowel rod. Make a hanging loop by tying a piece of string to both ends.

EVALUATION CHECKLIST

Be sure you did the following:

1. Made a cardboard loom, measuring carefully.
2. Attached the warp correctly.
3. Collected a variety of yarns.
4. Started with a thin, tight weave.
5. Used a variety of yarns and weaving techniques.
6. Wove in all loose ends.
7. Cut warp threads and tied them properly.
8. Attached the finished weaving to a rod for hanging.

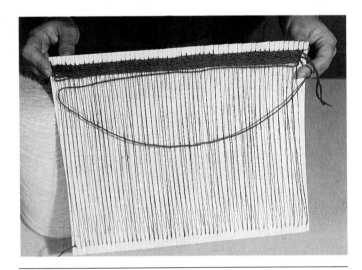

Figure 8.42 As you pull the weft through the warp, curve it slightly upward. Then, when you pack the weft tight, the warp threads will not be pulled in toward the center.

Figure 8.43 Packing the weft.

Figure 8.44 Weaving technique.

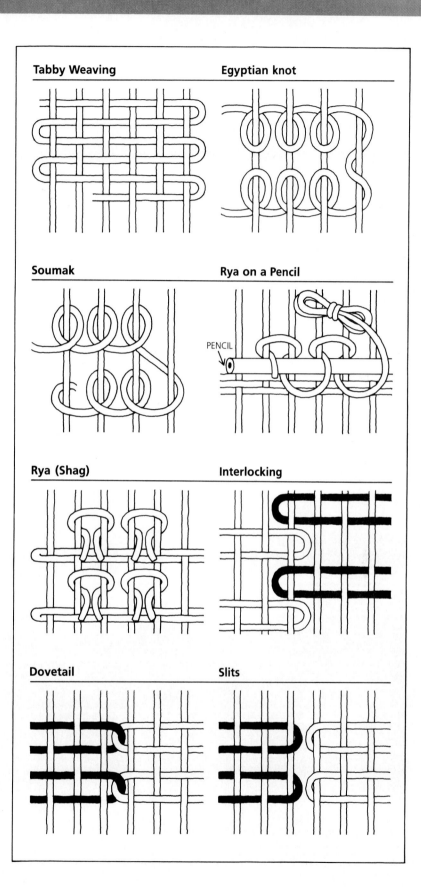

Figure 8.45   John Singleton Copley. *Paul Revere.* c. 1768–70.
Oil on canvas. 88.9 × 72.3 cm (35 × 28½"). Museum of Fine Arts,
Boston, Massachusetts. Gift of Joseph W., William B., and Edward
H. R. Revere.

A R T   C R I T I C I S M

Improving Your Critical-Thinking Skills

Description: What Do You See?

Study the portrait, *Paul Revere*, by John Singleton Copley (Figure 8-45). Read the credits to note the size of the work. How large would Revere's head be if you were standing in front of the work?

Describe exactly what you see in this painting. Look closely at Revere's face and describe his expression. Notice his hair, his clothes, and his position.

What other objects do you see in this painting?

Write down every fact you observe.

Analysis: How Is the Work Organized?

Before you study the textures in this work, describe the way the other elements affect the work. If you need help, review the earlier chapters.

Notice the lines. Do you see outlines or simply lines that appear on the edges of shapes? Do you see more static or active lines? Which ones have the strongest effect on the expressive quality of the work?

Now study the shapes and the spaces around them. Are there any areas of empty negative space? If so, where? What kinds of shapes do you see? How do they affect the expressive quality of the work?

Notice the values. Where are the lightest and darkest areas? Do you see any middle values? Has Copley used value to create the illusion of three-dimensional form? If so, where and how?

What colors do you see? Be careful. Look closely before you answer. Notice the table top. You know wood is brown, but Copley has used other colors as well. Why?

What has Copley done to make the silver teapot look silver? He has not used metallic paint, but it's obvious that the teapot is made of metal.

Do you find high- or low-intensity colors? Are they warm or cool? How do the colors affect the expressive qualities of the work?

Now look at the way Copley used texture. Did he use real or visual textures?

Do you see any brush strokes, or has he smoothed them away?

Did Copley reproduce textures as he saw them, or did he invent his own?

Locate and describe rough, smooth, matte, and/or shiny textured surfaces.

Do you see different degrees of texture? For example, are some things more shiny than others?

Interpretation: What Is Happening? What Is the Artist Trying to Say?

What has Copley said about Paul Revere in this painting? Is Paul Revere still the legendary man who rides a hobby horse through Grant Wood's toy town? (page 63). How does Copley's attitude about Paul Revere compare to Wood's?

Write a paragraph explaining your interpretation. Then write a new title for the work. Your title should sum up your interpretation.

Judgment: What Do You Think of the Work?

Do you like or dislike this work? Defend your answer using one or more of the three theories of art. See Chapter 2 to review these theories.

SOMETHING EXTRA

This painting was finished around 1770. Imagine that Revere is sitting across the table from another revolutionary leader. Who could be sitting with Revere? Write a dialogue for the two. End it with Revere in a thoughtful posture—his chin in his hand—thinking about the last statement or question made by his visitor.

A B O U T   T H E   A R T I S T

John Singleton Copley

Figure 8.46   John Singleton Copley, American, 1738–1815.

John Singleton Copley. *The Copley Family* (Detail). 1776–77. Oil on canvas. 188.4 × 229.7 cm (72½ × 90⅜"). National Gallery of Art, Washington D.C. Andrew W. Mellon Fund.

John Singleton Copley is generally considered the greatest portrait painter of the Colonial period in America. He was born on July 3, 1738, just one year after his parents had come to Boston from Ireland. His father died on a trip to the West Indies, but his mother was a strong, determined woman. She supported her family by running a tobacco shop.

When Copley was eleven, his mother married Peter Pelham, who was a painter, a printmaker, and a teacher. Pelham quickly discovered the young Copley's talent and gave him his first art lessons. The Pelham home was a gathering place for artists of that time. Copley saw prints of works by such famous artists as Raphael, Michelangelo, and Rubens.

In 1766 Copley sent *Boy with a Squirrel*, his portrait of his younger brother, to a London exhibition. Sir Joshua Reynolds, a leading artist in London, wrote to Copley and encouraged him to come to Europe to study. Copley was hesitant to leave America, but finally, in 1774, he sailed for London. He later toured the continent while studying art.

Copley had left his wife and children with her family in Boston. But his father-in-law was one of the importers of that famous shipment of tea that was dumped into Boston Harbor during the Boston Tea Party. Because of that incident, his father-in-law left the Colonies in anger, taking Copley's wife and children with him to London. Copley, who was then in Italy, joined them.

In the tradition of the New England Puritans, Copley placed truth above elegance. The portraits he painted revealed the personalities of his subjects. His strong value contrasts and his steel-like precision might have come from his early training as an engraver. He used strong lights to model the figure, which he placed before a solid, dark background. He also used hard edges—exactly opposite to the soft, Rococo style of European art at that time.

Copley enjoyed brief success in London. At first his art was appreciated and earned high prices. But he was not used to painting portraits in only five one-hour sittings, as was the custom in London. In America his models were willing to sit as long as ninety hours. As a result, he could not compete with the fashionable London painters.

Copley's life ended on a sad note, for he was constantly troubled by debts. For some reason he felt as if he had betrayed his original talent for honestly portraying people. In his old age he longed to return to America, but he remained in London until he died.

Chapter 8 Review: Talking about Art

USING THE LANGUAGE OF ART

For each new art term below, choose a work of art from this chapter. Then write a sentence about that work using the new term correctly in the sentence.

collages
decalcomania
frottage
grattage

matte surface
texture
visual texture

LEARNING THE ART ELEMENTS AND PRINCIPLES

1. With what senses do we perceive texture?
2. What is the difference between real and visual texture?
3. What is the difference between simulated and invented texture?
4. Name the four types of textures.
5. What determines how a surface looks?
6. By what can the roughness or smoothness of a texture be recognized?
7. What kind of a surface reflects light unevenly?
8. What kind of texture reflects light evenly?

INCREASING YOUR ART AWARENESS

1. Look at the photographs in Figure 8-2. Describe three of those photographs without naming any of the things in them. You may only describe the lines, shapes, spaces, values, and textures in the photographs. Your description should be so complete that another person could guess what you are describing.
2. What kind of visual texture is shown in Figure 1-2? What surfaces in this drawing appear to be rough? Which appear to be smooth?
3. How would you describe the different surface textures of St. George's armor in Figure 1-1? How would you compare these textures to that of the horse's body? How were the different effects created?
4. What textures do you see in Figure 2-10?

5. Compare the ways Ingres (Figure 8-3), Renoir (Figure 8-15), and Albright (Figure 8-16) have used texture in the representation of women.
6. Compare texture in Figures 3-19 and 8-17. What purpose does it serve in each?

UNDERSTANDING ART CULTURE AND HERITAGE

1. What is the title of the oldest work of art shown in Chapter 8? Name the artist.
2. In chronological order, list all of the artworks (with dates) shown in this chapter that were created in the nineteenth century. How are they alike? How are they different?
3. Which of the nineteenth-century paintings in this chapter is an example of the Neoclassic style (see Chapter 3)? Give reasons for your answer. Which is an example of Impressionism (see Chapter 3)? Give reasons for your answer.
4. What style of art is represented by Figure 8-18 (see Chapter 3)?

JUDGING THE QUALITY OF ART

Look at Vermeer's painting called *Woman Holding a Balance* (Figure 8-1). Use the four steps of art criticism to decide what message the artist was trying to convey. During analysis, be sure to examine not only texture, but all of the art elements you have studied so far. Can you interpret what Vermeer is saying? As you judge this work, be sure to use one or more of the art theories to defend your choice.

LEARNING MORE ABOUT ART

Artists have many special techniques to help them represent texture in painting. At the library find a book about painting techniques. Try to use some of the special tricks you discover to create the illusion of various textures. Present your findings to the class. Your report might take the form of a demonstration, or you might put up a bulletin board to illustrate your findings.

Joseph Stella. *The Brooklyn Bridge: Variations on an Old Theme.*
1939. Oil on canvas. 177.8 x 106.7 cm (70 x 42"). Collection of
Whitney Museum of American Art, New York, New York.

PART THREE

The Principles of Design

I t has been fairly easy to identify and isolate the elements of art. They have been pulled apart from each other and examined, one by one.

Have you ever taken apart a watch or a motor? If so, you know that it is much easier to take something apart than to put it back together. Putting art together is the purpose of the principles of design. In this part of *ArtTalk* you will learn about six principles. They are *rhythm, balance, proportion, variety, emphasis,* and *unity.*

The principles are *not* laws that have been handed down through the years. No master artist has ever recorded them for all time. They are simply guides that have been discovered by artists as they learned how people react to different visual effects. Artists have discovered that certain principles are a part of human nature—that they are necessary for people to experience visual comfort.

The principles of design will not guarantee success for an artist. The principles cannot inspire artists to new creative heights. The principles can only guide artists as they use the elements of art to solve visual problems and to express themselves.

Understanding the principles of design will help you understand how art objects are organized. It will also help you create successful works of your own. You will learn to recognize each principle in your natural environment and in works of art. You will then see how artists use a principle to express their feelings and ideas. At the same time, you will work at developing a skillful use of that principle in your own art.

As you did with the elements in Part Two, you will learn one principle at a time. At the end of each chapter you will add this new principle to your accumulated knowledge of elements and principles. After completing Chapter 12, you will have all the "words" and "grammar" you need to speak the language of art.

Gino Severini. *Dynamic Hieroglyphic of the Bal Tabarin.* 1912. Oil on canvas with sequins. 161.6 × 156.2 cm (63⅝ × 61½″). Collection, The Museum of Modern Art, New York, New York. Acquired through the Lillie P. Bliss bequest.

Rhythm and Movement

LEARNING OBJECTIVES

After reading this chapter and doing the exercises, you will be able to

- identify rhythms occurring in the world around you.
- understand how rhythm adds a sense of movement to a work of art.
- Identify and explain motif and pattern.
- Name and identify the types of rhythm.
- Use the principle of rhythm to create your own works.

WORDS TO LEARN

In this chapter you will learn the meanings of the words listed below.

kinetic sculpture

pattern

module

motif

rhythm

Rhythm is a hand-clapping, toe-tapping musical beat.

Rhythm is the throb of bass notes booming out of stereo speakers. It is the steady strumming on a guitar.

Rhythm is the synchronization of a marching band and a drill team making snappy moves.

Rhythm is the flashing lights and wailing sounds of fire engines.

Rhythm is the coming and going of the moon.

Rhythm is the steady beating of a heart.

Rhythm is tempo.

Rhythm is beat.

Life is full of rhythmic events. People crave the dependable rhythms of life. Rhythms are comforting. There is a rhythmic cycle to the seasons. Spring always follows winter, and when it does, people feel like celebrating. When you go to bed at night, you expect the next day. You are sure the earth will turn, the sun will rise, and day will follow night. The rhythmic routines of daily living give your life a sense of stability and security.

DEVELOPING YOUR SKILLS

1. Make a list of six events that are a part of your own daily rhythm, such as brushing your teeth.
2. Use a tape recorder to collect five non-musical, rhythmic sounds, such as footsteps, motors running, and typing.

Figure 9.2   This artist saw the meaning of existence in the changes of weather and seasons. He uses rhythms to express the living force in the natural environment. The elements in this painting seem to dance the dance of life.

Charles Burchfield. *October Wind and Sunlight in the Woods*. c. 1962–63. Watercolor on paper. 101.6 × 137.2 cm (40 × 54″). Georgia Museum of Art, The University of Georgia, Athens, Georgia. University purchase. Photography by Michael McKelvey.

Figure 9.3   This painting is based on a poem by a friend of the artist. The poem is about a shrieking fire engine tearing through darkened city streets on a wet night. Engine No. 5 is represented by the rhythmic repetition of the number five. Part of the name of the poet, William Carlos Williams, is hidden in the design. Can you find it?

Charles Henry Demuth. *I Saw the Figure 5 in Gold*. 1928. Oil on composition board. 91.4 × 75.6 cm (36 × 29¾″). The Metropolitan Museum of Art, New York, New York. The Alfred Stieglitz Collection, 1949. 49.59.1.

How We Perceive Visual Rhythm

Rhythm is the principle of design that indicates movement by the repetition of elements. The principle of rhythm is used in every art form.

In music, rhythm is created by the measure of time between musical sounds. There is a beat followed by a rest. **Visual rhythms** are rhythms you receive through your eyes rather than through your ears (Figure 9-4). Visual rhythm is created by repeated positive shapes separated by negative spaces. The positive areas are the "beats." Each beat is separated by negative spaces, which are the "rests."

Figure 9.4 Visual rhythms can be both natural and manufactured.

Photography by Robert Nix.

Everywhere you look you can see visual rhythms. Without even being aware of what you are seeing, you note the beats and the spaces between the beats. The books in a bookcase and the cars in a parking lot show visual rhythms. A line of people in the cafeteria has visual rhythm. Each person is a positive beat, and the spaces between the people are the negative areas.

A "beat" may be one element or a combination of elements. Look back one page at the photograph of the lily pads. The strongest beats are the round, flat shapes which vary in size. Each round shape has one split from its center to its edge. Each split is turned in a slightly different direction. Since this is a black-and-white photograph, you cannot see the colors of the round shapes, but you can see the value changes. Some leaves are very light—almost white. Most have a middle-gray value, and some are almost as dark as the negative spaces. But look

closely. There is a second, less noticeable beat: the thin curving and diagonal lines of the stems.

The negative space between the beats varies greatly. Some shapes touch and overlap, and in other areas the space between the shapes is wide. The value of the negative space varies from dark gray to black. The lightest areas of negative space are on the left and at the bottom of the photograph.

Visual rhythms create a sensation of movement as the viewer's eyes follow the visual beats through a work of art. Visual movement is different from real action, which involves a physical change in position. For example, a ball bouncing across a room is real action. Round shapes separated by negative spaces in a picture can create the same visual sensation as the movement of the ball because your eyes bounce from one round shape to the next. Artists use this type of visual movement to control the way the viewer looks at a work of art (Figure 9-5).

Figure 9.5 In this painting the horses are the beats of a rhythm that moves through the painting.

Rosa Bonheur. *The Horse Fair.* 1853–55. Oil on canvas. 244.5 × 506.7 cm (96¼ × 199½"). Metropolitan Museum of Art, New York, New York. Gift of Cornelius Vanderbilt, 1887.

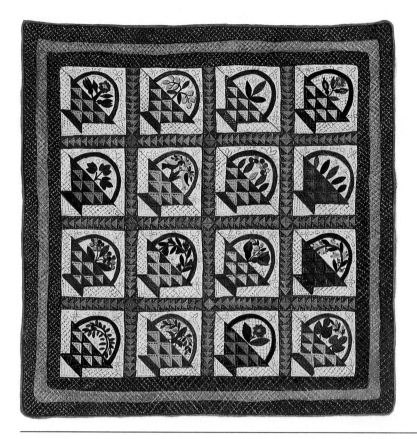

Figure 9.6 The motif in this design is the basket of flowers.

Unknown. *Basket of Flowers Quilt.* 1850. Index of American Design. National Gallery of Art, Washington, D.C.

DEVELOPING YOUR SKILLS

3. Look around you to find five visual rhythms that you see every day. List them and describe the elements that create the positive beats. Then describe the type of negative space that acts as the rests between the beats.

4. Look through newspapers and magazines for two advertisements that use rhythm to create visual movement. Indicate positive beats with a crayon or a marker.

SOMETHING EXTRA

A. Write a poem to express the differences between the rhythms of today's technological world and the pace of horse-and-buggy days gone by.

B. Make a chart illustrating the life cycle of a plant or animal. Emphasize the rhythmic quality of that cycle.

Repetition

Rhythm results from repetition. *Motif* and *pattern* are used frequently to talk about repetition in art.

Each unit that is repeated in visual rhythm is called a **motif** (Figure 9-6). Sometimes every motif is an exact duplicate of the first unit, and sometimes the repetitions vary from the original.

Look around and you will find examples of motif and repetition. In a marching band, one marcher is a motif, even though the marchers carry different instruments. On a grocery store shelf full of canned goods, one can is a motif. In a herd of cattle one cow is a motif.

Figure 9.7 This elevator grill is a delicate pattern of lines and round forms. It was once part of a large bank of elevators in the 1893 Chicago Stock Exchange. The building was torn down in 1972, but parts of it, such as this grill, have been saved in various museums.

Louis Sullivan. *Elevator Grille.* 1893. Bronze-plated cast iron. 185.4 × 78.7 cm (73 × 31″). High Museum, Atlanta, Georgia.

In sculpture and architecture a three-dimensional motif is sometimes called a **module**. Modular furniture is composed of standard, matching units.

Pattern is another word used to describe visual repetition. Pattern is a two-dimensional and decorative surface quality. All rhythms have a pattern; but not all patterns have rhythm.

You have seen a pattern of lines decorating fabric or a pattern used in construction (Figure 9-7). These patterns are functional or meant only as decoration. They tend to be stiff and rather dull. If you remember that rhythm is a repetition intended to create the feeling of movement, and that pattern is intended to be flat and decorative, you will have no trouble telling the difference between the two.

DEVELOPING YOUR SKILLS

5. Make a collection of decorative patterns. You may use photographs, clippings from magazines, scraps of fabric, etc. Identify the motif in each pattern by drawing a circle around one. Organize your pattern collection into a poster, a bulletin board, a booklet, or some other presentation.
6. Find a house in your neighborhood that has interesting visual rhythms. Make a pencil drawing of it, emphasizing the rhythmic areas. For example, you might draw the outer shape with a light line and then darken any rectangular shapes. Or, starting with a light line drawing, you might use a colored marker to accent vertical repetitions.
7. Make a design using shapes and lines to illustrate the difference between a 3/4-time **waltz** rhythm and a 4/4-time march rhythm. Ask a music teacher for advice if you need assistance.

SOMETHING EXTRA

C. Make a photo study of the visual rhythms in your home, your neighborhood, or your school.
D. Using a computer with graphic capabilities and the correct software, design a motif. Then create a variety of patterns with that motif. Either print the designs or photograph them as they appear on the monitor.

Types of Rhythm

Different visual rhythms are created with different arrangements of motif and space.

Random

A motif repeated in no apparent order, with no regular spaces, makes a random rhythm. One example is autumn leaves that cover the ground. Cracks in mud and splashes of paint are two more examples of random rhythm.

A crowd of people pushing into a subway train is full of rhythm. The motif is one person. Every person is different, and every space is slightly different.

Crowds often create random rhythms—think of Christmas shoppers, rush-hour commuters, and students in the halls between classes. See Figure 9-8.

Figure 9.8 Here you see the random arrangement of two motifs. What is your reaction to this arrangement?

Jennifer McCabe Carrasco. *Glads Rising Above Their Watermelons.* 1984. Watercolor. 57.2 × 76.2 cm (22½ × 30″). Private collection.

TECHNIQUE TIP

Stamp Prints

A stamp print is an easy way to make repetitive designs. The following are a few suggestions for making a stamp and printing with it. You may develop some other ideas after reading these hints. Remember, printing reverses your design, so if you use letters, be certain to cut or carve them backwards.

- Cut a simple design into the flat surface of an eraser with a knife that has a fine, precision blade.
- Cut a potato, carrot, or turnip in half. Use a paring knife to carve a design into the flat surface of the vegetable (Figure 9-9).
- Glue yarn to a bottle cap or a jar lid.
- Glue found objects to a piece of corrugated cardboard. Make a

design with paperclips, washers, nuts, leaves, feathers, or anything else you can find. Whatever object you use should have a fairly flat surface. Make a handle for the block with masking tape.

- Cut shapes out of a piece of inner tube material. Glue the shapes to a piece of heavy cardboard (Figure 9-9).

There are several ways to apply ink or paint to a stamp:

- Roll water-base printing ink on the stamp with a soft brayer.
- Roll water-base printing ink on a plate and press the stamp into the ink.
- Apply tempera paint or school acrylic to the stamp with a bristle brush.

Figure 9.9 Ideas for stamps.

DEVELOPING YOUR SKILLS

8. Make a stamp motif and print it in a random rhythm (Figure 9-10).
9. Place a leaf or a paper cutout under a sheet of newsprint and make a series of rubbings in a random manner (Figure 9-11).
10. Choose one letter of the alphabet. Look through newspapers and magazines for large examples of that letter. Neatly cut out twenty or more. Arrange them on a small piece of colored paper in a random pattern (Figure 9-12). (If you have trouble finding large letters, you might add some neatly drawn letters of your own to your design.)

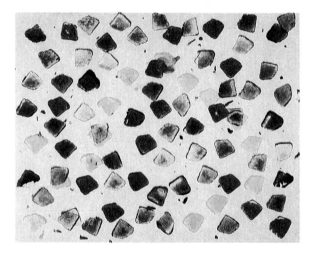

Figure 9.10 Student work. Stamp motif printed in a random rhythm.

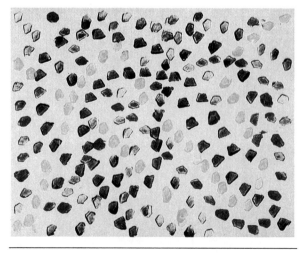

Figure 9.11 Student work. Random rhythm.

Figure 9.12 Student work. Random arrangement of letters.

Regular

Regular rhythm has identical motifs and equal amounts of space between (Figure 9-13). Regular rhythm has a steady beat.

Regular repetitions are used to organize things. Parking spaces and office mailboxes are laid out with regular rhythm. Stores organize merchandise into regular stacks and rows. This makes it easier for you to find things.

A grid is based on regular rhythm. It is a regular arrangement of parallel lines. A football field is laid out in a grid, as is a checkerboard. Skyscraper windows form a grid pattern on the side of a building (Figure 9-14). Today's artists use grids to explore new arrangements of space.

Regular rhythm can be boring if it is overdone. One note played on a piano over and over again is an example. Some modern Pop artists use this negative quality of regular rhythm to make social-protest statements (Figure 9-15 on next page).

Figure 9.13 This fern shows the regular rhythm found in nature.

Photography by Robert Nix.

Figure 9.14 The lights in these windows emphasize the gridlike arrangement of the windows. This is the Seagram Building in New York.

Ludwig Mies van der Rohe, and Philip Johnson. Seagram Building. 1957. New York, New York. Exterior at night. Photography by Sandak, Inc., Stamford, Connecticut.

Figure 9.15 One pair of lips on the face of Marilyn Monroe would be beautiful and appealing. What has Andy Warhol done to them by repeating them in a regular rhythm?

Andy Warhol. *Marilyn Monroe's Lips.* 1962. Synthetic polymer, enamel and pencil on canvas. Diptych. A (at left): 210.7 × 204.9 cm (82¾ × 80¾), B (at right): 210.7 × 209.7 cm (82¾ × 82⅜). Hirshhorn Museum and Sculpture Garden, Smithsonian Institution, Washington, D.C. Gift of Joseph H. Hirshhorn, 1972.

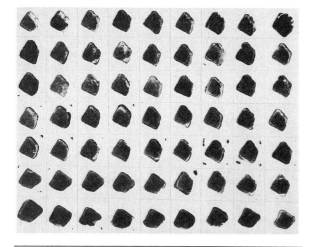

Figure 9.16 Student work. Checkerboard grid.

11. Create a regular rhythm by drawing a checkerboard grid with a pencil and ruler. After you have drawn your grid, choose one of the following motifs. Then add the motif to your grid. See Figure 9-16.
    - Using a stamp print, print one stamp print in each box.
    - Using crayon or pencil, make a rubbing of the same motif in each box. A coin or a key will produce a good rubbing.
    - Draw the same motif in each square.
    - Glue the same cut-paper motif in each square.

Alternating

Alternating rhythm can occur in several ways. One way is the use of a second motif. Another way is to make a change in the placement or content of the original motif. A third way is to change the spaces between the motifs. See Figures 9-17 and 9-18. Sometimes alternation is created by just changing the position of the motif. For example, the motif may be turned upside down.

Bricks are often laid in alternating rhythm. As a child, did you ever build with interlocking blocks? You had to use an alternating pattern to join the blocks.

An alternating rhythm using two motifs can still be very repetitive. Your eyes keep returning to the first motif even after the second motif joins the design. But the alternation does create interest.

Figure 9.17 The border design embroidered on this sidesaddle is an example of alternating rhythm using two motifs.

Child's sidesaddle. c. 1820. Unknown craftsperson from Monterey, California. Leather, velvet upholstery, and embroidered in silk. Index of American Design. National Gallery of Art, Washington, D.C.

Figure 9.18 The back of this bench shows an alternating rhythm created by changing the placement of the motif.

Brown and Owen. *Bench.* c. 1860–1900. Cast iron. 91.4 × 114.3 × 41.9 cm (36 × 45 × 16½"). High Museum of Art, Atlanta, Georgia.

Figure 9.19 Student work. Alternating rhythm with one motif.

Figure 9.20 Student work. Alternating rhythm with two motifs.

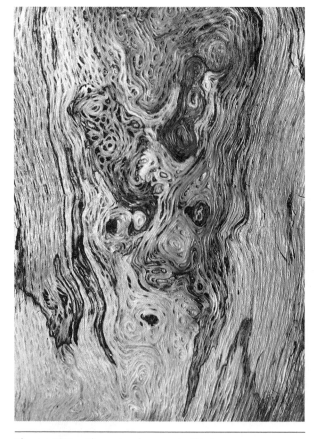

Figure 9.21 The natural curves in this tree create a flowing rhythm.

Photography by Robert Nix.

DEVELOPING YOUR SKILLS

12. Draw a checkerboard grid and create an alternating rhythm using one motif. Turn the motif upside down in every other box (Figure 9-19).
13. Draw a checkerboard grid and create an alternating rhythm using two motifs (Figure 9-20).
14. Use your imagination to create an alternating rhythm in a pencil drawing.

Flowing

Flowing rhythm is created by repeating wavy lines. Curved shapes, such as rolling hills or ocean waves, create flowing rhythms (Figure 9-21). Your eyes glide along a curving path that changes direction gradually (Figure 9-22). There are no sudden breaks in the movement of a flowing line.

Flowing rhythm is all upward swells and downward slides. You might think of the upward moves as the beats, and the downward moves as the rests. You feel calm as your eyes respond to flowing rhythms.

Figure 9.22 (facing page) The repetitions in this painting create rhythms that flow through the composition.

Giacomo Balla. *Swifts: Paths of Movement + Dynamic Sequences.* 1913. Oil on canvas. 96.8 × 120 cm (38⅛ × 47¼″). The Museum of Modern Art, New York, New York. Purchase.

DEVELOPING YOUR SKILLS

15. Look through magazines and newspapers for pictures that feature flowing rhythms. Be sure to look at all the advertisements as you search for the flowing rhythms. Mount and label at least five of the best examples that you find.

16. Create a relief design showing flowing rhythm. Glue 1/2-inch (1.3-cm) wide strips of construction paper on edge to a small piece of poster board. Use analogous colors for the strips and a complement of one of the colors for the background. Curl the strips so that they will hold a curve after you have glued them. Arrange the strips in sets of almost parallel ridges (Figure 9-23).

Figure 9.23   Student work. Relief design with flowing rhythm.

Figure 9.24   The light glowing from the street lamp is represented by a progressive rhythm of both line and color. Notice how the light close to the lamp is white and yellow in color and created with thin, small *V* lines. The light that is farther from the source gradually changes into mostly reds and lavenders and the V lines are wider and larger.

Giacomo Balla. *Street Light*. 1909. Oil on canvas. 174.7 × 114.7 cm (68¾ × 45¼″). Collection, The Museum of Modern Art, New York, New York. Hillman Periodicals Fund.

Progressive

In progressive rhythm there is a change in the motif each time it is repeated. The change is a steady one. It is like the number series *x plus 1*, *x plus 2*, *x plus 3*, and so on.

A progressive rhythm may start with a square as its motif. The size of the square may be changed by making it slightly smaller each time it is repeated. Or each square may be made a different color of the spectrum or a different step on the value scale. Shapes can be progressively changed. The sides of a square can be gradually rounded until it becomes a circle. See Figure 9-24.

DEVELOPING YOUR SKILLS

17. Choose a simple motif, such as a circle or a freeform shape. Then, starting with this motif, gradually change it to create a progressive rhythm (Figure 9-25). You may change the size, the value, or the color of the motif to create progression.

18. Starting with a simple geometric shape such as a square for your motif, create a progressive rhythm by gradually changing the square into a free-form shape (Figure 9-26).

19. Find a newspaper or magazine photograph of a full-length figure, complete from head to toes. Cut out the figure carefully and glue it to a piece of construction paper or poster board for reinforcement. Then trim the backing to make an accurate silhouette. Using this silhouette, trace a series of nine or more figures, overlapping them to create a feeling of depth. Then create a progressive rhythm. To create a progressive rhythm, use a pencil to draw a minimum of detail on the most distant figure. Then add more details to each figure until the closest figure is as completely detailed as possible. Shade the closest figure with values. Show hair, wrinkles, textures, blemishes, and so on.

Figure 9.25 Student work. Progressive rhythm.

Figure 9.26 Student work. Progressive rhythm.

Figure 9.27 Your eye is drawn through this photograph by the repeated diagonal lines.

Photography by Robert Nix.

Figure 9.28 The many repetitions of the legs, feet, tail, and chain in this work give the work a sense of actual movement.

Giacomo Balla. *Dynamism of a Dog on a Leash.* 1912. Oil on canvas. 89.9 × 109.9 cm (35⅜ × 43¼″). Albright-Knox Art Gallery, Buffalo, New York. Bequest of A. Conger Goodyear and gift of George F. Goodyear, 1964.

How Artists Use Rhythm

In Figure 9-27, a photograph of clothes on a line, nothing is really moving. Everything is frozen in time. But your eye is pulled to the right side of the photograph by the repetition of many diagonal lines and shapes that slant down to the right. Notice how all the clothes are being blown by the wind to slant to the right. Notice the slant of the clothespins. Notice how the bottom edges of the clothes slant up to the right. Everything in this composition is pulling your eyes through the photograph.

What memories does the photograph of the clothes blowing in the wind arouse for you? A windy day? The fresh smell of laundry? How does it make you feel? Tired from fighting the wind? Chilly? Refreshed? Happy? Sad?

Artists use rhythm in a work of art just as they use the elements and other principles of art—to communicate feelings and ideas. As your eyes follow the visual beats through a work of art, you experience the sensation of movement. Is the movement slow and easy, or quick and excited? Does it soothe you or make you nervous? An artist uses rhythms to create these feelings.

One group of artists tried to do more than control the way in which viewers looked at works of art. This group of artists, called the *Futurists* (Figure 9-28), used rhythm to capture the idea of movement itself. They used the word *dynamism* to refer to the forces of movement. They believed that nothing was solid or stable. They also believed that art should show such dynamism. They showed forms changing into energy by creating surfaces that seemed to be shaking apart. They slanted and overlapped surfaces.

Marcel Duchamp upset many people when he presented his *Nude Descending A Staircase* (Figure 9-29) at the Armory Show in New York City in 1913. The viewers were furious. What they didn't understand was that Duchamp was not painting a woman. Though he was not a Futurist, he too was painting motion. He portrayed an entire series of movements that had stopped at different stages. This is similar to the stop-action photography we see today.

Figure 9.29 Notice the "speed lines" around the legs of this moving figure. Duchamp probably took the idea of the lines from comic strips.

Marcel Duchamp. *Nude Descending a Staircase, No. 2.* 1912. Oil on canvas. 147.3 × 88.9 cm (58 × 35"). Philadelphia Museum of Art, Philadelphia, Pennsylvania. The Louise and Walter Arensberg Collection.

Umberto Boccioni was a Futurist. His works, such as the sculpture in Figure 9-30, portrayed movement in much the same way as did Duchamp's *Nude*. The forms in his sculpture seem to be shaped by the rush of flowing air. In some places the currents seem to pull the sculpture beyond its own form into space. In other places the air seems to pass through the sculpture itself.

When we talk about movement in visual art, we must talk about Alexander Calder. He was a mechanical engineer, but his father was a sculptor. Calder believed in what the Futurists were doing. He repeated abstract shapes, and he put them into real motion. He did this using the real forces of air currents and gravity. These works of art, which Calder created, are called **kinetic sculpture** (Figure 9-31).

Figure 9.30   Forms that seem to be shaped by rushing air.

Umberto Boccioni. *Unique Forms of Continuity in Space*. 1913. Cast 1931. Bronze. 111.2 × 88.5 × 40 cm (43⅞ × 34⅞ × 15¾″). Collection, The Museum of Modern Art, New York, New York. Acquired through the Lillie P. Bliss bequest.

Figure 9.31   Look closely at the places where the rods are joined by a carefully planned set of loops. Calder's works are so carefully balanced that the slightest air movement will set the sculpture in motion. Watching a Calder sculpture is like watching a graceful dancer.

Alexander Calder. *Lobster Trap and Fish Tail*. 1939. Hanging mobile: painted steel wire and sheet aluminum. About 2.60 × 2.90 m (8′ 6″ × 9′ 6″). Collection, The Museum of Modern Art, New York, New York. Commissioned by the Advisory Committee for the stairwell of the museum.

DEVELOPING YOUR SKILLS

20. Using what you have learned about the expressive qualities of the art elements, create two motifs. Make one calm and soothing; the other active and nervous. Then create two designs. Arrange the first motif in a calm rhythm that emphasizes the smooth qualities of the first motif. Arrange the second motif in an active, dynamic rhythm that emphasizes the nervous qualities of that motif.

I M A G I N E   A N D   C R E A T E

Painting with a Rhythmic Theme

MATERIALS

You will need the following:

Paper and pencil for sketching

Large white paper for painting

Color medium of your choice: wax crayons,
pastels, oil pastels, water-colors, tempera or school acrylics

Poster board

OBJECTIVE

Make a painting of a group of people involved in a rhythmic activity (Figure 9-32). Emphasize the theme by using a variety of visual rhythms to create a sense of visual movement. Prepare your finished work for display.

DIRECTIONS

Select a theme that interests you. Think of marching bands, athletic teams, children on a playground, dancers, joggers, and skaters. Do visual research for your painting. You can do this research by first observing people in the activity. After you observe the activity carefully, make several gesture drawings of each activity. Try several visual rhythms.

Select your best sketches. Organize your sketches into a composition. Your composition should reflect the rhythmic quality of the activity.

Add color using a medium of your choice. Use the rhythmic repetition of color to enhance the rhythmic quality of the painting.

Mount or mat the finished painting for display.

Figure 9.32 In this painting the artist has emphasized the rhythmic repetition of two elements—active lines and flowing color—to express different dance movements. If you look closely at the darker areas of the work, you will discover the shapes of two ballet dancers. They are almost lost in the excitement of line and color.

Rosalind Ragans. *Firebirds.* 1983. Dye on cotton. 91.4 × 121.9 cm (36 × 48″). Private collection.

MATERIALS

You will need the following:

Fifteen or more modular units, such as plastic or paper cups, paper-towel or toilet-tissue tubes, small boxes, paper plates, or units you invent (the modules may be two or three sizes)

Precision-blade or utility knife and scissors

White glue, pins, and tape

Poster board

Optional:

Spray paint or school acrylic paint

EVALUATION CHECKLIST

Be sure you did the following:

1. Selected a rhythmic theme.
2. Made a series of gesture drawings of people involved in the activity.
3. Organized the sketches into a composition that used more than one type of visual rhythm.
4. Selected a color medium.
5. Used the repetition of color to enhance the rhythmic quality of the work.
6. Prepared the finished work for display.

Modular Sculpture

OBJECTIVE

By joining a set of nine or more modules, create a three-dimensional, freestanding sculpture that displays a strong sense of rhythm (Figures 9-33 and 9-34 on the next page).

Make a base and attach the sculpture to the base for display.

DIRECTIONS

Choose a three-dimensional motif for the sculpture. Collect more modules than you need so that you can afford to experiment. Start with at least fifteen.

Create variations in the modules: cut some parts away; cut openings into some units; and add extra pieces to some.

As you begin to join the modules, study the work from all sides. Keep turning it, and don't rush. Take time to think.

When you are ready to begin gluing, apply glue to both surfaces to be joined. When the glue becomes tacky, press the two surfaces together. Straight pins or tape will help to keep the parts in place until the glue sets.

If you used modules that do not match, a coat of spray paint will help unify the sculpture. You may wish to paint the modules with acrylics, using a limited color scheme. Plan the colors so they, too, follow a rhythmic pattern.

Make a base by gluing your finished work on a piece of poster board that has been cut into a shape that repeats the shape of the sculpture.

EVALUATION CHECKLIST

Be sure you did the following:

1. Chose a three-dimensional motif for the sculpture.
2. Collected fifteen or more motif modules.

3. Created variations in the modules by cutting into or adding onto them.
4. Joined the modules using proper procedures.
5. *Optional*: Used paint to enhance the rhythmic quality of the work.
6. Mounted the work for display, using a base that repeated the shape of the sculpture.
7. Cleaned up the work area.

Figure 9.33 Student work. Modular sculpture.

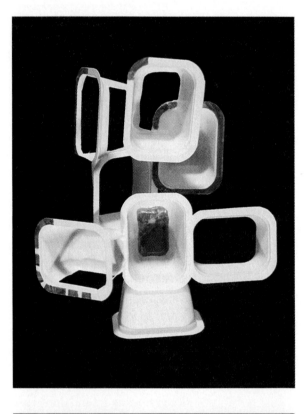

Figure 9.34 Student work. Modular sculpture.

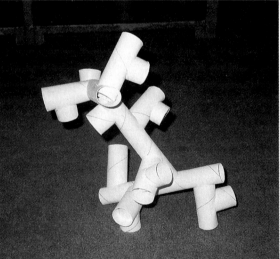

Printing a Rhythmic Fabric Design

MATERIALS

You will need the following:

Fabric

Stamp-making material (see the Technique Tip on page 217 for suggestions)

Paper, pencil, ruler, and crayons

Water-based, nontoxic textile paints and appropriate brushes

Newspaper-covered board or table on which the fabric can be stretched

Tape and/or pins

Iron and a padded surface for ironing

OBJECTIVE

Using one or two stamps, print an alternating design on a piece of fabric with water-based textile paints (Figures 9-35 and 9-36). Use the printed fabric to make something useful.

DIRECTIONS

Plan a design with an alternating rhythm for your fabric. First, make a design plan. Use a pencil and ruler to measure the spacing for the design on a sheet of paper. Draw the shapes for your stamps and color them with crayons to help you plan a color scheme for the design.

Prepare the stamps according to the Technique Tip directions. You will find these directions on page 217.

Wash the fabric to remove any sizing. Iron the fabric and stretch it over a newspaper-covered board or table. Tape or pin the fabric down.

Read carefully the manufacturer's directions for using the nontoxic textile paints. Collect any materials that you think you will need to print with the paints.

Using a ruler, measure the spaces you decided to use in your design plan and draw light pencil guidelines on the fabric.

Ink and print the stamps following your planned alternating rhythm. Be careful. Make sure that you avoid leaving fingerprints or smudges on the fabric.

Figure 9.35 Student work. Stamp print on fabric.

Figure 9.36 Student work. Fabric print.

Clean up the work area.

Follow the manufacturer's directions to set the textile paints and make them permanent.

Make something useful with the fabric such as a decorative pillow or something to wear.

EVALUATION CHECKLIST

Be sure you did the following:

1. Planned a design with an alternating rhythm.
2. Measured the spacing for the design properly.
3. Planned a color scheme using crayons.
4. Prepared the stamps according to directions on page 217.
5. Washed the fabric, ironed it, and stretched it out.
6. Read the paint manufacturer's directions carefully and prepared all of the necessary materials.
7. Sketched guidelines on the fabric.
8. Inked and printed the stamps, following the planned design.
9. Avoided smudges and fingerprints on the fabric.
10. Cleaned up the work area.
11. Set the textile paints according to directions.
12. Made something useful with the fabric.

Clay Coil Pot

MATERIALS

You will need the following:

Clay (approximately five pounds)

Cloth-covered board

Plastic bag (large enough to store work in progress)

Slip and brush

Scoring and modeling tools

Small bowl of water

Circular base pattern about 4 or 5 inches in diameter

Small found objects to press into the coils to add decoration

Optional:

Glaze

OBJECTIVE

Build a clay coil pot, emphasizing the rhythmic quality of coil construction (Figure 9-41).

DIRECTIONS

Collect all of your materials and determine where you will store your work between work sessions.

Make a base for your pot by flattening a small piece of clay about 1/2-inch thick. Using the pattern as a guide, cut it into a circle about four or five inches in diameter (Figure 9-42).

Begin a clay coil by shaping a small ball of clay into a long roll on the cloth-covered board until the roll is about 1/2-inch thick (Figure 9-43 on the next page). Your hands should be slightly damp so the clay remains damp and flexible and does not dry out.

Make a circle around the edge of the clay base with the roll of clay (Figure 9-44). Cut the ends on a diagonal and join them so that the seam does not show. Join this first coil to the base properly.

Make a second coil and place it on top of the first one. If you want the pot to curve outwards, place the second coil on the outside

TECHNIQUE TIP

Joining Clay

Use these methods for joining clay. First, gather the following:

- Clay
- Slip (a creamy mixture of clay and water)
- Brush
- Something for scoring clay, such as forks or combs
- Clay tools

1. Rough up or scratch the two surfaces to be joined (Figure 9-37).
2. Apply slip to one of the two surfaces using a brush or your fingers (Figure 9-38).
3. Gently press the two surfaces together so the slip oozes out of the joining seam (Figure 9-39).
4. Using clay tools and/or your fingers, smooth away the slip that has oozed out of the seam (Figure 9-40). You may wish to smooth out the seam as well, or you may wish to leave it for decorative purposes.

Figure 9.37 Score the clay.

Figure 9.38 Applying some slip.

Figure 9.39 Gently squeeze the two surfaces together.

Figure 9.40 Smooth the joined surfaces.

Figure 9.41 Student work. Coil pot.

Figure 9.42 Making the base.

edge of the first coil (Figure 9-45). If you want the pot to curve inward, place the second coil on the inside edge. Be sure to join each coil to the next using proper procedures. See the Technique Tip on the previous page for directions on how to join clay.

Do not smooth out all the seams. Leave some or all of the seams showing on the outside to emphasize the rhythmic quality.

Keep adding coils until the pot is a minimum of six inches high.

To add more interest to your pot, you may wish to press a simple motif into some of the coils (Figure 9-46). Try using your own finger tip. The shaped end of a tool, the curved end of a paperclip, a button, a sea shell, and the end of a spoon handle are other suggestions. Repeat the motif in a rhythmic pattern.

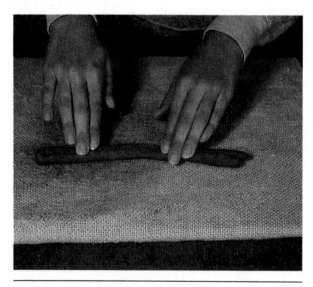

Figure 9.43   Rolling the clay coil.

Figure 9.44   Putting the first coil in place.

Figure 9.45   Adding a coil to the outer edge of a previous coil.

Figure 9.46   Pressing a pattern into the coil.

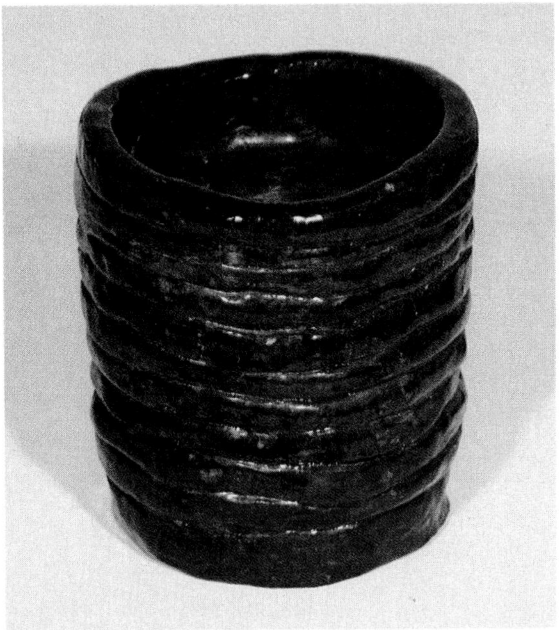

Figure 9.47 Student work. Glaze has changed the color and the surface of this coil pot.

SAFETY NOTE

Some ceramic glazes contain lead, which means they must not be used to hold food or drink. Be on the safe side: always use nonlead glazes on ceramic pieces.

If your clay is soft, do not add more than four or five coils during one work session or the pot might sag.

Seal your pot inside a plastic bag each day when you finish working so your work will not dry out.

When you have finished building your pot, allow it to dry slowly. It will become hard and brittle. You will need to fire it in a kiln. After the first firing, the pot may be glazed (Figure 9-47). Then it should be fired a second time.

EVALUATION CHECKLIST

Be sure you did the following:

1. Collected all of the necessary materials and planned a storage area.
2. Made the base 1/2-inch thick and cut it into a circle four or five inches in diameter.
3. Rolled the coils 1/2-inch thick and kept them flexible by working with damp hands.
4. Joined the coils to the base and to each other by using correct joining procedures.
5. Added coils until the pot was at least six inches high.
6. Allowed some or all of the coils to show on the outside.
7. *Optional:* Pressed a pattern into some of the coils.
8. Did not allow the pot to sag.
9. Between work sessions, kept the pot sealed in a plastic bag.
10. Dried the pot slowly.
11. Fired the pot in a kiln.
12. *Optional:* glazed the pot and refired it.

Figure 9.48 Vincent van Gogh. *The Starry Night.* 1889. Oil on canvas. 73.7 × 92.1 cm (29 × 36¼″). Collection, The Museum of Modern Art, New York, New York. Acquired through the Lillie P. Bliss bequest.

A R T   C R I T I C I S M

Improving Your Critical-Thinking Skills

Description: What Do You See?

Look at the credit line for *The Starry Night* by Vincent van Gogh. What medium was used to create this painting? How big is the painting? Look at the way the paint was applied to the canvas. What do you see?

Now describe everything you see in the painting. To help you organize your thoughts, start by listing the things you recognize in the foreground. Then list the things you see in the middle ground, the background, and the sky.

Analysis: How Is the Work Organized?

Before you study the way van Gogh uses rhythm, look at the different elements of art he uses.

Notice the lines. Which line direction seems to dominate? What is unusual about the way lines appear in this work?

Now look at the way the artist arranged the shapes, forms, and space. Is there any totally empty negative space? What is the expressive effect of the largest shapes?

The colors in this work are important. Where do you find the brightest colors?

Then study the textures. Is van Gogh trying to imitate the real textures of the objects? Does the texture of the brush strokes show?

Now you are ready to look at the visual rhythms in *The Starry Night*.

What elements and objects are used as motifs in this work? Describe them.

What kinds of rhythms did van Gogh use?

Can you find examples of regular rhythms?

Do you see any alternating rhythms?

Did van Gogh use random rhythms?

Are there any examples of progressive rhythm?

In how many places has he used flowing rhythms? Describe them.

Which rhythmic movement is dominant? Which area shows the most movement?

Interpretation: What is Happening? What Is the Artist Trying to Say?

The subject matter of this painting alone is unimportant. But the way van Gogh has included the elements of art and organized them using the principle of rhythm tells you a great deal about his feelings. Which part of the painting is alive with dancing rhythms? Which part is calmest? What does that tell you?

Put yourself in the painter's position—imagine the thoughts that were running through his mind as he painted. Write down the words or phrases he might have been thinking to himself.

Write a paragraph explaining your interpretation. Then create a new title that expresses your feeling about *The Starry Night*.

Judgment: What Do You Think of the Work?

Do you like the subject matter of this work? Do you like the way the artist has organized the elements of art and used the principle of rhythm? Does this painting touch your feelings?

Use one or more of the three theories of art to defend your reactions to this work.

SOMETHING EXTRA

Have you heard a pop song with the same name as this painting? Obtain a copy of it and listen to the lyrics. Do you think the song writer would feel the same way about this work as you do?

A B O U T   T H E   A R T I S T

Vincent van Gogh

Figure 9.49 Vincent van Gogh, Dutch, 1853–1890.

Vincent van Gogh. *Self Portrait*. 1889. Oil on canvas. (Dimensions unavailable.) SCALA/Art Resource, New York, New York.

Vincent van Gogh was born in a small Dutch village in 1853. He was only thirty-seven years old when he died in 1890, but his short and tragic life was a milestone in the world of art.

You may already be familiar with the story of van Gogh's life. It has been portrayed in a book, a movie, a popular song, and a play. You may know he went mad, cut off part of his ear, and committed suicide at the height of his creativity. Still, he left the world 1,600 extraordinary paintings and drawings.

Van Gogh was not interested in art when he was young. In fact, he spent twenty-seven years trying to find himself. He tried many different careers, including teacher, minister, and missionary, but failed at all of them. During these years, however, he wrote to his brother and best friend, Theo, illustrating his letters with many sketches. Theo admired the illustrations and offered to support Vincent in an attempt at an art career.

For the next ten years van Gogh painted and continued to write to Theo. In over 1,000 letters he explained all of the paintings he was working on. These letters have helped the world better understand the creative thinking processes of a genius.

Van Gogh's early paintings were brown and drab. Then, in 1886, he moved to Paris to be near Theo, and it was during this time that he was influenced by the colors of the Impressionists and the styles of Japanese woodcuts. He was not satisfied simply to paint a scene. He had to express his deep feelings about it. Painting was almost a religious expression for him.

He was fascinated by the sparkling sky of the southern nights. The first starry night he painted was painted from life. This was long before electricity and flashlights. Van Gogh's solution to the problem of seeing his paints in the dark was to attach a circle of candles to his broad-brimmed hat. He then set more candles around the canvas. He must have been a strange sight with his head ablaze in a circle of fire. *The Starry Night* in this chapter was painted from memory later while he was in an insane asylum.

No one really knows why van Gogh became ill. What is important is the work he left behind and the ideas he left to the artists who followed him.

Chapter 9 Review: Talking about Art

USING THE LANGUAGE OF ART

For each new art term below, choose a work of art from this chapter. Then write a sentence about that work using the new term correctly in the sentence.

kinetic sculpture	motif
pattern	rhythm
module	

LEARNING THE ART ELEMENTS AND PRINCIPLES

1. How is rhythm created in music?
2. In general, how is visual rhythm created?
3. How does rhythm add a sense of movement to a work of art?
4. What is the difference between rhythm and pattern?
5. In general, how are different rhythms created?
6. How is random rhythm created?
7. How is regular rhythm created?
8. How is alternating rhythm created?
9. How is flowing rhythm created?
10. How is progressive rhythm created?

INCREASING YOUR ART AWARENESS

1. Look at the photographs of rhythm in the environment in Figure 9-4. Choose one of the photos in 9-4 and describe the rhythmic repetitions in the photograph you choose. Discuss the lines, shapes, space, value, and texture of the repetitions. Describe the different types of rhythmic repetitions you find in the photograph.
2. Name one two- or three-dimensional work from Chapters 1 through 8 that contains a motif.
3. Name one work of art from Chapters 1 through 8 that contains a pattern.
4. From any chapter of this book except chapter 9, find a different work of art to illustrate each of the five types of rhythm. Tell how the artist used rhythm in each work.
5. What kind of rhythm is found in Figure 5-22? What feelings does this rhythm arouse?

UNDERSTANDING ART CULTURE AND HERITAGE

1. List the five works of art (with dates) in this chapter that were created in the nineteenth century.
2. Who were the Futurists and what was their aim (see Chapter 3)? Name one Futurist artist represented in Chapter 9 and list the titles of his works shown in this chapter.
3. Five paintings shown in this chapter were created between 1909 and 1913. Three of those paintings were painted by Giacomo Balla. Name the artists who painted the other two works from this time period. What similarities and differences do you see between their work and Balla's?
4. Duchamp's painting (Figure 9-29) created a sensation at the Armory Show of 1913. Why was this show so important (see Chapter 3)?
5. Which artist represented in this chapter do you think would be associated with the Pop Art movement (see Chapter 3)? Why?

JUDGING THE QUALITY OF ART

Imagine that you are a curator (person in charge) in a museum. You want the museum to purchase Severini's *Dynamic Hieroglyphic of the Bal Tabarin* (Figure 9-1). You must present your case to the Board of Directors. Your museum does not have a work of art in the Futurist style. Use the four steps of art criticism to explain why this painting would be such an excellent example of rhythmic movement. Point out how many different types of rhythm are used in this work.

LEARNING MORE ABOUT ART

Discuss the principle of rhythm with your music teacher. Find out if musicians use the same types of rhythms as visual artists. Try to find a work of music to illustrate at least two of the visual rhythms, or create a musical rhythm to match at least two of the visual rhythm types.

Figure 10.1 The true name of the Flemish artist who produced this work is not known. Music historians say that the painting is an accurate rendering of the musical instruments of the time. Even the finger positions on the instruments are correct.

Master of the St. Lucy Legend. *Mary, Queen of Heaven*. c. 1485. Painted wood. 215.9 × 185.4 cm (85 × 73″). National Gallery of Art, Washington, D.C. Samuel H. Kress Collection, 1952.

Balance

LEARNING OBJECTIVES

After reading this chapter and doing the exercises, you will be able to

☐ understand why people need balance and why it is important to a work of art.

☐ explain how visual weight is created and produce it in your own work.

☐ describe the types of balance and use them in your own work.

☐ tell what different types of balance can mean in a work of art.

WORDS TO LEARN

In this chapter you will learn the meanings of the words listed below.

balance

central axis

formal balance

informal balance

radial balance

symmetry

Balance is a principle of life. Every animal must balance breathing in and breathing out. The earth stays in orbit because the pull of the sun is balanced by the earth's spin. Without balance we feel uncomfortable (Figure 10-2). Artists use this feeling to communicate with us.

We all need to use balance to function from day to day. Standing up on a moving train or bus is a problem in balance. So is carrying a stack of books to your locker. Because of your ability to balance, you can stand erect and walk on two limbs instead of four.

Have you ever watched a toddler wobble, fall, and struggle to get back up? The toddler learns to use leg muscles and shifts in weight to overcome the effects of gravity. He or she learns to balance the force of gravity with muscle force.

DEVELOPING YOUR SKILLS

1. List and explain examples of balance that are mentioned in other school subjects. One example would be the "balance of power," which is discussed in history classes.

2. Think of everything you did yesterday. Make a list of the times you were concerned with balance. Here's a hint: You had to balance your breathing in with your exhaling, and you had to balance your body to stand still.

Figure 10.2 This building is known throughout the world, not because of its beauty or because the architect is well-known, but because it leans. The many diagonal lines tell the viewer that this building must either straighten up or fall. Because it remains off balance, defying gravity, it is famous.

Bell Tower of the Cathedral at Pisa. Begun in 1174.

Visual Balance

A work of art must contain **balance.** Balance is the principle of design concerned with equalizing visual forces, or elements, in a work of art. Visual balance causes you to feel that the elements have been arranged just right.

A visual *imbalance* creates a feeling of uneasiness. It makes you feel that something isn't quite right. You feel a need to rearrange the elements, in the same way that you feel a need to straighten a picture on the wall.

In the real world a balance scale can be used to measure equal weights. In visual art balance must be *seen* rather than weighed. The art elements become the visual forces, or weights, in an art object. A **central axis** is a dividing line that works like the point of balance in the balance scale.

Many works of art have a central vertical axis (Figure 10-3) with equal visual weight on both sides. Artists also use a horizontal axis. In works with a horizontal axis the weight is balanced between top and bottom (Figure 10-4).

There are basically two types of balance: formal and informal. They differ in how elements are arranged around the axis.

Formal Balance

Formal balance occurs when equal, or very similar, elements are placed on opposite sides of a central axis. The axis may be a real part of the design, or it may be an imaginary line, such as that in Figures 10-3 and 10-4.

Formal balance is the easiest type of balance to recognize and to create (Figure 10-5). After you find the axis, all you have to do is to match objects on each side and place them equally distant from the center.

Symmetry

Symmetry is a special type of formal balance. The two halves of a symmetrically-balanced composition are identical, mirror images of each other (Figure 10-6 on page 246). Other terms for this are *bilateral* and *two-sided* symmetry.

Figure 10.3 (at left) With a vertical axis there is equal visual weight on both sides.

Figure 10.4 (at right) Artists also use a horizontal axis, arranging the balance between top and bottom.

Figure 10.5 This painting was created by an American folk artist who had no art instruction. The use of formal balance was the easiest way to organize the visual elements. The formal balance also lends an air of importance to the large house sitting on the hill a little above the center of the composition.

Unknown American artist. *The Plantation.* c. 1825. Oil on wood. 48.6 x 74.9 cm (19⅛ x 29½"). The Metropolitan Museum of Art, New York, New York. Gift of Edgar William and Bernice Chrysler Garbisch, 1963. 63.201.3

The strong appeal symmetry has for us may be related to the bilateral symmetry of the human body. Things closely associated with our bodies, such as clothing and furniture, are usually symmetrical. Most traditional architecture, especially public architecture, is symmetrical (Figure 10-7).

Symmetry is very stiff. Artists use it to express dignity, endurance, and stability. But because formal balance is so predictable, it can be dull. Many artists avoid boring the viewer by using approximate symmetry, which is *almost* symmetrical.

Approximate symmetry has the stability of formal balance (Figure 10-8). Some small differences, however, make it more interesting than perfect symmetry. If you look carefully in a mirror, you may discover that your face has approximate symmetry. The two sides do not match perfectly.

Figure 10.6 (at left)   This body adornment is symmetrical to match the symmetry of the human body. The symmetry communicates dignity, which was the expressive intent of the artist who designed the adornment.

Leslie Mims Tichich. *Body Adornment*. c. 1970. Copper, brass, and leather with decorative ornaments applied. Collection of the artist.

Figure 10.7   This entrance to the Federal Reserve Building in Washington, D.C., is very important looking. The symmetrical arrangement of vertical and horizontal shapes gives the building a secure, stable look.

Cram, Goodhue and Ferguson. Federal Reserve Building. 1935. Washington, D.C. Facade. Photography by Sandak, Inc., Stamford, Connecticut.

Figure 10.8 This painting has become a symbol of everything that people mean when they say, "The good old days." It represents a Midwestern farmer and his daughter. The models were the artist's sister and his dentist. By using formal balance, Wood gives the work a stiff, serious mood. But by switching to approximate symmetry rather than pure symmetry, he adds that nostalgic, "folksy" look.

Grant Wood. *American Gothic.* 1930. Oil on beaverboard. 76 × 63.3 cm (29⅞ × 24⅞″). Collection, friends of American Art Collection. © 1987 The Art Institute of Chicago, Chicago, Illinois. 1930.934.

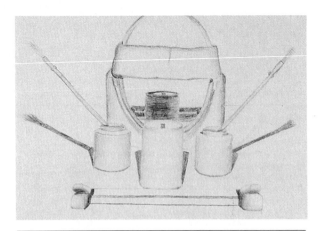

Figure 10.9A Student work. A symmetrical still life.

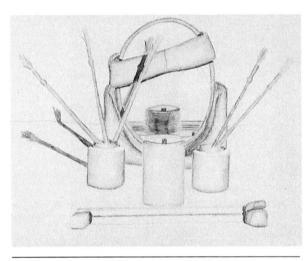

Figure 10.9B The same still life arranged with approximate symmetry.

DEVELOPING YOUR SKILLS

3. Study your own face carefully in a mirror to find the minor variations that create approximate symmetry. For example, is one eyebrow higher than the other? Describe the variations you see, or draw your face, emphasizing the variations.
4. Make a list of things you use that are designed with formal balance. Look around you at home, at school, and anywhere else you happen to be.
5. Using shapes cut from construction paper, create a symmetrical design on a small sheet of paper. Organize both sides into accurate mirror images of each other before you glue them down.

6. Arrange a symmetrical still life and make a drawing of the arrangement with pencil on a small sheet of paper (Figure 10-9A). Then rearrange or change the objects slightly to create approximate symmetry (Figure 10-9B). Make a drawing of the second arrangement. Mount the drawings side by side on a sheet of construction paper and label each drawing. Which one do you prefer? Survey your friends to find out their preferences.
7. Many objects associated with people are symmetrical when viewed from a specific point of view. Make some sketches of at least three such objects, emphasizing the symmetry you find. Look at chairs, cars, lamps, bicycles, and so on.

SOMETHING EXTRA

A. Discuss symmetry with your science teacher to find out about the structure of life forms. Which life forms are symmetrical? Report your findings to the class.
B. Discuss symmetry with your math teacher and report to the class about symmetry in mathematics.

Radial Balance

Radial balance occurs when the forces or elements of a design seem to come out (*radiate*) from

Figure 10.10 Radial balance.

Figure 10.11 Garrison designed this quilt for the anniversary of the Statue of Liberty. She used the traditional, radial design of the "Star of Bethlehem" pattern to represent the light of liberty. But then she surrounded it with scenes that celebrate liberty throughout our country. What parts of American culture do you see represented?

Elizabeth Garrison. *Long May Our Land Be Bright*. 1986. Quilt. Private Collection.

a central point. The axis in a radial design is the center point. In almost all cases the elements are spaced evenly around the axis to form circular patterns (Figure 10-10).

Radial balance is really a complicated variation of symmetry. While symmetry means just two matching units, four or more matching units may appear (Figure 10-11) in designs with radial balance.

The design in a kaleidoscope is a good example of radial balance. The continually changing shapes at the end of the tube radiate from a central axis (Figure 10-12).

Radial balance occurs frequently in nature. Most flower petals are arranged around a central axis and radiate outward (Figure 10-13). Many plants follow radial patterns of growth. For instance, if you cut an apple in half horizontally, you will see a radial star design. Cut an orange the same way and notice the radial pattern of the segments.

Figure 10.12 A kaleidoscope design.

Figure 10.13 The radial organization of the main blossoms in this painting is obvious. But notice how the artist has used lines and shapes in other areas to emphasize the radial balance of living, growing blossoms.

Sharon Hardin. *Blossoms*. 1984. Watercolor. 71.1 × 101.6 cm (28 × 40"). Private Collection.

Figure 10.14 Bulfinch emphasized the roundness of the dome by decorating the interior domed ceiling with a radial design.

Charles Bulfinch. Chamber ceiling, House of Representatives, State House, Boston, Massachusetts. 1795–98. Photography by Sandak, Inc., Stamford, Connecticut.

You can find many examples of radial balance in architecture. Domes and stained-glass windows (Figure 10-14) are designed on the principle of radial balance. Manufactured items such as gears, wheels, tires, kitchen tools, dials, and clocks are also radial in structure.

DEVELOPING YOUR SKILLS

8. Make a list of at least five objects you use or see every day that have radial balance.
9. Make a collection of magazine and newspaper photographs of at least six objects that have radial balance.
10. Make a series of drawings of five natural or manufactured objects that have a radial structure. Emphasize the radial quality of each object.

Informal Balance

Informal balance gives the viewer the same comfortable feeling as does formal balance, but in a much more subtle way. It involves a balance of unlike objects. This is possible because two unlike objects can have equal *visual weight* (Figure 10-15).

Informal, or *asymmetrical*, balance creates a very casual effect. It seems less planned than formal balance. However, it is not. What appears to be an accidental arrangement of elements can be quite complicated. Symmetry merely requires that elements be repeated in a mirror image. Informal balance goes beyond that. Artists consider all the visual weight factors and put them together correctly.

Of course gravity does not pull on an object in a two-dimensional work of art. The viewer does, however, perceive the objects in the work as if grav-

Figure 10.15   Barnet has used informal balance to make a statement about the relationship between husband and wife. Her size dominates the painting and reduces her husband to the size of a child. Barnet adds the cat to the husband's side of the painting to give that side equal weight. The husband is an architect, sculptor, and theatre designer. Which member of the family do you think handles the contracts and business deals? How can you tell?

Will Barnet. *Kiesler and Wife*. 1963–65. Oil on canvas. 121.9 × 181.6 cm (48 × 71½"). The Metropolitan Museum of Art, New York, New York. Purchase. Roy R. and Marie S. Neuberger Foundation, Inc. gift and George A. Hearn Fund, 1966. 66.66.

ity were in effect. Many factors influence the visual weight, or the attraction, that elements in a work of art have for the viewer's eyes.

Size and Contour

A large shape or form appears to be heavier than a small shape. Several small shapes or forms can balance one large one (Figure 10-16).

An object with a complicated contour is more interesting, and appears to be heavier, than one with a simple contour. A small, complex object can balance a large, simple object (Figure 10-17).

Color

A high-intensity color has more visual weight than a low-intensity color. The viewer's eyes are drawn to the area of bright color. What does this mean in terms of balance? It means that a small area of bright color is able to balance a larger area of a dull, more neutral color (Figure 10-18).

Figure 10.16 The many small shapes in the lower right corner of this painting balance the large shape of the stage with its closed curtain.

Edward Hopper. *First Row Orchestra*. 1951. Oil on canvas. 79 × 102 cm (31 × 40″). Hirshhorn Museum and Sculpture Garden, Smithsonian Institution, Washington, D.C. Gift of Joseph H. Hirshhorn, 1966.

Figure 10.17   In this wedding portrait of Frida and Diego Rivera, Frida depicts herself in the ribbons, jewels, and native Mexican costume that she often wore. Her small body, enveloped in all of the ruffles and folds, balances Diego's solid, heavy form.

Frida (Frieda) Kahlo. *Frieda and Diego Rivera*. 1931. Oil on canvas. 100 × 78.7 cm (39 × 31″). San Francisco Museum of Modern Art, San Francisco, California. Albert M. Bender Collection. Gift of Albert M. Bender.

Figure 10.18   In the stained glass window to the right, the bright colors of the geometric shapes balance the large area of clear glass.

Designed by Frank Lloyd Wright. American glass-stained window, one of a triptych. XX century. Glass, lead, wood. 219.7 × 71 × 5.1 cm (86¼ × 28 × 2″). The Metropolitan Museum of Art, New York, New York. Purchase. Edward C. Moore, Jr. gift and Edgar J. Kaufmann charitable foundation gift. 1967.

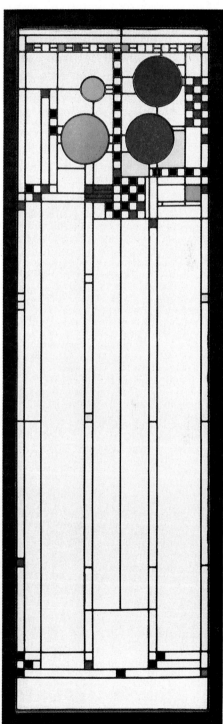

Warm colors carry more visual weight than cool colors. Red appears heavier than blue, and orange appears heavier than green (Figure 10-19).

Value

The stronger the contrast in value between an object and the background, the more visual weight the object has (Figure 10-20). Black against white has more weight than gray against white.

Dark values are heavier than light values. A dark red seems heavier than a light red.

Texture

As you know, a rough texture has an uneven pattern of light highlights and dark, irregular shad-

ows. For this reason a rough texture attracts the viewer's eye more easily than a smooth, even surface. This means that a small, rough-textured area can balance a larger area having a smooth surface (Figure 10-21). In a poster or advertisement, a

Figure 10.19 In this Rococo painting, Fragonard balances all of the cool, low-intensity colors with just one touch of warm, bright red on the dress in the foreground.

Jean-Honoré Fragonard. *A Game of Hot Cockles*. 1767–73. Oil on canvas. 115.5 × 91.5 cm (45½ × 36″). National Gallery of Art, Washington, D.C. Samuel H. Kress Collection.

Figure 10.20   The face and head scarf of the Virgin are no lighter in value than the Infant on His blanket or the shepherd's white skirt. Her face stands out so much more because it is placed against the dark value of the cave's interior, while the Infant and the shepherd are placed against the mid-value tan of the ground.

Giorgione. *The Adoration of the Shepherds.* c. 1505/1510. Paint on wood. 91 × 111 cm (35¾ × 43½"). National Gallery of Art, Washington, D.C. Samuel H. Kress Collection.

Figure 10.21   Student work. In this painting the small textured bush in the lower left balances the large, smooth hill shapes.

block of printed words has the quality of rough texture because of the irregular pattern of lights and darks. Poster designers must keep this in mind when balancing words and other visual elements.

Position

Children playing on a seesaw quickly discover that two friends of unequal weight can balance the seesaw by adjusting their positions. The heavier child moves toward the center; the lighter child slides toward the end. The board is then in balance (Figure 10-22).

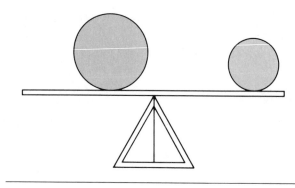

Figure 10.22 Does the see-saw look balanced?

Figure 10.23 The great wave close to the center is balanced by the smaller waves on the far right edge of this print. Study the three boats. How do they add to the informal balance of this work?

Katsushika Hokusai. *The Great Wave off Kanagawa* (from the series The Thirty-Six Views of Fuji). c. 1823–29. Woodblock print. 25.7 × 38 cm (10⅛ × 14¹⁵⁄₁₆″). The Metropolitan Museum of Art. Bequest of Mrs. H. O. Havemeyer, 1929. The H. O. Havemeyer Collection. JP 1847.

In visual art, a large object close to the dominant area of the work can be balanced by a smaller object placed far from the dominant area (Figure 10-23). A large, positive shape and a small, negative space can be balanced against a small, positive shape and a large, negative space.

Figure 10.24   Student work. Informal balance.

DEVELOPING YOUR SKILLS

11. Find five magazine illustrations, designs, or drawings that illustrate informal balance. Mount each example. Label the example, indicating how the visual weight is arranged in the illustration. Explain how the balance is achieved.

12. Create small designs using cut paper and/or fabric shapes to illustrate five weight arrangements that create informal balance (Figure 10-24). In each design keep all of the elements as alike as possible. Vary only the weight factors. For example, to illustrate differences in size, a large, red circle could be balanced by several small, red circles.

The Expressive Qualities of Balance

The type of balance used by an artist to organize a design has as strong impact on the feeling expressed by that design. Following are some general explanations of how artists use balance to express emotion.

Formal balance is a calm arrangement (Figure 10-25). It has been used to arrange people for

Figure 10.25   In this work the formal balance takes away from the violent impact of these "terrorists." How do lines and colors affect the feeling expressed by this work?

Bob Clements. *Evening Up the Score*. 1986. Painted wood. 274.3 × 152.4 × 15.2 cm (108 × 60 × 6″). Private collection.

dignified group portraits (Figure 10-26). Formal balance has also been used in some religious paintings. Paintings used as altarpieces in churches were designed to fit in with the formal balance of the church altar. Some modern works, such as Josef Albers' *Homage to the Square—Glow* (Figure 10-27), are symmetrical. This use of symmetry reduces complexity and allows viewers to concentrate completely on the element of color.

Government buildings, hospitals, and office buildings are designed using formal balance. One purpose for this type of balance is to imply that the people working in these buildings are stable and dignified. In Colonial times, homes were built with formal balance to make them dignified and calm-looking (Figure 10-28). This style is still popular today because people want their homes to look like a place to get away from the hustle and bustle.

With approximate symmetry, artists express the same sense of calm stability. But they avoid the rigid formality of pure symmetry (Figure 10-29).

Radial design is decorative. It appears in architecture, jewelry, pottery, weaving, and textile design. It is not used often by painters in its pure form. You can, however, find loose arrangements of radiating lines in many paintings (Figure 10-30). Artists use this technique to focus attention on an important part of the painting.

Figure 10.26 The formal arrangement of these figures adds to their dignity.

Unidentified artist. *Family Group.* Mid-17th century. Hanging scroll, colors on silk. 128.3 × 84.5 cm (50-1/2 × 33-1/4″). The Metropolitan Museum of Art, New York, New York. Anonymous gift, 1942. 42.190.1.

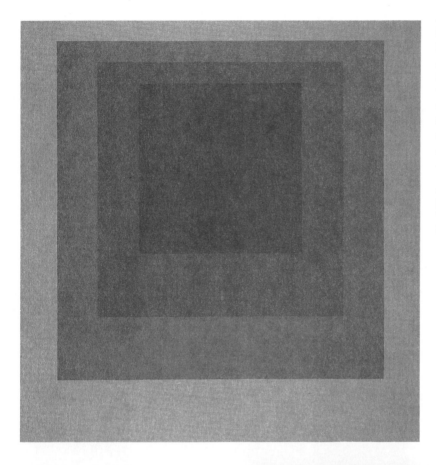

Figure 10.27 Albers had a strong influence on the development of American Hard Edge and Op art. He reduced line, shape, space, and texture to minimal importance and concentrated on color relationships. He created optical effects by changing the colors in the squares.

Josef Albers. *Homage to the Square: Glow.* 1966. Acrylic on fiberboard. 121.7 × 121.7 cm (48 × 48"). Hirshhorn Museum and Sculpture Garden, Smithsonian Institution, Washington, D.C. Gift of Joseph H. Hirshhorn, 1972.

Figure 10.28 Notice the architect's symmetrical arrangement of shapes on the front of this house. Imagine a vertical axis through the center. Do you see how the balance has been achieved?

John Vassall (Longfellow) House. 1759. Piazzas added later. Cambridge, Massachusetts. Facade. Photography by Sandak, Inc., Stamford, Connecticut.

Figure 10.29 How has O'Keeffe arranged the shapes in this painting to create approximate, not absolute, symmetry? Would you like the painting more if it were perfectly symmetrical? Why or why not?

Georgia O'Keeffe. *Lake George Window.* 1929. Oil on canvas. 101.6 × 76.2 cm (40 × 30"). Collection. The Museum of Modern Art, New York. Acquired through the Richard D. Brixey bequest.

Figure 10.30 The edges of the buildings and sidewalks, as well as the implied lines in the rows of windows and trees, radiate loosely from the vanishing point in this painting.

Maurice Utrillo. *Street at Corte, Corsica.* 1913. Oil on canvas. 60.8 × 80.7 cm (24 × 31¾"). National Gallery of Art, Washington, D.C. Ailsa Mellon Bruce Collection.

Figure 10.31 Constable has balanced the large mass of trees on the left with the small, busy contour of the cathedral and trees in the distance on the right.

John Constable. *A View of Salisbury Cathedral.* c. 1825. Oil on canvas. 73 × 91 cm (28¾ × 36″). National Gallery of Art, Washington, D.C. Andrew W. Mellon Collection.

Informal balance has a more natural look. When you look around your natural environment, you seldom find objects arranged with formal balance. To keep the natural quality of the real world in their works, artists use informal balance in arranging landscapes or groups of people (Figure 10-31).

Architects are using informal balance in many modern structures (see the David Wright house on page 9). Single-family, suburban homes have become the symbol of casual living, and these houses are designed with informal balance.

DEVELOPING YOUR SKILLS

13. Look through the rest of the chapters in this book to find examples of both formal and informal balance. Be sure to include symmetry, approximate symmetry, and radial balance. List the name of the work and describe how the type of balance used affects the feelings expressed.

14. Look around your neighborhood for buildings that have been constructed using formal or informal balance. Make a rough sketch of one building and describe the feeling it gives you. If you live in the city and all of the buildings are too tall, look at entrances and sketch one of those. The entrance includes the door and all of the decorative shapes around the doorway.

I M A G I N E   A N D   C R E A T E

Formal and Informal Group Portraits

MATERIALS

You will need the following:

Pencil and sketch paper

Two large, heavyweight sheets of white paper

Paint, of your choice, and brushes

Poster board

OBJECTIVE

Create two group portraits using drawings of your family, an imaginary family, or a group of your friends. Organize one drawing using formal balance. Organize the second using informal balance (Figures 10-32 and 10-33). Color both portraits with a medium of your choice.

DIRECTIONS

Use the pencil and sketch paper to make a set of drawings of your family, your friends, or an imaginary family. Humorous or fantasy drawings are acceptable. Use both formal and informal balance.

Be sure to pose the formal figures in stiff, vertical positions and dress them in formal or old-fashioned clothes. The informal figures should be posed casually and should be dressed in clothes such as jeans and T-shirts.

Draw appropriate backgrounds for each of the paintings. The formal figures might be in an old-fashioned parlor, while the casual figures might be at a picnic or watching TV together. Don't limit yourself to these suggestions; use your own ideas.

Using your best sketch ideas, paint both portraits on the heavyweight paper. Choose a color scheme to enhance the mood of each painting.

Mount or mat each of the paintings for display.

Figure 10.32   Student work. Formal portrait.

Figure 10.33   Student work. Informal portrait.

Write a short poem or essay about the two paintings, emphasizing similarities and differences. Don't be afraid to use humor if you think it is appropriate.

EVALUATION CHECKLIST

Be sure you did the following:

1. Made a set of drawings and chose the best examples of formal and informal balance.
2. Drew a formal arrangement of the figures on one sheet of heavy-weight paper; posed them in stiff, vertical positions; dressed them in formal or old-fashioned clothes.
3. Drew an informal arrangement of the figures on the second sheet of paper; posed them casually; dressed them in casual clothes.
4. Drew appropriate backgrounds for each picture.
5. Painted both portraits in a medium of your choice.
6. Cleaned up the work area properly.
7. Prepared both paintings for display.
8. Wrote a poem or essay about the two paintings, emphasizing similarities and differences.

SAFETY NOTE

Remember to read the labels on your paints. Look for *AP*, *CP*, *HL*, or *Nontoxic* on the label.

Fabric Medallion

MATERIALS

You will need the following:

Pencil, ruler, compass, and sketch paper for planning

Fabric for round medallion (size depends on intended use)

Embroidery thread and fine yarn.

Scissors

Needles and pins

Fabrics that will not unravel for appliqué shapes

Materials to which the medallion will be attached

A container in which to store the medallion, threads, and other equipment while working

Optional:

Embroidery hoop

OBJECTIVE

Design and make a round fabric medallion decorated with appliqué and stitchery as a gift for someone you know. *Appliqué* is the technique of attaching fabric shapes to a fabric background by gluing or sewing. Use radial balance to organize your design (Figure 10-34).

DIRECTIONS

Choose the person for whom you will design the medallion. Think of symbols that represent the personality and interests of that individual. Sketch all of your symbol ideas. Choose the best symbol or symbols for the medallion.

Using pencil, ruler, and compass, plan a radial design that uses the symbols. You may want to build the individual's name or initials into the design. Make several plans and choose the best.

Select fabric for the background, the shapes to be appliqued, and the threads and yarns you will need. Be sure to consider the relationship of colors and textures as you select materials. Collect your tools. Place everything in the container.

Draw the radial design on the fabric.

Cut out the appliqué shapes and pin them in place.

Refer to the stitchery chart on page 198. If necessary, practice some stitches on scrap fabric. If you are planning to use the medallion

Figure 10.34 Student work. Fabric medallion.

on clothing, be sure to use small stitches so they will not snag and tear when worn.

Sew the appliqué shapes in place, and remove the pins.

Finish your design by using a variety of decorative stitches.

Decide how you will turn the medallion into a useful object. Collect the necessary materials and finish it.

EVALUATION CHECKLIST

Be sure you did the following:

1. Designed the medallion as a gift.
2. Experimented with a variety of symbols.
3. Chose the best symbols for the medallion.
4. Planned a radial design. Made several sketches and selected the best.
5. Selected fabrics, threads, and yarns needed.
6. Drew the radial design on the fabric.
7. Cut out the appliqué shapes and pinned them in place.
8. Referred to the stitchery chart on page 198, and practiced some stitches on scrap fabric.
9. Sewed the appliqué shapes in place.
10. Finished the design using a variety of decorative stitches.
11. Turned the medallion into a useful object.
12. Cleaned up the work area.

Round Plaster Relief

MATERIALS

You will need the following:

Moist clay

Slip

Plaster

Plastic dish pan or bucket

Nine-inch pie pan

An assortment of discarded and found objects, such as spools, nails, screws, bolts, nuts, keys, clothespins, pieces of rope or cord, dowels, plastic forks and spoons, coins, twigs, pine cones, acorns, nuts, seashells, and bark

Clay carving tools

Paperclip

Soft, discarded toothbrush

Sandpaper

White glue

Staining materials, commercial metallic finishes, or school acrylics

Newspaper-lined trash can

Storage container

OBJECTIVE

Create a round plaster relief using radial balance (Figure 10-35). Finish the surface by painting or staining.

DIRECTIONS

Collect your supplies and keep them in your storage container.

Press a small amount of clay into a flat slab and practice making impressions in the clay with the found objects and carving tools you have collected. Decide which of the impressions you like and note them for use in your final design. Avoid those that produce undercuts.

Use a large portion of clay to prepare your mold (Figure 10-36). Line the pie pan or cardboard with a "crust" of clay one inch (2.54 cm) thick. To make the relief thick enough, you may wish to build clay walls higher than the pan walls.

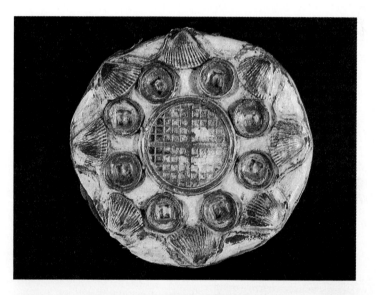

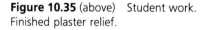

Figure 10.35 (above)   Student work. Finished plaster relief.

Figure 10.36 (at right)   The clay mold.

Figure 10.37 Stick a paperclip into the plaster.

Using the tools you selected, create your radial design. Join any raised areas to the slab with slip. Smooth the edges carefully so no plaster will get caught in the seams (see the Technique Tip below).

Use just enough water to fill your mold. Mix it with the plaster in the plastic container. Follow the directions on page 128. Pour the plaster into your mold. When the plaster is almost set, place a bent paperclip (Figure 10-37) into the plaster so one end is sticking out. This will be the hanger for your relief when it is finished.

Dispose of excess plaster in a newspaper-lined trash can.

Allow enough time for the plaster to set. Leaving it overnight is fine. Just be sure that you have a safe place to store it.

When the plaster is set, pry apart the pie pan and separate the clay from the plaster. Since pieces of plaster will be stuck in the clay, the clay cannot be used for ceramics. But it can be saved for another project like this.

Smooth out any sharp plaster edges with sandpaper.

Wash the relief with water to remove any clay. An old toothbrush works well to clean the clay out of the indentations.

Allow time for the plaster to dry.

TECHNIQUE TIP

Clay Mold for a Plaster Relief

When making the clay mold for a plaster relief, everything you press *into* the clay will be raised in the plaster design. If you build up areas, those areas will become indentations in the final product (Figure 10-38).

Do not make any impressions that have undercuts (Figure 10-39). An undercut traps the plaster, and the plaster will break off when removed from the mold. When you make an impression, the deepest part must be the narrowest.

When you create a raised area of clay to form an indentation in the plaster relief, you must make sure that the opposite type of undercut does not occur (Figure 10-30).

If you make any mistakes in the clay design, simply smooth out the area with your fingers.

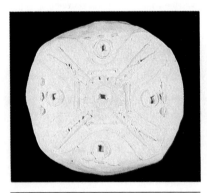

Figure 10.38 Remove the relief.

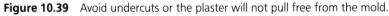
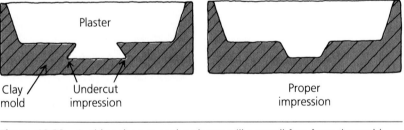

Figure 10.39 Avoid undercuts or the plaster will not pull free from the mold.

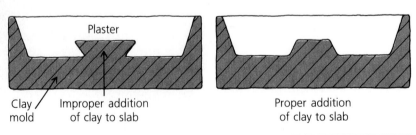

Figure 10.40 Be careful when adding raised clay areas.

Figure 10.41 Staining the surface.

Before staining, coat the surface of the relief with slightly diluted white glue.

Stain the surface with wood or shoe stains (Figure 10-41). Apply the stain generously, allowing it to sink into the indentations. Before the stain dries, wipe off the raised areas with a cloth or a paper towel to bring out the highlights. Be careful not to wipe off all of the stain. For further decoration, try commercial gold or silver metal patinas.

Hang the relief for display by tying a strong string to the paperclip on the back.

EVALUATION CHECKLIST

Be sure you did the following:

1. Collected materials and supplies and kept them in the storage container.
2. Practiced making impressions and selected those for the design. Avoided undercuts.
3. Created the clay mold according to directions.
4. Created a radial design.
5. Mixed the plaster properly and poured it into the mold.
6. Added a bent paperclip while the plaster was setting.
7. Allowed enough time for the plaster to set.
8. Separated the plaster from the clay carefully.
9. Smoothed out sharp edges with sandpaper.
10. Washed the plaster and cleaned out the crevices.
11. Allowed time for the relief to dry.
12. Coated the relief with slightly diluted glue.
13. Stained the surface, following directions.
14. Hung the relief for display.
15. Cleaned up the work area after each work session.
16. Disposed of excess plaster in a newspaper-lined trash can.

SAFETY NOTE

If you have a breathing difficulty, remember to avoid plaster and clay dust. Use a dust mask, if necessary.

Figure 10.42   O'Keeffe, Georgia. *Cow's Skull: Red, White, and Blue*. 1931. Oil on canvas. 101.3 × 91.1 cm (39⅞ × 35⅞"). The Metropolitan Museum of Art, The Alfred Stieglitz Collection, 1952.

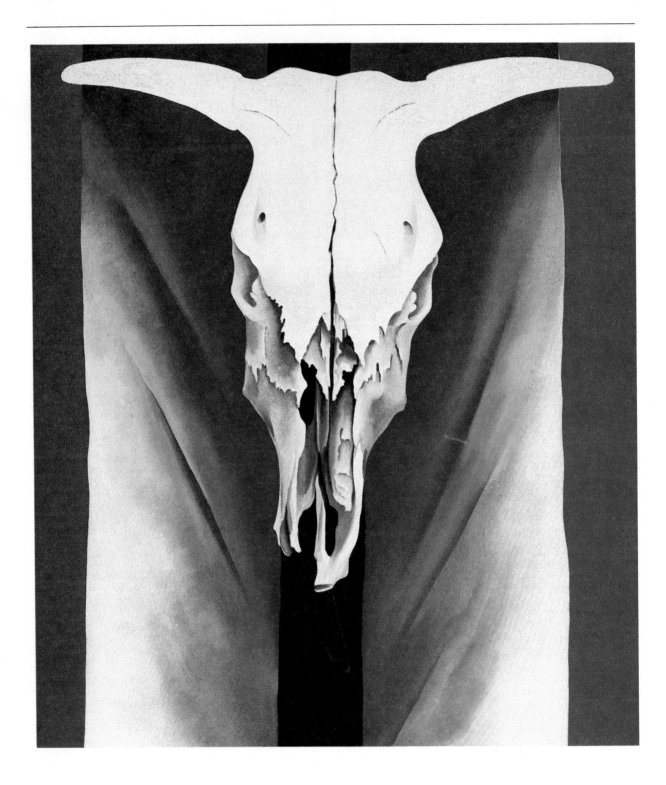

A R T   C R I T I C I S M

Improving Your Critical-Thinking Skills

Description: What Do You See?

Read the credit line to determine the size and medium of *Cow's Skull—Red, White, and Blue* by Georgia O'Keeffe.

There are not very many objects or shapes in this work. Do not be fooled, however, by its seeming simplicity. Write down every fact you observe.

Analysis: How Is the Work Organized?

What kind of lines do you see? Locate and describe them. Notice the thick and thin variations of line, and study the contour lines. Do the lines seem more static or more active? What line directions do you see? Does one direction seem to dominate?

Now examine the shapes used in the painting. Are there any geometric shapes? Where are they? Describe them.

Do you find free-form shapes? Where are they? Describe them.

Study the shapes within the skull carefully. What do you notice? Do you see flat shapes?

Are there any negative areas? If so, where?

Does the artist use perspective to create the illusion of space? If so, what kind of space? Which area seems closest to the viewer and which seems the most distant? Examine the painting carefully again to make sure your answers are based on visual facts.

Next, examine the colors O'Keeffe uses. What colors can you find? What do these colors symbolize? What color intensities and values do you notice? Where is the area of lightest value? Where do you see the darkest value?

Now examine the painting for its textures. Has O'Keeffe imitated any real textures? Has she invented any? Describe the textures you see. Do not confuse contour with surface. Are there any variations in texture? Is the contrast strong or subtle?

There are many different rhythms in this work. What kinds of visual rhythms can you find? Describe them and explain the expressive qualities of the various rhythms.

Which type of balance has the artist used to organize the objects in this painting? What sort of feeling does this arrangement give?

Interpretation: What Is Happening? What Is the Artist Trying to Say?

The subject matter of this painting is very simple. However, look at all your clues from analysis before you try to read the meaning.

Consider the expressive qualities of the elements and principles. What do they tell you? Can you find symbolic meanings? Does the skull look frightening? Why do you feel it does (or doesn't)? Concentrate on the lines and shapes in the skull—what begins to happen as you do so?

Go beyond storytelling to discover the feelings and moods expressed in this painting. What is the artist telling you about the skull? What does "Red, White, and Blue" symbolize?

Does this painting remind you of a book, a play, a movie, a poem, or a song you know?

Write a paragraph explaining your interpretation. Then write a new title for the painting. Your title should sum up your interpretation.

Judgment: What Do You Think of the Work?

Does this painting appeal to you? Does it say something to you? Would you like to see it in your home or your school? Does it make you think? Do you like it?

Use one or more of the theories of art to defend your opinion.

A B O U T   T H E   A R T I S T

Georgia O'Keeffe

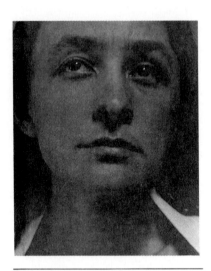

Figure 10.43   Georgia O'Keeffe, American, 1887–1986.

Alfred Stieglitz. *Georgia O'Keeffe*. 1919. Palladium print. 24.1 × 18.8 cm (9⅝ × 7⅜"). Collection, The Museum of Modern Art, New York. Gift of Georgia O'Keeffe.

Georgia O'Keeffe was a leader in the world of twentieth-century art. Her strong, personal vision of nature and the western desert made her a pioneer.

She was born on November 15, 1887 on a small dairy farm near Sun Prairie, Wisconsin. She died in the spring of 1986 in her beloved New Mexican desert.

As a young child she developed an interest in music, but by the time she was ten she knew that she wanted to become a painter instead. She took her first art lessons in a convent school in Wisconsin. She continued to study art as an adult but soon lost interest in European art styles. After awhile she quit painting to take a job as a commercial artist.

In 1912 she studied abstract design and took a job teaching art in a high school in Amarillo, Texas. The beauty of the dry, open landscape inspired her as nothing else had. The rocks and mountains had fantastic shapes, and the colors were breathtaking. She loved the wind, the open spaces, and the emptiness.

When she was twenty-nine she destroyed all of the work she had done up to that time and started over. She began to paint only to please herself, and she painted the West.

O'Keeffe sent some of her new drawings to a friend in New York. The friend showed them to Alfred Stieglitz, whose gallery was to become a gathering place for many artists.

Stieglitz liked O'Keeffe's work and gave her her first solo show. He also gave her the needed financial aid to give up teaching to devote all of her time to painting. Eventually Stieglitz and O'Keeffe married, and the marriage made each more famous. Stieglitz photographed O'Keeffe 500 times. Her face became famous before her paintings did.

It was at this time that O'Keeffe shocked the art world. She decided to paint something that people were too busy to notice. She painted flowers, but she painted them so large that they could not be ignored. She changed the meaning of the flowers by changing their size. She left out details in order to express her inner feelings. Her paintings say more about her emotions than about the subjects she painted.

O'Keeffe did not want to remain in New York. The western plains were calling her to paint. She began to spend summers in New Mexico, and, after Stieglitz died, she left New York for good.

O'Keeffe painted *Cow's Skull* because she wanted to create something that was uniquely American. Do you think she succeeded?

Chapter 10 Review: Talking about Art

USING THE LANGUAGE OF ART

For each new art term below, choose a work of art from this chapter. Then write a sentence about that work using the new term correctly in the sentence.

balance   informal balance
central axis   radial balance
formal balance   symmetry

LEARNING THE ART ELEMENTS AND PRINCIPLES

1. Why is balance important to a work of art?
2. What are the visual forces, or weights, in art?
3. What is the difference between bilateral and approximate symmetry?
4. What factors in a work of art influence the visual weight of the art elements?
5. Which carry more weight, warm or cool colors?
6. How can value affect visual weight?
7. What does a formally balanced building express?

INCREASING YOUR ART AWARENESS

1. Is the balance in 6-40 formal or informal?
2. Is the balance in 6-26 formal or informal?
3. Name one visual weight factor used to create informal balance in Figure 8-1?
4. Place your feet together and look down at your shoes. What kind of symmetry do you see?
5. Excluding Chapter 10, find artworks that illustrate each of the five visual weight factors. Give the title of each work, the artist's name, and the visual weight factor used.

UNDERSTANDING ART CULTURE AND HERITAGE

1. List one work of art from each of the following centuries: 15th, 16th, 17th, 18th, 19th, and 20th.
2. What does the work of art in Figure 10-1 reveal about the society in which it was created?

3. List two works of art from non-Western cultures (see Chapter 3) reproduced in this chapter.
4. Why is Figure 10-19 a good example of the Rococo style (see Chapter 3)?
5. Name three works of art in this chapter that convey something about American life and culture. What does each work express?

JUDGING THE QUALITY OF ART

Look at Figure 10-1, *Mary, Queen of Heaven.* Use art criticism to become acquainted with more than the religious story being told.

During description, notice the musical instruments that were painted with such accuracy. Also notice all of the angels' wings. You are sure to see something unusual if you look closely. Finally, notice the landscape at the bottom of the painting. What period of history is represented there?

During analysis, study all the elements first. Then consider how this unknown artist has used rhythm and balance to organize the lines, shapes, spaces, colors, and textures in this work. How does balance affect the work's expressive quality?

Use interpretation to explain what this painting is communicating to you. Open up your senses. Forget that this is a Medieval painting for a church. Allow your eyes to linger over the painting and try to sense its spirit.

During judgment, be sure to defend your conclusions.

LEARNING MORE ABOUT ART

How many athletic activities depend upon balance? Look this up in the library or schedule a conference with your physical education teacher to discuss the subject. Are different kinds of balance involved? Is there any relationship between the kinds of visual balance and the athletic types of balance? Present your findings in a report. Use a poster or some photographs to illustrate your findings.

Figure 11.1 Whistler was concerned with the abstract arrangement of elements. He referred to his works as arrangements, symphonies, and nocturnes. The painting below is a portrait of a woman for whom Whistler had a great deal of affection.

James McNeill Whistler. *The White Girl (Symphony in White, No. 1)*. 1862. Oil on canvas. 214.7 × 108 cm (84-1/2 × 42-1/2"). National Gallery of Art, Washington, D.C. Harris Whittemore Collection.

Proportion

LEARNING OBJECTIVES

After reading this chapter and doing the exercises, you will be able to

☐ understand how we perceive proportion and scale.

☐ explain and recognize the Golden Mean.

☐ measure and draw human faces and bodies with correct proportions.

☐ understand how artists use proportion and distortion to create meaning.

WORDS TO LEARN

In this chapter you will learn the meanings of the words listed below.

distortion

exaggeration

Golden Mean

proportion

scale

sighting

"I wish my nose weren't so big!"
"This desk is too small for me!"
"You put too much salt in the stew!"
All of these complaints are about problems with proportion. **Proportion** is the principle of art concerned with the size relationship of one part to another.

The size of an object by itself has no meaning (Figure 11-2). We can't tell how big or small an object is unless we can compare it with something else. If you are over six feet tall, you must approach a doorway with caution. When shopping for clothes, you look for the sizes designed to fit the proportions of your body. When cooking, you must be sure that the proportions in your recipes are correct.

DEVELOPING YOUR SKILLS

1. Measure the chairs and tables in a kindergarten classroom and a third-grade room. Measure the chairs, desks, and tables in your classroom. Make a chart to illustrate and compare differences.
2. Imagine that you are an interior designer. List all of the measurements you would have to consider to properly design one of the following:
   • A walk-in closet in which all of your clothing and linens must be stored
   • The cooking space in a kitchen
   • A lunch counter in a short-order restaurant

Figure 11.2 Look very closely at these cliffs. Without anything to compare them to, can you tell how high they are?

Photography by Robert Nix.

The Golden Mean

You have just read about the importance of proportion to the function of products. Proportion is also important in creating the beauty of art objects (Figure 11-4).

Through the ages, people have sought an ideal of harmony and beauty. They have looked for a ratio (a mathematical comparison of sizes) that would produce an ideal form for figures and structures.

The ancient Greek philosopher Pythagoras found that he could apply mathematical equations to both geometric shapes and musical tones. If this

Figure 11.3 This chair was created by an artist famous for his designs. Besides being a comfortable form to support your body, it is a piece of sculpture that has symbolic qualities.

Ludwig Mies van de Rohe. "Barcelona" Chair. 1929. Chrome-plated flat steel bars with pigskin cushions. 75.9 × 74.9 × 75.2 cm (29⅞ × 29½ × 29⅝"). Collection, The Museum of Modern Art, New York, New York. Gift of Knoll International.

Figure 11.4 This painting is beautiful, but a mystery. This famous heiress from the fifteenth century has some odd proportions. She is too thin. The red silk belt emphasizes her painfully thin waist. Her lips are too thick. They symbolize a sensuous person. Her forehead is too high. That is thought to be a sign of an intellectual woman. She is a combination of conflicting symbols. Even though her individual features might be considered ugly, they combine in an unusual way to make a stunning female.

Rogier van der Weyden. *Portrait of a Lady.* c. 1460. Oil on wood. 37 × 27 cm (14½ × 10¾"). National Gallery of Art, Washington, D.C. Andrew W. Mellon Collection.

is so, he thought, there must also be a way to explain other things—even the universe—in mathematical terms.

Euclid, another Greek, discovered that he could divide a line into two parts so that the smaller line had the same proportion, or ratio, to the larger line as the larger line had to the whole line. This ratio was called the *Golden Section* or the **Golden Mean** (Figure 11-5). With this ratio, the ancient Greeks felt they had found the ideal proportion. It was used to control the relationship of parts in sculpture, architecture, and even pottery. In math, this ratio is written 1 to 1.6.

Figure 11.5 The ratio of the Golden Mean is 1 to 1.6.

The Golden Rectangle (Figure 11-6) had sides that matched this ratio. The longer sides were a little more than half again as long as the shorter sides. This was thought to be the most pleasing shape.

One of the many fascinating facts about the Golden Mean is its relationship to the human figure. If you divide the average adult male body at the navel, the two body measurements that result (head to navel = A, navel to toes = B) have a ratio of 1 to 1.6 (Figure 11-7).

The secret of the Golden Mean was forgotten with the fall of Ancient Greece. The ratio was rediscovered, however, during the Renaissance, and a book was written about it. This time it was called the *Divine Proportion,* and it was thought to have magical qualities.

Since that time, some artists have chosen to use the Golden Mean as the basis for their compositions. Others, unaware of the mathematical ratio, used the Golden Mean just because that arrangement of parts looked good. Most artists now reject the idea that only this one rule could fit the "correct" proportions for all works of art. But the ratio is found so often in every aspect of visual art that it is hard to ignore its importance (Figure 11-8).

Many people looked at the human body as a source for perfect proportions. As you know, artists during the Golden Age of Greece believed that the human body was the true expression of order. Statues created during this time were not realistic portraits of real people. The artists of this period showed the ideal form rather than reality (Figure 11-9 on page 278).

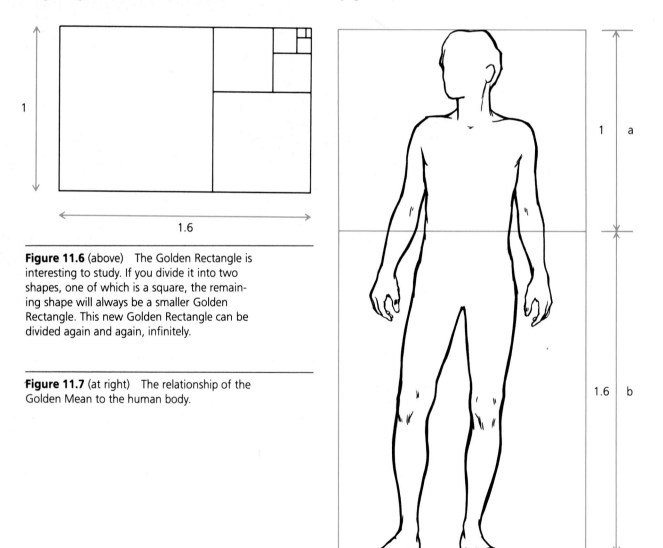

Figure 11.6 (above)   The Golden Rectangle is interesting to study. If you divide it into two shapes, one of which is a square, the remaining shape will always be a smaller Golden Rectangle. This new Golden Rectangle can be divided again and again, infinitely.

Figure 11.7 (at right)   The relationship of the Golden Mean to the human body.

Figure 11.8 Can you find the proportions of the Golden Mean in this work?

Reginald Marsh. *Why Not Use the L?* 1930. Egg tempera on canvas. 91.4 × 121.9 cm (36 × 48″). Collection of Whitney Museum of American Art, New York, New York. Photo by Geoffrey Clements.

In the first century B.C., Vitruvius, a Roman writer, set down ratios for human proportion. These were later used by Leonardo da Vinci and other artists. The modern-day architect Le Corbusier applied human dimensions to architecture and city planning (Figure 11-10 on the next page).

DEVELOPING YOUR SKILLS

3. Study the illustration of the Golden Rectangle (Figure 11-6). Look through this book to find works of art that have been organized using the proportions of the Golden Rectangle. List two and make simple diagrams showing the use of the Golden Rectangle in each composition.

4. Notice the rectangles in your home. List and describe five that use proportions close to those of the Golden Rectangle.

A. Read about one of the following topics and report your findings to the class. Use charts, diagrams, and pictures to help explain your findings.
  - If you are interested in music, read about the Pythagorean theories of music. Ask your music teacher for help, if needed.
  - If you are interested in mathematics, find out more about the Golden Mean, or find out what Fibonacci's number sequence has to do with the Golden Mean. Ask your math teacher for help, if needed.

Figure 11.9 (at left) This sculpture is idealized. The facial features and all the proportions are so perfect, you would not recognize the model if she stood next to the work.

Greece (from Alexandria?). *Dancing Lady.* c. 50 B.C. Peloponnesus marble. 85.4 cm (33⅝″) high with base; 78.7 cm (30¹⁵⁄₁₆″) high without base; base 32.1 cm (12⅝″) wide, 6.7 cm (2⅝″) high; diameter at sides: 21.6 cm (8½″). The Cleveland Museum of Art, Cleveland, Ohio. John L. Severance Fund.

Figure 11.10 (at right) The sculptural form of this building is based on human dimensions.

Le Corbusier. Chapelle Notre-Dame-du-Haut, Ronchamp. 1955. Giraudon/Art Resource, New York, New York.

Scale

Scale is much like proportion, but there is a difference. Proportion refers to the relationship of one part to another. **Scale,** on the other hand, refers to size as measured against a standard reference, such as the human body. A seven-foot (213 cm) basketball player may not look big next to other basketball players. The player will look big, however, when you see him in scale—that is, compared with a crowd of average people.

In art, there are two kinds of scale to consider. One is the scale of the work itself. The other is the scale of objects or elements within the design.

The pyramids of Egypt are of such a large scale that ordinary people are overwhelmed by their size. These pyramids were designed to be so large to express the eternal strength of Egypt.

Wall paintings inside a pyramid depict the body of the pharaoh in very large scale. His servants, however, are very small in scale to emphasize their low status. This use of scale to emphasize rank has appeared in the art of many cultures.

Actual works of art are usually much larger or much smaller than they appear to be when you look at photographs of them. You may have seen photos with a human hand or a human figure added for the purpose of showing the size of the objects in relation to human scale. Without some sort of measure, no illustration in any book can convey the effect of the scale of a work of art.

Some works that seem monumental in quality are really quite small in size. This is why the dimensions are always listed in the credits of the work. Try to visualize the size of a work in relation to your size. Imagine how it would look if it were in the room with you.

The picture of Claes Oldenburg's *Falling Shoestring Potatoes* (Figure 11-11) is not very impressive until you realize that the sculpture is 9 feet (274 cm) tall. If you could stand beside it, the potatoes would be as tall or taller than you are, and the bag would tower an additional 3 feet (91 cm) up. The scale of this work compared with a real bag of shoestring potatoes is enormous. It is also big compared with a human being.

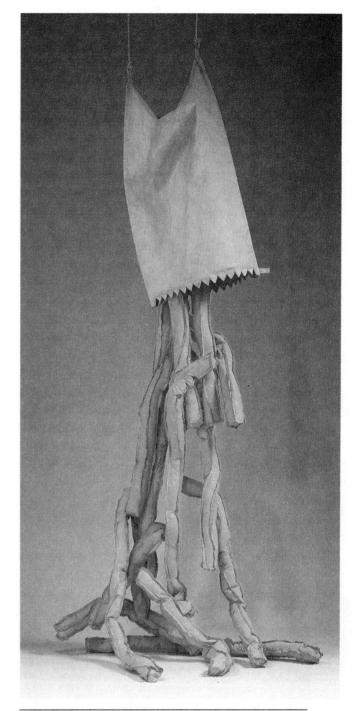

Figure 11.11   This soft sculpture is 9 feet tall. This type of exaggerated scale is one method Pop artists use to make viewers see ordinary objects in a new way.

Claes Oldenburg. *Falling Shoestring Potatoes.* 1965. Painted canvas, kapok. 274.3 × 116.8 × 106.7 cm (108 × 46 x 42"). Walker Art Center, Minneapolis, Minnesota. Gift of the T. B. Walker Foundation, 1966.

Variations in scale within a work can change the work's total impact. For example, the scale of furniture to be placed in a room is the concern of interior designers. The designer considers the scale of the space into which the furniture will be placed. The needs of the people who will use the space must also be considered. An oversized, overstuffed sofa would crowd a small room with a low ceiling. However, the same sofa would fit comfortably in a large hotel lobby with a four-story ceiling. The large scale of the lobby would make the size of the sofa look right.

Figure 11.13   Student work. Unrealistic scale.

Figure 11.12   Student work. Realistic scale.

DEVELOPING YOUR SKILLS

5. Find works in this book that show how scale was used to create special effects.

6. Create two small collage scenes using magazine cutouts of people, furniture, and hand-held objects, such as books, combs, pencils, hair dryers, and dishes. Arrange the cutouts on a small sheet of paper using the following relationships:

   • Realistic, accurate scale: All the things in the scene are in scale with the people and all of the people are in correct proportion to each other (Figure 11-12). You may have to employ perspective techniques and arrange things in depth to use all of your cutouts.

   • Unrealistic scale: The objects and furniture are not in scale with the people (Figure 11-13). A mysterious or humorous effect is created through the change in normal scale relationships. Draw a background environment for each scene using water-base markers, colored pencils, or crayons.

7. Carry a tape measure with you for a full day. List, measure, and describe every chair you use. Measure each chair's seat height and depth, and the height of the arm rest, if there is one. Rate each chair on the quality of the back support. Does the chair support the small of your back? Describe the cushioning, if there is any.

   Make a chart that creatively presents your findings. Include sketches of the chairs, or magazine pictures that closely resemble the chairs, in the report. Arrange the chairs in order, from the most comfortable to the least comfortable. Study your chart and write a statement summing up the conclusions you reach about the chairs' comfort and proportions.

8. If you have access to an antique car, list all of the measurements relating to the driver's proportions. Include the relationship between the seat, the steering wheel, pedals, dashboard, windshield, floor, and roof. Compare those measurements with the same measurements in the late-model cars. Make a chart, diagram, or model to present your findings. Write a statement summing up your conclusions regarding car design and the relationship of proportion to comfort and efficiency.

Drawing Human Proportions

Different cultures have set different standards for human beauty. People from the Middle Ages would look upon us as giants (Figure 11-14). The rounded females in Rubens' Baroque paintings would seem fat by today's standards (Figure 11-15). Even today there are dramatic differences between the desirable proportions of a high-fashion model and the average person.

Fig. 11.14 (at right)   The man who wore this armor was about 5'5" tall. Would many men today fit into this armor?

English (Greenwich School). Armor of George Clifford, Third Earl of Cumberland, K.G. 1590. Photograph courtesy of the Metropolitan Museum of Art, Munsey Fund, 1932.

Figure 11.15 Rubens' Virgin looks much chubbier than those in most other paintings of the Virgin Mary. But hefty proportions were the favored style in the time of Rubens, so he painted Mary in that manner.

Sir Peter Paul Rubens. *The Assumption of the Virgin.* c. 1626. Oil on wood. 125.4 × 94.2 cm (49⅜ × 37⅛″). National Gallery of Art, Washington, D.C. Samuel H. Kress Collection.

Figures

People come in a variety of sizes and shapes. Categories for clothes sizes—"slim," "husky," "petite," "tall"—are just one indication of the many different shapes and sizes of people.

Although they vary in size and shape, most people do not vary with regard to proportion. The 7-foot (213-cm) basketball player and the 5-foot (152-cm) dancer might have the same proportions. The tall basketball player's arms, legs, and torso

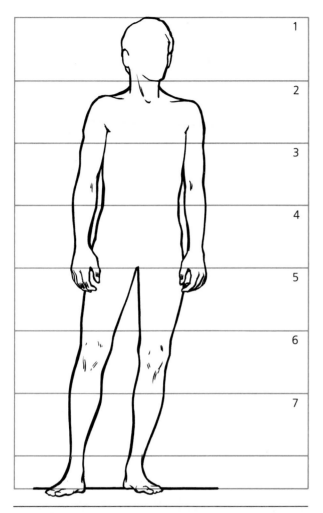

1
2
3
4
5
6
7

Figure 11.16 (above)   Average body proportions.

have the same ratio to each other as the arms, legs, and torso of the dancer. Body proportions cannot be explained in inches or centimeters. They can only be defined in ratios of one body part to another.

The unit usually used to define the proportions of an individual figure is the length of the head from the chin to the top of the skull. The average adult is seven and one-half heads tall (Figure 11-16); a young child is five or six heads tall; and an infant is only three heads long (Figure 11-17). Many amateur paintings of children look strange because the artist has drawn the head too small in proportion to the rest of the body. When this happens, the child looks like a miniature adult.

DEVELOPING YOUR SKILLS

9. Measure your head from the top of your skull to the bottom of your chin. Since the top of your head is round, hold something flat, such as a piece of cardboard, across the top of your head to obtain an accurate measurement.

Use the length of your head as a unit against which to measure the rest of your body. In this way you can figure the relationship, or ratio, of all parts of your body to your head. You may need a friend to help you obtain accurate measurements. Determine the number of head lengths that each of the following represents:

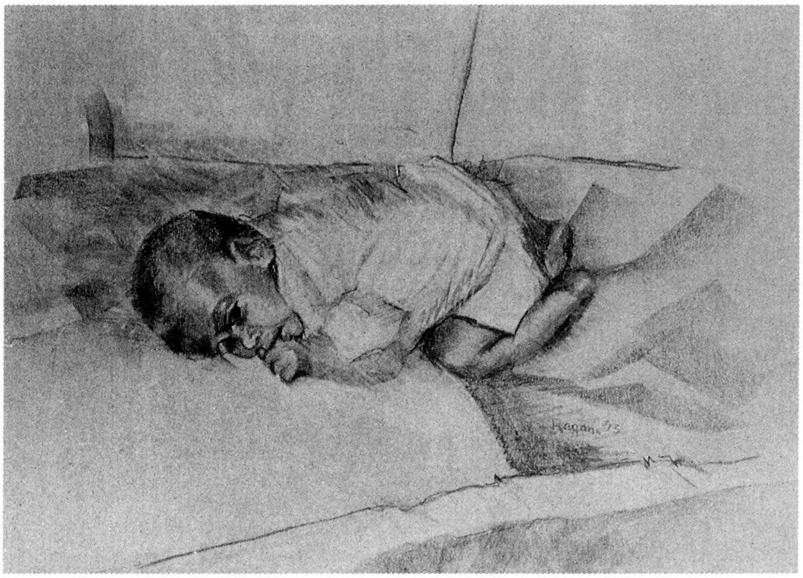

Figure 11.17   Notice the ratio of head to body in this sketch of an infant. Does the ratio differ from the usual adult ratio?

- Total height
- Chin to waist
- Waist to hip
- Knee to ankle
- Ankle to bottom of bare heel
- Underarm to elbow
- Elbow to wrist
- Wrist to tip of fingers
- Shoulder to tip of fingers

Record the ratios and create a diagram or chart to show your findings. Compare your findings with those of your classmates. Find averages for the class, since the ratios will not be exactly alike.

10. Look through magazines and newspapers for full-length photographs of adults, children, and infants. Using head ratios, measure the

proportions of the people. How do the proportions compare with your own proportions?

11. Look through the newspaper for ads that use drawings of full-length fashion models. How do their proportions compare with your own proportions?

12. Make a series of figure drawings using a live model. Use the sighting technique (see below) to help you see proportions. Remember, as your model's poses change, the proportions will look different. Measure what you see, not what you think you should see.

If your model is sitting facing you, the length from hip to knee may be *foreshortened*. This means that the amount of leg you see from hip to knee will depend upon your point of view (Figure 11-19).

TECHNIQUE TIP

Sighting

Sighting is a method that will help you determine proportions (Figure 11-18).

Hold a pencil vertically at arm's length in the direction of the object you are drawing. Close one eye and focus on the object you are going to measure. Slide your thumb along the pencil until the length of the pencil above your thumb matches the length of the object. Now, without moving

your thumb or bending your arm, hold the pencil parallel to the widest part of the object. Compare the length of the object with its width. You can determine the ratio of width to length by seeing how many times the width fits

into the length. This method can be applied either to different parts of the same object or to two or more different objects. Use one measurement as a base measurement and see how the other measurements relate to it.

Figure 11.18 This girl is using a pencil to sight proportions. Have you seen artists do this in movies and t.v. shows and wondered what they were doing?

Heads and Faces

As you read this section, look in a mirror or at a friend to check the examples discussed.

The front of the head is approximately oval. No one has a head that is perfectly oval—some people have narrow chins, and some have square jaws.

Since a face is approximately symmetrical, it has a central vertical axis when seen from the front (Figure 11-20). If the face turns away from you, the axis curves over the surface of the head.

You can divide the head into four sections along the central axis. This is done by drawing three horizontal lines that divide the axis into four equal parts, as shown in Figure 11-20.

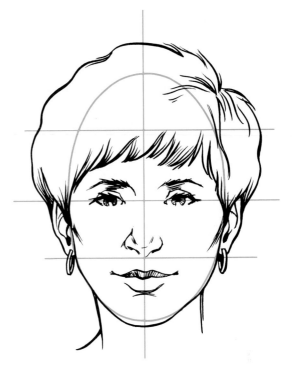

Figure 11.20 Facial proportions.

Figure 11.19 This recruiting poster is a famous example of foreshortening. You don't see most of the finger that is pointing at you because of your point of view.

Montgomery Flagg. *I Want You.* 1917. Recruiting poster.

The top fourth of the head is usually full of hair. The hair may start above the top horizontal line, or it may fall below it, as happens when a person wears bangs.

The eyes usually appear on the central horizontal line. They are at the center of a person's head. Notice the width of the space between the eyes. How does it relate to the width of one eye? The bottom of the nose rests on the lowest horizontal line, and the mouth is closer to the nose than to the chin. Use the sighting technique to determine other relationships, such as nose width, mouth width, and ear placement. Remember that the facial proportions of infants are a little different, as shown in Figure 11-22 on the next page.

When you view a head in complete profile (side view), all of the vertical proportions remain the same as in the front view. However, both shape and contour change. Try to discover the new ratios (Figure 11-21). Notice the relationship between the distance from the chin to the hairline and the distance from the front of the forehead to the back of the head. Can you find a ratio to help you locate the ear in profile? Study the contour of the front of

Figure 11.21 Profile proportions.

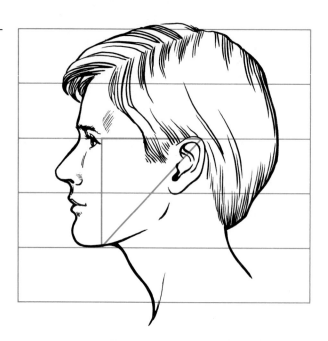

Figure 11.22 As with body proportions, the facial proportions of infants are different from those of adults. The skull is large. The infant's features seem to be squeezed together in the lower third of his face.

Albrecht Dürer. *Virgin and Child with Saint Anne.* 1519. Tempera and oil on canvas, transferred from wood. 60 × 49.9 cm (23⅝ × 19⅝"). The Metropolitan Museum of Art, New York, New York. Bequest of Benjamin Altman, 1913.

the face. Which part protrudes the most? Notice the jawline from the chin to the ear and the relationship of the neck to the head (Figure 11-23).

Figure 11.23 The artist has placed these heads one behind the other so we get a clear idea of the relationship between front and profile views. What feeling has Bishop produced with this organization? What does it tell you about the girls?

Isabel Bishop. *Two Girls*. 1935. Oil and tempera on composition board. 50.8 × 61 cm (20 × 24″). The Metropolitan Museum of Art, Arthur Hoppock Hearn Fund, 1936.

DEVELOPING YOUR SKILLS

13. Use a mirror to study the proportions of your head. Draw a self-portrait with charcoal or pencil. Use sighting to help find accurate size and shape relationships.

14. Look through magazines for large photographs of heads. Look for adults, children, and babies. Remember that a head is not flat, and when it is turned, the central axis moves and curves around the shape of the head. You can always find the axis because it goes through the center of the nose, lips, and between the eyes. Draw the central axis and the three horizontal dividing lines on each face you have selected. Do you find any proportional differences among the faces of adults, children, and infants?

How Artists Use Proportion and Distortion

Many artists use correct proportions in their work. They want every viewer to recognize the person, place, or thing being shown. These artists use correct proportion to create illusions of reality. This ability to show objects as though they were real seems almost like magic to many viewers.

Most Americans have favored works of art that are accurate, realistic views of life. Early American artists were hired to paint portraits—not so much to create art as to record accurate information about real people (Figure 11-24). George Catlin recorded the life of the American Indian (Figure

Figure 11.25 As a young man Catlin visited forty-eight Indian tribes, and he lived with Indians in both North and South America. His paintings are an accurate record of Indian life.

George Catlin. *See-non-ty-a, an Iowa Medicine Man.* c. 1845. Oil on canvas. 71.1 × 58.1 cm (28 × 22⅞"). National Gallery of Art, Washington, D.C. Paul Mellon Collection.

Figure 11.24 (below)   The earliest American artists were self-taught folk artists. They painted anything from tavern signs to family portraits. This painting shows a group of neighbors getting together to prepare flax for weaving into linen.

Linton Park. *Flax Scutching Bee.* 1885. Paint on bed ticking. 79.4 × 127.6 cm (31¼ × 50¼"). National Gallery of Art, Washington, D.C. Gift of Edgar William and Bernice Chrysler Garbisch.

Figure 11.26 The intensity of feeling in this painting is almost unbearable. The twisted, tortured hands and feet of Christ are visual symbols of the entire Crucifixion. Grunewald has used just enough distortion to express the suffering without losing the reality of the moment.

Mathias Grunewald. *The Small Crucifixion*. c. 1510. Oil on wood. 61.6 × 46.0 cm (24¼ × 18⅛"). National Gallery of Art, Washington, D.C. Samuel H. Kress Collection.

11-25). Do you remember reading in Chapter 3 about the "Ashcan School?" The Ashcan painters were so labeled because they painted realistic city scenes, ashcans and all (Figure 7-13).

Some artists use exaggeration and distortion rather than real proportion to convey their ideas and feelings. **Exaggeration** and **distortion** are deviations from the expected, normal proportions. They are powerful means of expression. Artists can lengthen, enlarge, bend, warp, twist, or deform parts or all of the human body. By making these changes they can show moods and feelings that are easily understood by viewers (Figure 11-26).

In the past, movie stars of the silent screen had to exaggerate facial expressions and body language to convey meaning without words. If you have ever seen an old silent movie, you have probably laughed at the strange eyelid movements, mouth twisting, and awkward gestures. Today, mimes use face and body movements that are larger than life to express meaning. The mimes move with graceful control that comes from years of training. Even though exaggerated or distorted, the movements a mime makes can convey a sense of truth (Figure 11-27).

It takes study and skill to use exaggeration and distortion effectively. Artists who do so have first practiced the use of accurate proportion.

Edward Munch and Pablo Picasso are two artists who use exaggeration and distortion in their work. Horror radiates from the figure in the center of *The Shriek* by Munch (Figure 11-28). Picasso's poor, undernourished couple in *Frugal Repast* is far from depressing because the lengthened hands

Figure 11.27   A mime.

Photograph courtesy of Owen Flynn, mime.

Figure 11.28   Here you see how Munch used distortion to express horror.

Edvard Munch. *The Shriek.* 1895, signed 1896. Lithograph. 35.4 × 25.4 cm (13¹⁵/₁₆ × 10″). Collection, The Museum of Modern Art, New York. Matthew T. Mellon Fund.

Figure 11.29 In this work Picasso uses distortion to exaggerate the atmosphere of poverty and starvation.

Pablo Picasso. *The Frugal Repast.* 1904 (printed 1913). Etching. 46 × 37.6 cm (18³⁄₁₆ × 14¹³⁄₁₆″). Collection, The Museum of Modern Art. New York, New York. Gift of Abby Aldrich Rockefeller.

and arms of the lovers weave the withered bodies into an expression of tender togetherness (Figure 11-29).

Chagall uses distortion to present a happier theme in his painting, *Birthday* (Figure 11-30). The subjects of this work are the artist himself and Bella, his fiancée. The birthday is the artist's. Instead of simply showing himself leaning over to kiss Bella, Chagall used distortion. It looks as if he leaped backwards, stretched his neck like a swan, curved it around, and gave Bella a kiss as he floated by. Do you think that Chagall might have had the expression, "I'm so happy, I'm floating on air," in mind when he created this work?

Figure 11.30 (above)   Chagall's painting shows a child-like belief in love's power to "conquer all." He created distorted fantasies full of bright colors that look like joyful dreams.

Marc Chagall. *Birthday.* 1915. Oil on cardboard. 80.6 × 99.7 cm (31¾ × 39¼"). Collection, The Museum of Modern Art, New York. Acquired through the Lillie P. Bliss bequest.

Figure 11.31 (at right)   Lachaise's sculpture looks like today's "Super Mom." This monumental work is powerful without losing its feminine quality.

Gaston Lachaise. *Walking Woman.* 1922. Bronze. 48.8 × 26.9 × 18.9 cm (19¼ × 10⅝ × 7½"). Hirshhorn Museum and Sculpture Garden, Smithsonian Institution, Washington, D.C. Gift of Joseph H. Hirshhorn, 1966.

Artists can create feelings of great stability and calm by placing a small head on a large body. A monumental, or large and imposing, quality results. This is due mainly to placing a small head on a large, stable base. The monumental quality of Gaston Lachaise's *Walking Woman*, Figure 11-31, is due to exaggerated proportions and spacing rather than to large scale.

Another use of exaggeration can be seen in the features of a mask. Masks have been used in all societies from early primitive tribes to our modern computer age (Figure 11-32). A mask allows a person to hide his or her real self and become someone, or something, else.

Masks were worn by primitive tribes as part of their rituals. The masks were thought to attract and please the gods, ancestral spirits, and animals. These tribes believed that, when a mask was put on, magic turned the wearer into the person or animal that the mask represented.

Cartoons are another way in which exaggeration can be used. Editorial cartoonists use this technique to make caricatures of famous people. The caricatures emphasize unusual facial features. Likewise, characters in comic strips are often made by using proportions that are larger than life. The most distorted comic-strip characters are often the funniest ones.

DEVELOPING YOUR SKILLS

15. Cut two ovals about 9 inches (23 cm) long from any color of construction paper. Using parts cut from magazines, create one face using accurate proportions. On the second oval, create a distorted face (Figure 11-33).

16. Collect comic strips and classify them according to whether they use accurate proportions or distortions. Analyze the distorted comics. How does the artist use the distortion to express meaning?

17. Find caricatures (cartoons in which certain features are exaggerated) of one well-known per-

Figure 11.32 Some masks were worn and some were held, but most were created for ceremonial purposes.

Primitive. South American, Peru, Moche. *Ornamental Mask*. I-III century. Silvered copper with shell inlay. 9.5 cm (3¾") high. The Metropolitan Museum of Art, New York, New York. Gift of Jane Costello Goldberg from the collection of Arnold I. Goldberg, 1980.

IBO (Federation of Nigeria). *Three-Faced Mask*. c. 1900. Wood. 40.6 cm (16") high. The High Museum of Art, Atlanta, Georgia. The Fred and Rita Richman Collection of African Art. Gift of Mr. and Mrs. Fred M. Richman, 1972.

Iroquois. *False Face Mask*. 1860. Courtesy of the Museum of the American Indian, Heye Foundation, New York.

Figure 11.33 Student work. Accurate and distorted proportions.

son done by two different artists. The editorial page of a newspaper is a good source. Find a photograph of the same person. Compare the three pictures by describing similarities and differences.

SOMETHING EXTRA

B. Look through the illustrations in the other chapters of *ArtTalk* to find and list reproductions of paintings and sculptures that fit the following categories:
  1. Works showing realistic, accurate use of proportion.
  2. Works in which human proportions are exaggerated or distorted to create special effects.
C. Choose one work from each of the categories above. Write a brief statement to explain how the artist has used proportion or scale to enhance the meaning of the work.

TECHNIQUE TIP

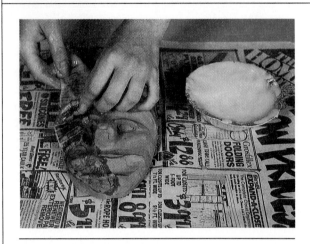

Figure 11.34 Applying strips.

Figure 11.35 The sheet method.

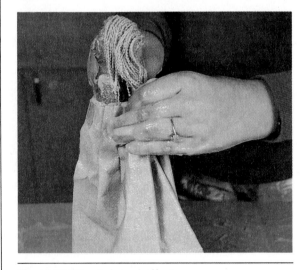

Figure 11.36 A draped effect.

Papier-Mâché

Papier-mâché is a French term that means "mashed paper." It refers to sculpturing methods that use newspaper and liquid paste. These methods can be used to model tiny pieces of jewelry or creatures larger than life. The wet newspaper and paste material are molded over supporting structures that can vary from a small wad of dry paper to a large wood and wire frame. The molded newspaper dries to a hard finish. The following are the three basic methods for working with papier-mâché:

Pulp Method   Shred newspaper, paper towels, or tissue paper into tiny pieces and soak them in water overnight. (Do not use slick magazine paper, as it will not soften.) Then mash the paper in a strainer to remove the water, or wring it out in a piece of cloth. Mix the mashed paper with prepared wheat paste or white glue until the material is the consistency of soft clay. Four sheets of shredded newspaper will require about 4 tablespoons (60 ml) of white glue, or a cup (240 ml) of prepared wheat paste. A few drops of oil of cloves prevents spoiling. A spoonful (5 ml) of linseed oil makes the mixture smoother. If necessary, this mixture can be stored in a plastic bag in the refrigerator.

Use the mixture to model small shapes. When it is dry, it can be sanded and holes can be drilled through it.

Strip Method   Tear newspaper into strips. Either dip the strips in a thick mixture of paste, or rub paste on the strips with your fingers. Decide which method works best for you. Use wide strips to cover wide forms. Very thin strips will lie flat on a small shape. After applying, rub your fingers over the strips so that no rough edges are left sticking up (Figure 11-34).

If you do not want the finished work to stick to the support structure, first cover the form with plastic wrap or a layer of wet newspaper strips.

You can store any unused paste mixture in the refrigerator to prevent spoiling.

If you are going to remove the papier-mâché from the support structure, you need to apply five or six layers of strips. Change directions with each layer so that you can keep track of the number. If you are going to leave the papier-mâché over the support structure, then two or three layers may be enough.

Sheet Method   Brush or spread wheat paste on a sheet of newspaper or newsprint (Figure 11-35). Lay a second sheet on top of the first and smooth out the layers. Add another layer of paste and another sheet of paper. Repeat this process until you have four or five layers of paper. This method is good for making drapery on a figure (Figure 11-36). If you let the layers dry for a day until they are leathery, they can be cut and molded any way you wish. Newspaper strips dipped in the paste can be used to seal any cracks that may occur.

Support Structures   Just as there are several methods for working with papier-mâché, there are also various types of support structures. In fact, there is no limit to the types of materials that can be used to form the inside of a papier-mâché object. Dry newspaper can be wadded up and wrapped with string or tape (Figure 11-37). Wire armatures can be padded with rags before the outside shell of papier-mâché is added.

Clay can be modeled as a base, but if this is done, be sure there are no undercuts that would keep the paper layers from lifting off easily when dry. Also, all kinds of found materials, such as boxes, tubes, and plastic bowls, can be arranged and taped together to form a base (Figure 11-38).

For large figures, a wooden frame covered with chicken wire makes a good support. Push and pinch the wire into the shape you want.

Drying Papier-Mâché   If the weather is humid, or the layers thick, papier-mâché takes longer to dry. An electric fan will keep air moving and speed up the drying process.

Figure 11.37   Newspaper wrapped with string.

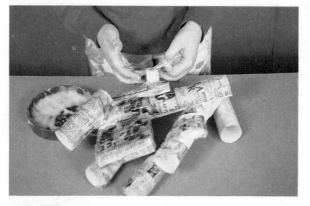

Figure 11.38   Boxes tied together.

I M A G I N E   A N D   C R E A T E

Modern Spirit Mask

MATERIALS

You will need the following:

Paper, pencil, and ruler

Storage container

Newspaper and paper towels

Nontoxic wheat paste

Mixing bowl

Materials to build the substructure

Brushes and tempera or school acrylic paint

Small drill and sandpaper

Lightweight items to decorate the mask

Polymer medium

Optional:

Plastic wrap for protection

OBJECTIVE

Imagine that you are the spiritual leader of a tribe. Modern problems, such as pollution, nuclear power, drug abuse, oil shortages, generation gaps, and world hunger, are worrying your people. Choose one such issue that is of concern to you. Create a mask that can be worn in a ceremony to appease the "spirits" responsible for this problem.

Design and construct a mask that you can wear using papier-mâché, paints, and lightweight found materials (Figure 11-39). In designing your mask, exaggerate and distort the shape and features of the face to increase its expressive force. Write and act out a ceremony in which the mask can be used.

Figure 11.39   Student work. Papier mâché masks.

DIRECTIONS

Choose a contemporary issue that concerns you. Then think of and draw symbols related to it.

Design a mask to incorporate these symbols. Distort and exaggerate the shape and features of the face to express your feelings.

Next, plan the colors you will use for decoration. Choose a color scheme that enhances the expressive quality of the mask.

Draw a plan for constructing the mask. Measure your head so the mask will fit. Draw up a list of materials you will use. List the color scheme. In your plan, include the method you will use to attach the mask to your head. Plan for breathing and viewing holes. These do not have to be associated with the proper features. It is very possible that you will plan to look out through a mouth.

Collect all of the materials you need and keep them in a container. Plan for a drying and storage area.

Construct a supporting structure over which you will form the papier-mâché. Choose one of the following methods or think of some other way that you prefer.

Press heavy-duty aluminum foil over your face so that it shapes itself to your face and head. Stuff wads of newspaper under the foil so that it will not collapse when you apply the papier-mâché.

Use clay.

Use found materials taped together.

Build the mask over an old football helmet.

Cover the support structure with plastic wrap or wet strips of newspaper so the papier-mâché won't stick.

Now, mix the wheat paste. If you mix too much, store the unused portion in a cool place so it won't sour.

Use any or all of the papier-mâché techniques to construct your mask. See the Technique Tip on pages 294 and 295.

When the mask is dry, lift it off the support structure. Trim the edges and add the items for holding the mask in place on your head. Drill and cut holes in it as necessary and sand any rough places.

Now you can paint and decorate the mask. If you use tempera, you may want to add a coat of polymer medium to make the paint waterproof.

Finally, write a ceremony in which to use your mask. You may wish to create a song, a dance, or a poem for the ceremony. Or you may choose to read something from your literature book or from another appropriate source. Ask friends to help you perform the ceremony before the rest of the class.

SAFETY NOTE

Do not use commercial wallpaper paste for papier-mâché. These pastes contain poisons for the purpose of repelling bugs and mice. Toxic materials can be absorbed through the skin. Be sure to use paste that has a nontoxic label.

EVALUATION CHECKLIST

Be sure you did the following:

1. Chose an issue.
2. Planned and drew symbols related to the theme.
3. Used distortion and exaggeration in designing the mask.
4. Incorporated symbols into the mask's design.

5. Chose a color scheme to enhance the expressive quality of the mask.

6. Measured and drew plans so the mask would fit, when finished.

7. Planned a way to wear the mask, with breathing and viewing holes.

8. Planned an area for drying and storing.

9. Constructed a support structure for the mask.

10. Prevented the mask from sticking to the support structure.

11. Worked with papier-mâché properly and smoothed the surface as the layers were built up.

12. Trimmed edges and added materials to hold the mask in place when worn.

13. Drilled and cut breathing and viewing holes.

14. Painted and decorated the mask.

15. Wrote a ceremony in which to use the mask, and presented it to the class.

Life-size Papier-Mâché Figure Environment

MATERIALS

You will need the following:

Paper, pencil, and ruler

Storage container

Wood or chicken wire and tools needed to work with them

Newspaper, paper towels, non-toxic or other commercial papier-mâché adhesive, wheat paste, and bowl

Brushes and tempera or school acrylic paint

Polymer medium

Props and furniture to create setting

Clothes and wig to finish figure

Tape recorder and tapes

OBJECTIVES

Design and build a life-size, papier-mâché figure using correct human proportions, and place it in a real environment (Figure 11-40).

DIRECTIONS

Choose an idea for your life-size sculpture. A school athletic event may provide inspiration. You may design a self-portrait, a character from fiction, or make a statue representing your favorite school subject. Another possible idea would be for the whole class to divide into small groups and develop a set of figures that belong together, such as the members of a favorite musical group or the characters in a popular TV show. Plan each figure so that it is involved in an activity, such as a sport, cooking, writing, or car repair.

Make many sketches to plan your figure. Use a live model in the pose you wish to create. Draw the model from every point of view. The more drawings you make, the more you will understand your subject.

Now make a list of all the materials you will need, including furniture, props, and clothing.

Next, draw plans to scale so you can build from the plans. Let 1 inch (2.5 cm) equal 1 foot (30 cm). Plan the support structure carefully. For a large figure you will probably need a wood and wire frame. Use correct proportion.

Figure 11.40 Segal is concerned with everyday themes. He creates his ghostly figures by wrapping real people in plaster-imbedded gauze bandages. As soon as each section dries, it is cut off. When he has cast all of the parts of one person, they are reassembled. The mystery of his work is that on the inside each work is a perfect mold of the model. But Segal alters the exterior. He always combines these ghostly forms with real, ordinary objects to create scenes of people doing very ordinary activities.

George Segal. *The Bus Driver.* 1962. Figure of plaster over cheesecloth; bus parts including coin box, steering wheel, driver's seat, railing, dashboard, etc.; wood platform 13 × 131.1 × 192.1 cm (5⅛″ × 51⅝″ × 75⅝″), figure 135.9 × 68.3 × 114.3 cm (53½ × 26⅞ × 45″). Overall height 190.5 cm (75″). Collection. The Museum of Modern Art, New York, New York. Philip Johnson Fund.

Find a work space that will not be disturbed. Locate all of the materials you will need before you begin. Gather your materials and keep them in a storage container.

Now build the support structure; get help, if necessary.

When you have completed the structure, cover the entire form with two or more layers of papier-mâché. Be sure that you smooth the surface so rough edges don't spoil the final effect.

Now you are ready to put the finishing touches on the figure. First paint the areas of the figure that will not be covered with clothes. Next, dress and decorate the figure. When you have completed this, place the figure in the planned environment. If you wish, record sounds, music, or poetry that can be played to enhance and explain your statue.

Finally, make a sign showing the title of the work and your name.

EVALUATION CHECKLIST

Be sure you did the following:

1. Selected the subject and theme.
2. Made many sketches from a live model.
3. Drew construction plans to scale, letting 1 inch (2.5 cm) equal 1 foot (30 cm).

4. Planned construction of the support structure carefully.
5. Used correct body and face proportions.
6. Built the support structure.
7. Covered the form with two or more layers of papier-mâché.
8. Avoided rough edges by smoothing the papier-mâché as it was added.
9. Painted the areas that were going to be uncovered.
10. Dressed and decorated the figure.
11. Placed the figure in the planned environment.

Life-size Soft Sculpture–Variation of Papier-Mâché Figures

OBJECTIVES

Use the preceding directions, but construct your figure using soft sculpture materials and procedures (Figure 11-41). See page 129 for soft sculpture directions.

Figure 11.41 By creating this soft-sculpture family without using color, Bayless is forcing us to notice the solid forms and the texture of the stitches. All of the clothes can be removed for washing and ironing.

Florence Bayless. *Family.* 1980. Muslin and stuffing. Life size. Private collection.

Expressive Painting

MATERIALS

You will need the following:

Sketching paper and pencils

Large sheet of heavyweight paper

Yellow chalk and soft eraser

Painting medium of your choice and appropriate tools

Poster board

OBJECTIVE

Create an emotional, expressive painting using distortion to emphasize the meaning of the work (Figures 11-42 and 11-44).

DIRECTIONS

Study El Greco's use of distortion in Figure 11-43. Also look back to the expressive works of art in this chapter that use distortion. Notice especially Figures 11-28, 11-29, 11-30, and 11-31. Study how each artist has used distortion to create an emotional effect.

Choose an emotion that you would like to express. You might consider including contentment, joy, celebration, togetherness, love, sadness, grief, despair, anger, anxiety, frustration, exhaustion, and panic.

Make some rough sketches of figures to express the emotion you choose. Think of the expressive qualities of line and shape, and choose those that express the emotion you wish to use. For example, anxiety might be shown with a zigzag line. You could arrange the line movements of the figure to emphasize a nervous quality. Plan the entire composition around the emotional content. For instance, you might draw trees with the same zigzag lines. Select your best idea.

Figure 11.42 Student work. Expressive painting.

Select a paint medium that you think would be appropriate for your work. Some media you might consider are tempera, school acrylic, watercolor, oil pastel, pastel, or even wax crayon.

Collect your materials and plan for storage and drying space.

Lightly sketch your plan on the paper with yellow chalk. Use the soft eraser, if necessary. Be careful not to tear the surface of the paper when erasing, especially if you are going to use watercolor paints.

Figure 11.43 El Greco was three hundred years ahead of his time when he distorted human proportions to express emotions. These elongated figures with small heads and sweeping, flame-like forms express the mystical, religious feelings of his times. Notice the mysterious cherubs who surround the Virgin. They seem to be emerging from and fading into the cloudy atmosphere.

El Greco. *Madonna and Child with Saint Martina and Saint Agnes.* 1597/1599. Oil on canvas. 193.5 × 103.0 cm (76⅛ × 40½"). National Gallery of Art, Washington, D.C. Widener Collection.

Figure 11.44 Student work. Distortion for expressive effect. The exaggeration from small head to large legs creates the illusion.

Consider the expressive effect and symbolic meaning of color and select colors to strengthen your idea.

Paint your work. Use the movement of your color strokes to accent the emotional quality of your work.

When your painting is finished, mount or mat it for display.

EVALUATION CHECKLIST

Be sure you did the following:

1. Studied the expressive works of art in this chapter.
2. Chose an emotion as a theme.
3. Considered the expressive qualities of line and shape in making rough sketches.
4. Selected a medium that seemed appropriate for the theme.
5. Planned a storage and drying space.
6. Sketched the final idea with yellow chalk.
7. Selected colors with an expressive effect and symbolic meanings.
8. Used the movement of the color strokes to accent the emotional quality.
9. Prepared the finished painting for display.
10. Cleaned up the work area.

Figure 11.45 Marisol. *The Family.* 1962. Painted wood and other materials in three sections. 209.9 × 166.4 cm (82⅝ × 65½"). Collection, The Museum of Modern Art, New York, New York. Advisory Committee Fund.

ART CRITICISM

Improving Your Critical-Thinking Skills

Description: What Do You See?

Study *The Family* by Marisol. Use the credit line to determine its medium and size.

Describe the objects and people in the work. Note everything you observe about each person in detail, including body position, facial expression, clothing, and hairstyle.

Write down every fact you observe.

Analysis: How Is the Work Organized?

Now consider the following questions:

What type of line do you see outlining the figures? What type of line outlines the wooden panels?

Imagine an axis through the center of each figure. What kind of line would it be?

Do the lines look active or static?

Locate the free-form and geometric shapes and forms. Does one type dominate? What is the relationship between the free-form and geometric shapes and forms. Does the arrangement of positive figure forms create a closed or an open group?

Since you cannot walk around the real sculpture, use the shadows that the sculpture casts to help you determine whether a section is two- or three-dimensional.

Each person in this sculpture has a different amount of two-dimensional and three-dimensional area. Which figure has the most area in three dimensions? Rank the figures according to how much area in three dimensions they have, beginning with the figure having the most.

Is the depth in this work real or is it an illusion? Now ask yourself the following questions:

Does the work have a special color scheme?

How does Marisol handle surface textures? Can you find rhythmic repetitions that lead your eyes around the work? What type of balance has Marisol used? What do the proportions of the five people tell you about their ages?

Now think about the scale of this piece. Check the measurements. If you were standing before this work, how would the scale of the figures relate to human scale? Are the figures distorted or are they in proportion? Are they in scale with one another and with the other parts of the work?

Interpretation: What Is Happening? What Is the Artist Trying Say?

Let the clues you collected during analysis help you discover the meaning of this piece. What is the expressive meaning of the line direction of the body axis? Why are the free-form shapes confined within geometric rectangles? Why do some parts protrude three-dimensionally from the rectangles? Is there any meaning to the ratio between the three-dimensional and the two-dimensional parts in each figure? What does the amount of negative space between the figures tell you about the family relationships? Do the colors and textures add to the meaning? How do balance and rhythm work in this sculpture? Finally, what does Marisol's use of proportion and scale say about the people and objects?

Write a paragraph explaining your interpretation of *The Family*.

Judgment: What Do You Think of the Work?

Now it is time to express your personal opinion. Would you like to see this sculpture in your home? In your school? Would you like to visit it in a museum just to see it once? Does it make you think? Do you like this work? Why or why not?

You may use one or more of the theories of art to defend your opinion. Look back to Chapter 2 to review the theories.

A B O U T   T H E   A R T I S T

Marisol Escobar

Figure 11.46 Marisol Escobar; born in Paris, France, American citizen; 1930—

Courtesy Sidney Janis Gallery, New York.

Marisol Escobar was born in Paris in 1930 of Venezuelan parents. Her family moved from Paris to Venezuela, back to Europe, and then, when her mother died in 1941, back to Venezuela again. Her final move was to the United States in 1950.

Her development as an artist was influenced by her childhood travels. Traveling made more of an impact on her work than all of the art schools she attended.

While she was in school at the Art Student's League in New York, Abstract Expressionism was the "in" style. This style was, however, too serious for Marisol, so she created funny things to amuse herself. She collected discarded objects she found on the streets, such as pieces of wood, toys, and fabrics and used them in her work. The work you have just studied, *The Family*, is based on a photograph that had been thrown away. She found it among waste-papers near her studio.

By 1953 she had given up painting to spend all of her time on sculpture. Her first works were small clay figures enclosed in boxes. Then she added other materials. Gradually her works became assemblages that got larger and larger. Finally she combined carving, modeling, painting, drawing, and found objects.

When she first showed her sculptures in 1958, she became a celebrity. She stopped using her last name so that she would stand out from the crowd. But it was her work and not her name that made her famous. Everyone waited to see what her next humorous idea would be. Her trademark became the interweaving of two- and three-dimensionality.

Marisol was considered a Pop artist, because Pop artists were poking fun at the American way of life and its dependence on material things. Marisol's work was full of humor, but she was really more influenced by folk art and Pre-Columbian, South American pottery.

In all her early works, she was the subject. It was not vanity that caused her to do this. It was a matter of practicality. Her best ideas always came in the middle of the night, and she was the only model available.

Today her work is more serious. She uses the same techniques of combining two- and three-dimensionality, but her subjects have changed. In 1982 she created a life-size version of Leonardo da Vinci's *The Last Supper*. Her version is made of plywood, fabric, and plaster, except for the figure of Christ. This she carved from stone to accent its calm stability and to contrast it to the other figures.

Chapter 11 Review: Talking about Art

USING THE LANGUAGE OF ART

For each new art term below, choose a work of art from this chapter. Then write a sentence about that work using the new term correctly in the sentence.

distortion   proportion
exaggeration   scale
Golden Mean   sighting

LEARNING THE ART ELEMENTS AND PRINCIPLES

1. What is the Golden Mean ratio?
2. Explain the difference between scale and proportion.
3. What was the name for the geometric form that had sides matching the ratio of the Golden Mean?
4. What are the two kinds of scale in art?
5. What unit is usually used to define the proportions of any individual figure?

INCREASING YOUR ART AWARENESS

1. Notice some TV or magazine advertisements in which a figure or object stands out because all else is either too big or too small in comparison. Write a paragraph about the message conveyed in each case.
2. Compare the use of exaggeration in Figures 11-4 and 7-13. In which painting does exaggerated color play a key role? In which painting are exaggerated facial expressions important to the meaning of the work? In which work does exaggeration of human body proportions contribute to the work's effect?
3. What effect does distortion have in Figure 5-21?
4. Compare Figures 11-22 and 11-26 in terms of their use of proportion or distortion.
5. Does Figure 3-5 show any exaggeration or distortion? What do you think was the artist's aim in this portrait?

UNDERSTANDING ART CULTURE AND HERITAGE

1. In chronological order, list all of the artworks (with dates) shown in this chapter that were created before the 16th century. List the culture or country in which each was created.
2. List the artworks (with dates) shown in this chapter that were created in the 19th century.
3. Both Figures 11-22 and 11-26 were created by sixteenth-century German artists. Which work is more closely tied to Renaissance ideas (see Chapter 3)? Give reasons for your answer.
4. What are the features of El Greco's art (Figure 11-43) that identify him as a Mannerist (see Chapter 3)?
5. What are the features of Rubens' art (Figure 11-15) that identify him as a Baroque artist (see Chapter 3)?

JUDGING THE QUALITY OF ART

James NcNeill Whistler was an American artist who spent most of his life in Europe. He often worked with black, white, and gray. His most famous work, commonly known as *Whistler's Mother,* is really called *Arrangement in Gray and Black, No. 1: The Artist's Mother.*

Look back to Figure 11-1 by Whistler. Imagine that you are a critic writing about this work in 1863. Use the four steps of art criticism to attack or defend this work. During analysis, notice how the artist has used the expressive effect of proportion to glamorize his girlfriend. You must also discuss his limited color scheme.

LEARNING MORE ABOUT ART

Do some library research to determine how scale has been used in the art of many cultures to emphasize a person's rank and importance. Try to find examples from as many different cultures as you can, both ancient and modern. Report on your findings.

Figure 12.1 Stuart began painting when he was thirteen. Later he travelled to London, where he studied under another American, Benjamin West. The painting below was the turning point in Stuart's career. It brought him instant fame and fortune.

Gilbert Stuart. *The Skater (Portrait of William Grant).* 1782. Oil on canvas. 245.5 × 147.6 cm (96⅝ × 58⅛"). National Gallery of Art, Washington, D.C. Andrew W. Mellon Collection.

Variety, Emphasis, and Unity

LEARNING OBJECTIVES

After reading this chapter and doing the exercises, you will be able to

- identify and describe variety, emphasis, and unity in your environment and in a work of art.

- understand how artists use variety and emphasis to express their ideas and feelings.

- understand how artists use the elements and principles of art to create unified works of art.

- use variety, emphasis, and design to create your own works of art.

WORDS TO LEARN

In this chapter you will learn the meanings of the words listed below.

contrast

dominant

emphasis

focal point

harmony

subordinate

unity

variety

You have already learned about the principles of rhythm, balance, and proportion. In this chapter you will learn about two additional principles: *variety* and *emphasis*. Even more important, you will learn about the principle of *unity*. It is only when all of the elements and all of the principles work together that you achieve a unified work of art.

Unity and variety complement each other in the same way that positive and negative spaces complement each other. Unity and variety are like two sides of one coin. Unity controls and organizes variety, while variety adds interest to unity.

Unity is also related to emphasis. Artists frequently emphasize one element of art or one part of a work over other elements and parts. They cannot do this successfully, however, without making sure that all of the elements and parts are unified.

DEVELOPING YOUR SKILLS

1. Write several paragraphs explaining how variety is present in some area of your life, such as school, the TV shows you watch, or the clothes you wear. Read your composition in class.
2. Find three examples of emphasis in your daily experiences. Key words underlined or circled in a letter, fanfares for TV introductions, and gestures people make are some common types of emphasis. List and describe your examples for the class.

Variety

People cannot stand sameness for too long. They need variety in all areas of their lives. Imagine how bored you would be if your daily routine were *exactly* the same every day of the week, for a whole year. Imagine how visually boring the world would be if everything in it—everything—were the same color. Even if the color used were your favorite color, you would soon want to see any color—even your least favorite—to break the monotony.

People put a great deal of time and effort into creating variety in their environment. They may buy all new furniture or paint the walls, not because the furniture is old or the paint is peeling, but simply because they need a change. New clothes, new foods, new friends—the list of items that we seek out to relieve the sameness or boredom of life is endless.

Just as you must add variety to your life to keep it interesting, so must artists add some variety to their works. **Variety** is the art principle concerned with difference. *Contrast* is another term used to talk about difference.

A work that is too much the same can become dull and monotonous. For example, a work composed of just one shape may be unified, but it will not hold your attention. Variety, or contrast, is achieved by adding something different to a design to provide a break in the repetition (Figure 12-2). When different elements are placed next to each other in a work of art, they are in contrast (Figure 12-3 on the next page). This type of contrast, or variety, adds interest to the work of art.

Almost every artist uses contrasting elements to balance unifying elements. Wide, bold lines complement thin, delicate lines. Straight lines contrast with curves. Free-form shapes differ from geometric shapes. Rough textures add interest to a smooth surface. The number of contrasts that can be introduced through color seems endless. The degree of contrast may range from bold to subtle. The amount of difference between the elements depends on the artist's purpose.

Figure 12.2 MTV has used variety to maintain interest in its logo. The shape of the logo is always the same: a heavy, rock-like, solid "M" decorated with a small, light, thin "TV." But every time you see the logo, the colors and patterns on it change. Repetition reassures the viewer that this is the same station, but variety stirs the viewer's curiosity.

Courtesy of MTV Networks.

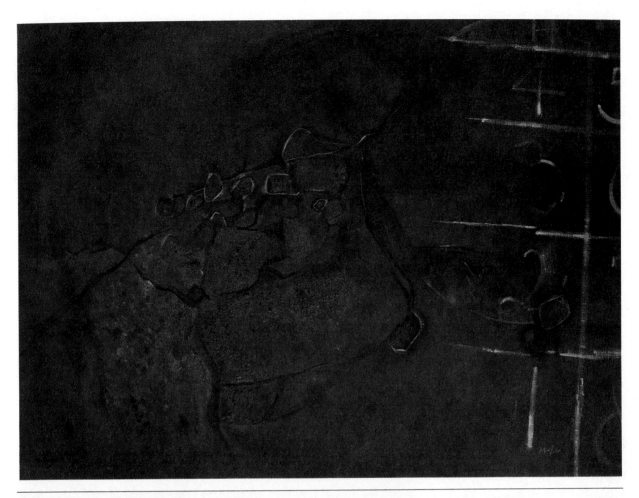

Figure 12.3 The title explains the subject of this work. Identify and describe the unifying and contrasting elements. Is there more to this than a childhood game scratched on a sidewalk? What do the contrasts tell you?

Loren MacIver. *Hopscotch*. 1940. Oil on canvas, 68.6 × 91.1 cm (27 × 35⅞"). Collection, The Museum of Modern Art, New York, New York. Purchase.

DEVELOPING YOUR SKILLS

3. Use media of your choice to make a set of small designs showing strong contrast of each of the following elements:
   - Line
   - Shape and form
   - Space
   - Color
   - Value
   - Texture

4. Select one of the bold contrast designs that you completed in Skill 3 and copy it, changing the amount of contrast from strong to subtle.

5. Look through the works you have produced in this course. Find one that seems dull. Study it and tell how you could add variety without destroying the unity.

6. Look through *ArtTalk* for works of art that show bold contrast of line, shape, color, value, and texture. List one work for each kind of contrast. Explain how the contrast was created.

SOMETHING EXTRA

A. Using your camera, make a set of six photos illustrating visual variety in your neighborhood.

B. Arrange a bulletin-board display of student works that are all the same size. Add interest to the display by varying the size of the negative areas.

Emphasis

Have you ever underlined an important word or phrase several times in a letter? Have you ever raised the volume of your voice to make sure the person you were talking to understood a key point?

These are just two ways that people use emphasis to focus attention on the main points in a message. In advertisements, music, news stories, your lessons at school, and your day-to-day communications, you see and hear certain ideas and feelings being emphasized over others.

Emphasis is the principle of art that makes one part of a work dominant over the other parts. Artists use this principle of emphasis to unify a work of art. Emphasis controls the sequence in which the parts are noticed. It also controls the amount of attention that a viewer gives to each part.

There are two major types of visual emphasis. In one type, a certain element of art dominates the entire work. In the other type of emphasis, one area of the work is dominant over all of the other areas.

Emphasizing an Element

If the artist chooses to emphasize one element, all of the other elements of the work are made **subordinate** (less important). The **dominant** (most important) element affects the viewer's perception of the total work. This element also affects the way in which all of the separate items and elements in the work are perceived.

Sometimes the dominant element is made so strong that the whole work seems to be drenched in that element. For instance, Bronislaw Bak's *Interpenetrations in Red*, Figure 12-4 below, is saturated with the color red. In this painting the redness takes on a meaning all its own. It affects the viewer's perception of the painting as a whole, as well as the viewer's perceptions of the separate parts.

Emphasizing an Area

When an entire area in a work of art is emphasized, this area is called a **focal point.** The focal point is the first part of a work to attract the attention of the viewer. The other areas are subordinate to the focal point (Figure 12-5).

Figure 12.4 Redness overwhelms this painting. There is no focal point— your eyes dance from one red to another.

Bronislaw Bak. *Interpenetrations in Red.* 1980. Oil on canvas. 120 × 150 cm (4 × 5′). Private Collection.

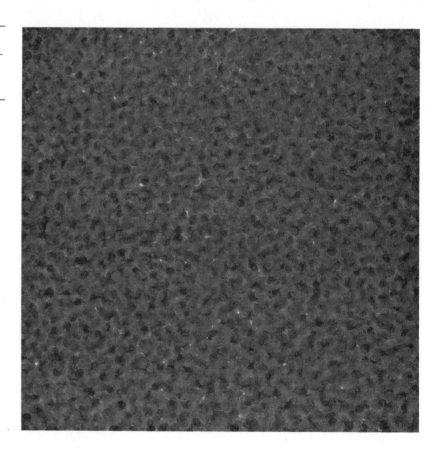

Figure 12.5 Rembrandt uses contrasting values to give this work a focal point. He lights the face but lets most of the work sink into darkness. Only the old, gnarled hands emerge from the darkness as a secondary point of interest.

Rembrandt van Rijn. *Self-Portrait*. 1659. Oil on canvas. 84 × 66 cm (33¼ × 26″).
National Gallery of Art, Washington, D.C. Andrew W. Mellon Collection.

It is possible for a work of art to have more than one focal point. Artists must be careful about this, however. Too many focal points will confuse the viewer.

Artists must decide on the *degree* of emphasis needed to create a focal point. This usually depends on the purpose of the work. Of course, a focal point is not necessary, and many artists don't create a focal point in their works (Figure 12-6).

When artists do create focal points, they are usually careful not to overdo the emphasis. They make certain that the focal point is unified with the rest of the design.

Artists use several techniques to create a focal point in a work of art. Following are brief explanations of these techniques.

Contrast

One way to create a focal point is to place an element that contrasts with the rest of the work in that area. One large shape, for example, will stand out among small ones. One angular, geometric shape will be noticed first among rounded, free-form shapes. A bright color will dominate in a design of low-intensity colors, while a light area will dominate in a dark design (Figure 12-7). An object with rough texture becomes a focal point in a design of smooth textures. The list of ways that contrast can be used to create a focal point is endless.

Isolation

Artists sometimes use *isolation* to create a focal point, and thereby emphasize one part of their work. They do this by putting one object alone, apart from all of the other objects (Figure 12-8). This draws the viewer's eye to the isolated object.

Location

Location is another method used to create a focal point for emphasis. A viewer's eye is normally drawn toward the center of a visual area. Thus, something near this center will probably be noticed first. Since the exact center is a dull location, most

Figure 12.6 The artist has designed this work without a focal point. In this detail you can see how one shape leads your eyes to another. Your eyes cannot find one place to rest that is more important than another. Something else of equal interest is always drawing you on.

Lois Dvorak. *The Lizards.* 1982. Hand-made, hand-dyed papers and opera cloth stitched and interwoven on four layers of dowels, accented with metallic marking pen and metallic threads. 81.3 × 101.6 cm (32 × 40″). Courtesy of the artist.

Figure 12.7 Tanner used value contrast to create a focal point. The people in this painting are preparing a meal. You hardly notice their action because the bright light of the lamp attracts your attention first. Then the objects in the darker areas begin to take form because curiosity draws your eyes into the dark. How does this relate to your normal viewing habits? If you came upon this scene, what would attract your attention first? What would you have to do to be able to see the people?

Henry Ossawa Tanner. *Etaples Fisher Folk.* 1923. Tempera and oil on canvas. 120.7 × 94 cm (47½ × 37"). The High Museum of Art, Atlanta, Georgia. J. J. Haverty Collection.

Figure 12.8 (below)   Church has made the large, white iceberg the center of attention by setting it apart. What other methods has this artist used to make that iceberg the center of attention?

Frederick Edwin Church. *The Icebergs.* 1861. Oil on canvas. 163.8 × 285.4 cm (64½ × 112⅜"). Dallas Museum of Art, Dallas, Texas. Anonymous gift.

artists place the objects they wish to emphasize a bit off center. They use a point a little to the left or right of center and a little above center (Figure 12-10 on the next page).

Convergence

When many elements in a work point to one item, that item becomes the focal point. This technique, called *convergence*, can be created with a very obvious radial arrangement of lines. It can also be achieved through a more subtle arrangement of people who are staring and pointing at the point of emphasis (Figure 12-9 below).

The Unusual

In a work of art, an object that is out of the ordinary can become the focal point (Figure 12-11). In a row of soldiers standing at attention, the one standing on his head will be noticed first. The unexpected will always draw the viewer's attention.

Figure 12.9 In this painting all of the people are staring at the preacher and the girl. The viewer becomes one of the crowd and stares too. Can you find lines in this painting that are also pointing to the two figures?

John Steuart Curry. *Baptism in Kansas.* 1928. Oil on canvas. 101.6 × 127 cm (40 × 50″). Collection of Whitney Museum of American Art, New York, New York. Photograph by Geoffrey Clements.

Figure 12.10 The young woman appears to be in the center of this painting. If you measure, however, you will see that her head is to the left of the vertical axis and far above the horizontal axis. What devices has Morisot used to make the woman's face the center of interest?

Berthe Morisot. *In the Dining Room.* 1886. Oil on canvas. 61.3 × 50 cm (24⅛ × 19¾"). National Gallery of Art, Washington, D.C. Chester Dale Collection.

Figure 12.11   Siqueiros has used the unusual to create his center of interest. Enlarging the head of the screaming infant and placing it behind the child is definitely unexpected. What other techniques has he used to emphasize the screaming head?

David Alfaro Siqueiros. *Echo of a Scream*. 1937. Duco on wood. 121.9 × 91.4 cm (48 × 36"). Collection, The Museum of Modern Art, New York, New York. Gift of Edward M. M. Warburg.

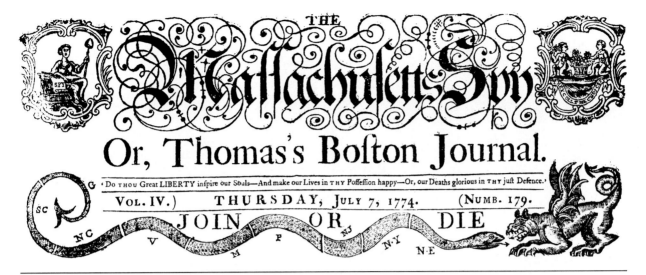

Figure 12.12 It is said that this cartoon was drawn by Ben Franklin. How did he use unity to convey his message? What do the parts of the snake symbolize?

Ben Franklin (attributed to). *Join or Die*. Cartoon. 1774. 5 × 7.25 cm (2 × 2⅞″). Courtesy of the Library of Congress.

DEVELOPING YOUR SKILLS

7. Look through the other chapters of *ArtTalk* for examples of works in which the artist has emphasized one element, making all of the others subordinate to it. Make a list of these works.

8. Make a series of small designs with strong focal points, using each of the following:
   - Contrast of shape
   - Contrast of color
   - Contrast of value
   - Contrast of texture
   - Isolation
   - Convergence
   - Location
   - The unusual

9. Collect a set of five magazine or newspaper advertisements that have a strong focal point. Identify the focal point in each.

Unity

Unity is oneness. It brings order to the world. Without it, the world would be chaotic.

Countries made up of smaller parts are political unities. The United States is such a country. Its fifty states are joined by a single federal government. As a whole unit, the United States is a world power far stronger than the combined power of the separate states (Figure 12-12).

A tree is a unity in nature composed of roots, trunk, bark, branches, twigs, leaves, blossoms, and fruit. Each part has its own purpose that adds to the living, growing tree. An electric lamp is a manufactured unity composed of a base, electric wire, sockets, bulbs, shades, and so on. All of the separate parts of the lamp work together as a unity to provide light.

DEVELOPING YOUR SKILLS

10. List five different kinds of unified objects that you might find in your world. Name the unity: describe its various parts and explain how and why the separate parts are joined into a unified whole.

Figure 12.13   Rodin created this monument to honor six citizens who gave their lives in 1347 to save the city of Calais. Rodin showed the six men getting ready to see the king, who was laying siege to the city. Rodin spent two years modeling faces and bodies to express the men's tension and pain. Each figure would be successful as an individual statue. But Rodin has placed them so that unity results. The work was designed to be placed at street level, not on a pedestal above the heads of the people.

Auguste Rodin. *The Burghers of Calais.* 1886. Bronze. 209.6 × 241.3 × 198.1 cm (82½ × 95 × 78″). Hirshhorn Museum of Sculpture Garden, Smithsonian Institution. Washington, D.C. Gift of Joseph H. Hirshhorn, 1966.

Creating Visual Unity

In art, **unity** is the principle of design that allows you to see a complex combination of elements, principles, and media as a complete whole. Unity is like an invisible glue. It joins all of the separate parts so they look as if they belong together.

Unity is difficult to understand at first because it is not easily defined. It is a quality that you *feel* as you view a work of art (Figure 12-13). As you study a work, you may think that you would not change one element or object. When this happens, you are receiving an impression that the work is a unified whole.

Unity helps you concentrate on a visual image. You cannot realize how important this is until you study a work that lacks unity. Looking at a work that lacks unity is like trying to carry on a serious discussion while your little sister is practicing the violin, your brother is listening to the stereo, and your mother is running the vacuum cleaner. It would be difficult to concentrate on your conversation with all of these distractions. It is the same with a work of art that lacks unity. You can't concentrate on the work as a whole because all of the parts demand separate attention.

To create unity, an artist adjusts the parts of a work so they relate to each other. A potter adjusts decorations on a bowl to complement the bowl's shape, size, and purpose (12-14). Clothing designers choose fabrics that complement the design and purpose of each outfit (Figure 12-15). Painters ad-

Figure 12.14 (above)   Notice how the curves of the blue slip decorations match the curves of the unusual handles. What other devices has this potter used to unify his work?

Bob Owens. *Covered Jar with Fluid Handles.* 1985. Ceramics. Private Collection.

Figure 12.15   The designer of these clothes travels around the world looking for fabrics with unusual colors and textures. She then designs and creates unique patterns for her wearable art.

Florence Bayless. *Thai Silk Shirt and Vest.* 1986. Silk. Private collection.

Figure 12.16 Johns combines the loose brushwork of Abstract Expressionism with the commonplace objects of American Realism. His map of the United States could be "pulled apart" by the wild action painting. But it is unified by the harmonious, limited color scheme of a primary triad.

Jasper Johns. *Map.* 1961. Oil on canvas. 198.2 × 307.7 cm (78 × 123⅛"). Collection, Museum of Modern Art, New York, New York. Gift of Mr. and Mrs. Robert C. Scull.

just the elements in a work to each other. A "busy" work with a variety of shapes and textures can be unified with a limited color scheme, for example (Figure 12-16).

Following are several techniques that artists use to create unity.

Harmony

Some people consider harmony to be a principle of design. You may have heard *harmony* used in place of *unity*. The two terms, though, are not really alike. Unity describes the whole work. **Harmony,** on the other hand, is concerned with agreement among the elements of a work. It describes the separate but related parts. While it could be considered a principle from this standpoint, here we will discuss it as a way to achieve the more important principle of unity.

In musical harmony, related tones are combined into blended sounds. Harmony sounds pleasing because the tones agree with each other. In visual harmony, related art elements are combined. The result looks pleasing because the elements agree with each other.

Used in certain ways, color can produce harmony in a work of art. The use of a monochromatic or analogous color scheme can create harmony. Repetition of shapes that are related, such as rectangles with different proportions, produces harmony (Figure 12-17). A design that uses only geometric shapes appears more harmonious than a design using both geometric and free-form shapes.

Figure 12.17   Notice how often Degas repeats round shapes in this work: the hats, the ring of flowers, the round-looking bows, the young woman's head, her bodice, and her skirt. He then creates a second harmony of vertical lines. He uses thin lines in the foreground and thick ones in the background.

Edgar Degas. *The Millinery Shop*. c. 1879/84. Oil on canvas. 100 × 110.7 cm (39⅖ × 43⅗"). © 1987 Art Institute of Chicago, Chicago, Illinois.

Even space used in a certain way can produce harmony. If all of the parts in a work of art are different sizes, shapes, colors, and textures, the space between the parts can be made uniform to give the work a sense of order.

Simplicity

Another way to create unity is through *simplicity*. Simplicity is not, however, easy to achieve. An artist must plan very carefully to create a good, simple design. This is done by limiting the number of variations of an element. The fewer variations the artist uses, the more unified the design will seem (Figure 12-18).

A painting in which the entire surface is covered with a single, even layer of one hue will appear strongly unified. A sculpture of a single person expresses a simple unity (Figure 12-19). A weaving with a limited color scheme will have a much stronger sense of unity than a weaving with a full range of hues, values, and intensities (Figure 12-20).

Repetition

The repetition of objects and elements can be an effective way to unify a work of art. Louise Nevelson's assemblages are a good example. As you know from reading Chapter 6, Nevelson collects objects that are not alike. This presents a problem of unity, which she solves in one or more ways. Often she places the objects in a series of box-like containers (Figure 12-21 on page 326). The boxes help to unify the work. She sometimes paints the entire structure the same color. Sometimes she repeats both container shape and color to unify her work.

Figure 12.18 How has Malevich simplified this work? Which elements have been limited? Which elements vary?

Kasimir Malevich. *Suprematist Composition: White on White*. 1918. Oil on canvas. 79.4 × 79.4 cm (31¼ × 31¼"). Collection, The Museum of Modern Art, New York, New York.

Figure 12.19 (above)   Why was it much easier for Barlach to unify this sculpture than it was for Rodin to unify *The Burghers of Calais* (Figure 12-13)?

Ernst Barlach. *Singing Man.* 1928. Bronze. 49.5 × 55.6 × 35.9 cm (19½ × 21⅞ × 14⅛″). Collection, The Museum of Modern Art, New York, New York. Abby Aldrich Rockefeller Fund.

Figure 12.20   Student work. Which elements did the artist use to unify this weaving? Which elements were used to introduce variety?

Figure 12.21 The use of one color and the repetition of the box shapes add to the unity of this work.

Louise Nevelson. *Sky Cathedral.* 1958. Assemblage: wood construction painted black. 3.4 × 3.1 × .5 cm (11'3½" × 10'¼" × 1'6"). Collection, The Museum of Modern Art, New York, New York. Gift of Mr. & Mrs. Ben Mildwoff.

Figure 12.22 Wright was a genius who dared to be different. In 1936 he was asked to design a house close to this waterfall. Instead, he placed the house right over the falls. Terraces hang suspended over the running water. Even though they are made of reinforced concrete, the terraces repeat the shapes of the natural stone terraces below. The stones that make up the walls come from the building site, which ties the house even closer to its surroundings.

Frank Lloyd Wright. Falling Water House. Bear Run, Pennsylvania. 1936. Photography by Sandak, Inc., Stamford, Connecticut.

Many architects are concerned with unity. Their aim is for the homes they design to blend with the land (Figure 12-22). They may use materials that repeat the colors and textures found in the home's environment. They may also use materials that reflect the surroundings. For instance, mirrored outside walls have been used on skyscrapers. The mirrors reflect the shapes and colors of the clouds and sky, and the buildings seem to blend with the atmosphere.

Proximity

Proximity, or closeness, is another way of unifying very different shapes in a work (Figures 12-23 and 12-24 on the next page). This is achieved by limiting the negative space between the shapes. Clustering the shapes in this way suggests unity and coherence. The sense of unity can be made even stronger if the cluster of unlike items is surrounded by an area of negative space.

Figure 12.23 (above)   The artist has created unity by grouping the women and children close together. There is no negative space between the figures. Each one touches the next. They are surrounded by a dark background of negative space. However, each figure is different. Study the figures carefully. List all of the differences you can find.

Elisabeth Vigee-Lebrun. *The Marquise de Peze and the Marquise de Rouget with Her Two Children.* 1787. Oil on canvas. 123.4 × 155.9 cm (48⅝ × 61⅜"). National Gallery of Art, Washington, D.C. Gift of the Bay Foundation in memory of Josephine Bay Paul and Ambassador Charles Ulrick Bay.

Figure 12.24   Soyer has created a strong center of attention by crowding a group of people very close together.

Raphael Soyer. *Farewell to Lincoln Square (Pedestrians).* 1959. Oil and conte crayon on canvas. 153.2 × 140 cm (60⅜ × 55⅛"). Hirshhorn Museum and Sculpture Garden, Smithsonian Institution, Washington, D.C. Gift of Joseph H. Hirshhorn Foundation, 1966.

Continuation

Sometimes shapes can be arranged so that a line or edge of one shape continues as a line or edge of the next shape (Figure 12-25 below). This type of arrangement allows the viewer's eye to flow smoothly from one element to the next, along the continuing contour. This continuity links the different parts into a unified group.

11. Look at the reproductions in the other chapters of *ArtTalk*. Find examples of works that have been unified through each of the following techniques:
    • Simplicity
    • Harmony of color

Figure 12.25 Gris uses continuity to tie this composition together. Find out how many lines have been continued. Hold the straight edge of a ruler over a strong line direction to see how many times that line is continued throughout the painting. For example, look at the line that starts in the upper left corner. Hold a ruler against that point and line it up with the inner edge of the guitar. Follow that line and notice how it appears again as a very subtle change in value in the lower right corner. See how many lines you can find that continue through the composition in one way or another.

Juan Gris. *Guitar and Flowers*. 1912. Oil on canvas. 112.1 × 70.2 cm (44⅛ × 27⅝″). Collection, The Museum of Modern Art, New York, New York. Bequest of Anna Erickson Levene in memory of her husband, Dr. Phoebus Aaron Theodor Levene.

Figure 12.26   Student work. A unified window display.

- Harmony of shape
- Repetition
- Proximity
- Continuation

12. Using any media you wish, create small designs to illustrate the following *unifying* devices:
    - Simplicity
    - Harmony of color
    - Harmony of shape
    - Harmony through space
    - Proximity
    - Continuation

13. Suppose you have been hired to create a window display for a gift shop that sells many unrelated objects. Cut out photographs from magazines of fifteen unrelated objects that represent the merchandise for sale. Use as many unifying techniques as you can to create the display. Draw the window and the design for the display and glue the cutouts where the objects would be placed in the design (Figure 12-26).

How Artists Use Variety and Emphasis to Enhance Unity

As you know, artists use variety and emphasis to make their works more interesting and appealing. If carried to extremes, however, these two principles can destroy the unity of a visual work. This means that artists must be careful to balance the contrasting qualities of variety and emphasis with their attempts to create unity. Otherwise the end result will not be a unified work of art.

When you first look at *Blam*, it looks as though Lichtenstein copied a comic strip picture (Figure 12-27). While the artist did base his idea on an actual newspaper comic strip, this work is a totally new painting. Lichtenstein simplified, limited, and reorganized the shapes. He omitted all writing except "BLAM" and the number "3" on the plane. He repeated certain shapes, such as the ovals in the nose of the plane and the cockpit. Notice how many times curved shapes are repeated, and that they are repeated with variations.

Figure 12.27 Lichtenstein gets many of his ideas for paintings from comic strips. He turns the comics into abstract arrangements of line, shape, color, and texture to create totally new art.

Roy Lichtenstein. *Blam.* 1962. Oil on canvas. 172.7 × 203.2 cm (68 × 80″). Courtesy of Yale University Art Gallery, New Haven, Connecticut. Lent by Richard Brown Baker.

You can find several examples of line continuity in *Blam*. For example, the bottom line of the right wing is continued in the bold, black line of the yellow explosion on the left. If you hunt, you can find many continued lines, some of which are curved.

To keep the work interesting, Lichtenstein has used the principles of emphasis and variety. He has introduced color to add contrast, but he has limited his colors to the three primaries. In this way he has kept the color from destroying the work's unity.

Another element used for contrast is texture. All of the positive shapes are smooth, but the negative spaces in the background have been textured in an exaggerated imitation of the dots used to print color. To reduce the degree of contrast, Lichtenstein has made the dots match the blue of the plane.

Notice how a focal point, or area of emphasis, has been created at the center of the exploding lines. But there are several secondary areas of importance: the word "Blam," the nose of the plane, and the inhuman-looking, free-form figure falling out of the cockpit. Were it not for these subordinate areas, the unity of the work might have been destroyed.

Blam is unified because Lichtenstein has achieved a successful balance between the harmonizing and contrasting devices in the painting.

You will also find a successful balance between harmonizing and varying devices in Isabel Bishop's *Bootblack* (Figure 12-28). The woman is the focal point of the work. Bishop has created this focal point by using isolation, line continuation, the unusual, and contrast. The woman, with her back to us, is isolated from the other figures. She stands alone against the large horizontal wall shape. The fact that she is standing alone, and that she is the only female in the work, creates a feeling of isolation.

Bishop has used line in two ways to add to the area of emphasis. Notice that the woman is almost vertical, while all the other figures slouch. Also notice the S-curve that starts at the bottom of the painting with the bootblack's left shoe. The line curves through his bent body to the seated customer, then runs up through the customer's newspaper to the man in the brown suit, who is staring across the empty space at the isolated woman. This gradual curve directs our attention to the woman.

Color is another contrasting element. The woman is dressed in a warm, blue-green color. All other colors in the work are browns, tans, grays, and blue-grays. Again, this contrast adds emphasis to the woman.

To balance the emphasis on the woman, Bishop has harmonized all of the colors, using low intensities and light values. He has used repetition with the elements of line and shape. The round hat on the woman is repeated in many round shapes, such as the other hats, the curve of the bootblack's back, and the round wall on the left. The vertical position of the woman is repeated in the vertical lines of the buildings in the background. Without this repetition to balance the emphasis on the woman, Bishop's work might not have been the unified work that it is.

DEVELOPING YOUR SKILLS

14. Look back at the different artworks you have created during this course. Find one work that seems to lack unity. Study it to decide which unifying devices might improve the composition. Write a brief statement describing how you would use these devices to improve the work.

SOMETHING EXTRA

C. Using your camera, make a set of six photos illustrating visual unity in your neighborhood.

Figure 12.28 (facing page)   Bishop has spent her artistic career recording the people and scenes that she has observed from her studio window in New York City.

Isabel Bishop. *Bootblack*. c. 1933–34. Oil on paper mounted on fiberboard. 50.5 × 43.2 cm (19⅞ × 17"). Hirshhorn Museum and Sculpture Garden, Smithsonian Institution, Washington, D.C. Gift of Joseph H. Hirshhorn, 1966.

I M A G I N E   A N D   C R E A T E

MATERIALS

You will need the following:

Sketching paper and pencils

Heavyweight white paper

Colored tissue paper in a variety of colors

Colored pages from magazines

Colored construction paper

Scissors

Liquid laundry starch, slightly diluted white glue, or polymer medium

Large brushes

Water-base markers, crayons, or paints

Storage container

Poster board

Tissue and Found-Paper Collage

OBJECTIVE

Plan and create a two-dimensional tissue and found-paper collage to illustrate the concept of unity (Figures 12-29 and 12-30). Use several unifying devices to make your message strong.

Figure 12.29   Student work. A tissue and found-paper collage expressing the unified wish of all students that a football team win "One more time."

DIRECTIONS

Choose an idea such as *togetherness*, *school spirit*, or *world peace*, to express unity (Figures 12-29 and 12-30).

Plan your composition with rough sketches. Plan to use as many unifying devices as you can. Select your best plan.

Draw your final plan lightly on the heavyweight white paper.

Collect the materials and tools you will need, and place them in your storage container. Plan for a drying area.

Look through magazines to find areas of color and visual textures that you can use for accents. For example, a large photograph of chocolate cake might yield enough textured brown material to make a tree trunk. Or a large area of blue sky might become a cheerleader's outfit. You do not want to fill your design with magazine-cutout colors, but they will make excellent accents.

As you add the magazine colors and the tissue paper, remember that you do not need to make everything fit your drawing perfectly. Feel free to overlap tissue colors to create new colors. You do not have to stay neatly inside all the lines.

Figure 12.30 Student work. This student work was one of fifty-two works selected to represent the theme of world peace at the Good Will Games in 1986.

Poster. *Together We Can Make Things Happen.* Courtesy of Turner Broadcasting System.

TECHNIQUE TIP

Tissue Paper Collage

For your first experience with tissue, make a free design with the tissue colors. Start with the lightest colors of tissue first and save the darkest for last. It is difficult to change the color of dark tissue by overlapping it with other colors. If one area becomes too dark, you might cut out a piece of white paper, glue it over the dark area carefully, and apply new colors over the white area.

Apply a coat of adhesive to the area where you wish to place the tissue. Place the tissue down carefully over the wet area (Figure 12-31). Don't let your fingers get wet. Then add another coat of adhesive over the tissue. If your brush picks up any color from the wet tissue, rinse your brush in water and let it dry before using it again.

Experiment by overlapping colors. Allow the tissue to wrinkle to create textures as you apply it. Be sure that all the loose edges of tissue are glued down.

Figure 12.31 Applying art tissue.

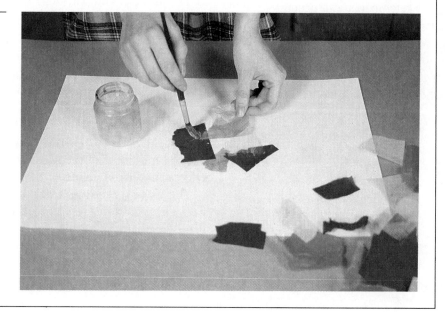

When all of the collage materials are dry, accent the main lines of the design by going over them with the markers, crayons, or paints. You may add some interesting textures by rubbing the crayons over some tissue areas.

Mount or mat the finished work for display.

EVALUATION CHECKLIST

Be sure you did the following:

1. Chose a theme requiring unity.
2. Made several rough sketches using as many unifying devices as possible.
3. Selected the best plan.
4. Drew the final plan lightly on the heavyweight paper.
5. Planned a drying area.
6. Selected some magazine cutouts to add visual texture.
7. Overlapped tissue colors.
8. When everything was dry, accented the main lines of the work with drawing or painting materials.
9. Prepared the finished work for display.
10. Cleaned up the work area.

Mixed-Media Collage Combining Visual and Verbal Symbols

MATERIALS

You will need the following:

Sketch paper and pencils

Heavyweight paper in a color of your choice

Found materials

Magazines

Scissors

White glue

Drawing and painting materials of your choice

Poster board

OBJECTIVE

Create a mixed-media collage combining visual symbols. Use found materials and part of a favorite poem or phrase.

DIRECTIONS

Study the mixed-media collage in Figure 12-32. Notice how the artist has combined words and phrases with visual symbols. If you understand French you will notice that the words are a humorous play on the artist's name. Some of the visual symbols are directly related to the words. Others just fit the design. Some visual symbols have been drawn by the artist. Others are decals, rubber stamps, lace, and stamps. Some of the letters are written and printed by the artist. Others are stick-on letters or those cut from magazines and glued on.

Think of some lines from a favorite poem or a saying that you like. The words may be your own or something you have read. Write them down and think about them. Think of visual symbols that will go with the words.

Find a storage container, and plan a storage place where your work can dry safely.

Figure 12.32   This mixed-media collage combines words and visual symbols so that they are unified into a complete visual idea.

Barbara Aubin. *I Dreamed I Saw a Pink Flamingo in the Salle de Bain.* 1982. Mixed media: decals, rubber stamp; stamps; lace; drawing with crayon, pencil, ink on charcoal paper. 53.3 × 71.1 cm (21 × 28″). Photo courtesy of Fairweather Hardin Gallery, Chicago, Illinois. Photography by Anne Clark.

Collect the materials you will use to create your collage. Think about the textures as well as the shapes, sizes, and colors of the materials you collect. Keep everything in your container.

Make some rough sketches of your idea. Notice how Barbara Aubin (Figure 12-32) has used the words as design elements. They are not written in neat rows that are easy to read but are woven into the surface of the work. Select your best idea.

Place the objects you have collected on your paper, but do not glue them down right away. Think about them. Take time to arrange and rearrange your words and images until you are satisfied. Then glue them down. Add drawn and painted images and words as you need them.

When you have finished, mount or mat your work for display.

EVALUATION CHECKLIST

Be sure you did the following:

1. Studied the mixed-media collage by Barbara Aubin.
2. Selected the poem or words to be used.
3. Planned the visual symbols.

4. Found a storage container and a drying area.
5. Collected materials with a variety of shapes, sizes, colors, and textures.
6. Made some rough sketches to plan the collage and selected the best idea.
7. Took time to organize the visual and verbal symbols on the background. Arranged and rearranged them before gluing.
8. Added drawn and painted images and words as needed.
9. Prepared the finished work for display.
10. Cleaned up the work area.

Special-Occasion Calendar

MATERIALS

For this project you will choose your own materials.

OBJECTIVES

Design and make a calendar for a special person or group of people (Figure 12-33). Use unifying devices to hold the total design together. Use variety to emphasize special days. Try to free your calendar design from the ordinary calendar form. Use new systems and unusual materials.

DIRECTIONS

Select the person or group for whom you will make the calendar. It may be for a family, a club, or a school. The calendar may look far into the future, or it may be a memory calendar looking back into the past.

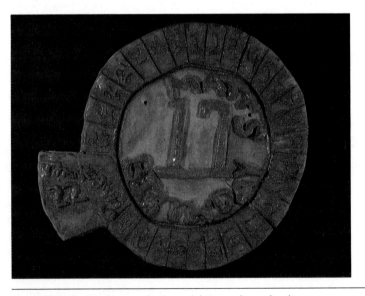

Figure 12.33 Student work. A special November calendar emphasizing Mark's birthday and Thanksgiving.

into a design that is in scale with the wall area to be painted (Figure 12-37 on the next page).

You should consult with your teacher to learn how to prepare the walls, to decide what medium to use, and determine how your project will be paid for.

Measure the area to be painted (see the Technique Tip below). Make scale drawings and color renderings of the drawings.

EVALUATION CHECKLIST

Be sure you did the following:

1. Asked the administrator to select a wall for the mural.
2. Brainstormed ideas for the mural.
3. Made some sketches to show to people during the survey.
4. Presented ideas and asked appropriate people about their preferences.
5. Assembled all of the ideas and, as a team, voted on the best theme.
6. Asked everyone to make sketches for some part of the mural.
7. Decided on unifying devices to hold the work together.
8. Elected leaders to collect and organize the sketches into a final design.
9. Consulted with the teacher concerning ways to prepare the wall, chose an appropriate medium, and arranged for financing.
10. Measured the area carefully.
11. Made scale drawings and color renderings.
12. Presented the final plans to the appropriate person for final approval.
13. Divided responsibilities among the team members.
14. Enlarged the drawings onto the wall.
15. Planned a work schedule.
16. Protected the work area properly.
17. Painted the mural.

TECHNIQUE TIP

Using a Grid for Enlarging

Sometimes you must take a small drawing and enlarge it. To do this, you must first measure the size that the large, finished product will cover. Then, using proportional ratios, reduce that size to something you can work with.

For example: If you want to cover a wall 5 feet high (152 cm) and 10 feet (305 cm) wide, let 1 inch (2.5 cm) equal 1 foot (30 cm). Then make a scale drawing that is 5 inches (12.7 cm) high and 10 inches (25.4 cm) wide. After you have completed your small drawing, draw vertical and hori- zontal grid lines one inch (2.5 cm) apart on the drawing. On the wall, draw vertical and horizontal grid lines one foot (30 cm) apart.

Number the squares on the wall to match the squares on the paper and enlarge the plan, one square at a time.

Figure 12.34 This quilt is not a calendar, but it was designed to celebrate a very special occasion, the 250th birthday of the state of Georgia. Everything on the quilt symbolizes a part of the state. How many symbols can you identify?

Elizabeth Garrison. *Georgia*. 1983. Quilt. 120 × 157.5 cm (4 × 5¼'). Private Collection. 12-38

When you have selected the subject of your calendar, do research to find out which days should be emphasized.

Select a unique medium—think about a quilt, a mobile, three-dimensional shapes, clay slabs, a fiber hanging, or a soft sculpture project (Figure 12-34). Consider the amount of time you have. Don't choose something you cannot complete.

Plan the system you will use to present the days. Plan the unifying device(s) as well as variety to emphasize special days.

Now draw working plans for your project.

Make a list of all the materials you will need, and plan for work and storage space.

Collect all of the materials and place them in the storage container.

When you have done this and are ready to begin, execute your plans.

Finally, prepare the work for presentation to the person or group for whom you made it.

EVALUATION CHECKLIST

Be sure you did the following:

1. Selected the subject of the calendar.
2. Did research to find out which dates needed to be emphasized.
3. Selected a unique medium of choice.
4. Planned a system to present the dates on the calendar.
5. Planned unifying devices as well as variety to emphasize the special dates.
6. Drew working plans for the project.
7. Made a list of all materials needed.
8. Found a storage container and collected the materials for the project.
9. Prepared the finished work for presentation to the person or group for whom it was made.
10. Cleaned up the work area.

Group Project Mural

MATERIALS

You will need the following:

A specific wall area to be painted

Sketch paper and pencils

Tape measures, yardsticks, and rulers

Chalk

Acrylic paints

Brushes

Drop cloth

Safe ladders

Cleaning materials, such as sponges, soap, and buckets of water

OBJECTIVE

Design and execute a painted mural for a wall in your school (Figure 12-35).

DIRECTIONS

Even though this is a public project and you should consider the needs and interests of your "customers," you might present some ideas of your own to help your customers begin thinking.

Ask the principal or administrator to choose a wall area for the mural.

As a group, brainstorm some ideas you would like to use for the mural. Make some sketches, because most people will find it difficult to visualize your ideas.

Show your ideas to the administrators, teachers, and students. Ask them which colors, themes, and styles they prefer.

Assemble all of the ideas you have collected and, as a team, vote on the best theme.

Everyone in the group should make some of the sketches of items to be included in the mural (Figure 12-36).

Since the mural will be created by several people, you should decide on specific unifying devices to hold the work together. Color harmony is one such device.

Everyone cannot work on planning the final composition. One or two people need to collect all of the sketches and organize them

Figure 12.35 Student work. Rainforest mural from a school lunchroom.

Figure 12.36 Student working on a mural.

18. Used safe procedures.
19. Cleaned up between work sessions and took care of the materials and tools properly.
20. Presented the mural to the school in a planned ceremony.

SAFETY NOTE

If you must use a ladder, it should be strong and steady, with a shelf for paint or other tools. Never play with someone on a ladder. Accidents can happen too easily.

Figure 12.37   Student working on a mural. Notice how the floor is protected.

Figure 12.38 Winslow Homer. *The Gulf Stream.* 1899. Oil on canvas. 71.4 × 124.8 cm (28⅛ × 49⅛"). The Metropolitan Museum of Art, New York, New York. Catharine Lorillard Wolfe Collection. 06.1234.

18. Used safe procedures.
19. Cleaned up between work sessions and took care of the materials and tools properly.
20. Presented the mural to the school in a planned ceremony.

SAFETY NOTE

If you must use a ladder, it should be strong and steady, with a shelf for paint or other tools. Never play with someone on a ladder. Accidents can happen too easily.

Figure 12.37   Student working on a mural. Notice how the floor is protected.

Figure 12.38   Winslow Homer. *The Gulf Stream*. 1899. Oil on canvas. 71.4 × 124.8 cm (28⅛ × 49⅛"). The Metropolitan Museum of Art, New York, New York. Catharine Lorillard Wolfe Collection. 06.1234.

Figure 12.34 This quilt is not a calendar, but it was designed to celebrate a very special occasion, the 250th birthday of the state of Georgia. Everything on the quilt symbolizes a part of the state. How many symbols can you identify?

Elizabeth Garrison. *Georgia.* 1983. Quilt. 120 × 157.5 cm (4 × 5¼'). Private Collection.
12-38

When you have selected the subject of your calendar, do research to find out which days should be emphasized.

Select a unique medium—think about a quilt, a mobile, three-dimensional shapes, clay slabs, a fiber hanging, or a soft sculpture project (Figure 12-34). Consider the amount of time you have. Don't choose something you cannot complete.

Plan the system you will use to present the days. Plan the unifying device(s) as well as variety to emphasize special days.

Now draw working plans for your project.

Make a list of all the materials you will need, and plan for work and storage space.

Collect all of the materials and place them in the storage container.

When you have done this and are ready to begin, execute your plans.

Finally, prepare the work for presentation to the person or group for whom you made it.

EVALUATION CHECKLIST

Be sure you did the following:

1. Selected the subject of the calendar.
2. Did research to find out which dates needed to be emphasized.
3. Selected a unique medium of choice.
4. Planned a system to present the dates on the calendar.
5. Planned unifying devices as well as variety to emphasize the special dates.
6. Drew working plans for the project.
7. Made a list of all materials needed.
8. Found a storage container and collected the materials for the project.
9. Prepared the finished work for presentation to the person or group for whom it was made.
10. Cleaned up the work area.

Group Project Mural

MATERIALS

You will need the following:

A specific wall area to be painted

Sketch paper and pencils

Tape measures, yardsticks, and rulers

Chalk

Acrylic paints

Brushes

Drop cloth

Safe ladders

Cleaning materials, such as sponges, soap, and buckets of water

OBJECTIVE

Design and execute a painted mural for a wall in your school (Figure 12-35).

DIRECTIONS

Even though this is a public project and you should consider the needs and interests of your "customers," you might present some ideas of your own to help your customers begin thinking.

Ask the principal or administrator to choose a wall area for the mural.

As a group, brainstorm some ideas you would like to use for the mural. Make some sketches, because most people will find it difficult to visualize your ideas.

Show your ideas to the administrators, teachers, and students. Ask them which colors, themes, and styles they prefer.

Assemble all of the ideas you have collected and, as a team, vote on the best theme.

Everyone in the group should make some of the sketches of items to be included in the mural (Figure 12-36).

Since the mural will be created by several people, you should decide on specific unifying devices to hold the work together. Color harmony is one such device.

Everyone cannot work on planning the final composition. One or two people need to collect all of the sketches and organize them

Figure 12.35   Student work. Rain-forest mural from a school lunchroom.

Figure 12.36   Student working on a mural.

into a design that is in scale with the wall area to be painted (Figure 12-37 on the next page).

You should consult with your teacher to learn how to prepare the walls, to decide what medium to use, and determine how your project will be paid for.

Measure the area to be painted (see the Technique Tip below). Make scale drawings and color renderings of the drawings.

EVALUATION CHECKLIST

Be sure you did the following:

1. Asked the administrator to select a wall for the mural.
2. Brainstormed ideas for the mural.
3. Made some sketches to show to people during the survey.
4. Presented ideas and asked appropriate people about their preferences.
5. Assembled all of the ideas and, as a team, voted on the best theme.
6. Asked everyone to make sketches for some part of the mural.
7. Decided on unifying devices to hold the work together.
8. Elected leaders to collect and organize the sketches into a final design.
9. Consulted with the teacher concerning ways to prepare the wall, chose an appropriate medium, and arranged for financing.
10. Measured the area carefully.
11. Made scale drawings and color renderings.
12. Presented the final plans to the appropriate person for final approval.
13. Divided responsibilities among the team members.
14. Enlarged the drawings onto the wall.
15. Planned a work schedule.
16. Protected the work area properly.
17. Painted the mural.

SAFETY NOTE

You will probably work on the mural after school or on Saturdays. If you will want a snack while you work, always take time to clean your hands before you eat. Many paints contain pigments that are toxic. If you handle food with paint on your hands, you take the risk of accidentally consuming some toxic materials.

TECHNIQUE TIP

Using a Grid for Enlarging

Sometimes you must take a small drawing and enlarge it. To do this, you must first measure the size that the large, finished product will cover. Then, using proportional ratios, reduce that size to something you can work with.

For example: If you want to cover a wall 5 feet high (152 cm) and 10 feet (305 cm) wide, let 1 inch (2.5 cm) equal 1 foot (30 cm). Then make a scale drawing that is 5 inches (12.7 cm) high and 10 inches (25.4 cm) wide.

After you have completed your small drawing, draw vertical and horizontal grid lines one inch (2.5 cm) apart on the drawing. On the wall, draw vertical and horizontal grid lines one foot (30 cm) apart.

Number the squares on the wall to match the squares on the paper and enlarge the plan, one square at a time.

A R T   C R I T I C I S M

Improving Your Critical-Thinking Skills

Description: What Do You See?

Before you describe *Gulf Stream* by Winslow Homer, remember to read the credit line to find out the size and medium of this work.

Now study the work carefully, and list everything you find. The water is a very important part of this painting. Be sure that you describe it thoroughly. Start with the foreground and describe everything you find there. Then move back into the middle ground. Finally, study the background.

Analysis: How Is the Work Organized?

Look at each element carefully.

What types of lines do you see? Does one type of line direction seem stronger than another? Are the lines active or static? What is the effect of the lines you have found?

What shapes do you find? Are they geometric or free-form? What are the effects of the shapes you find? Are they the same as the line effects?

How has Homer used space? Can you find positive and negative areas? Has he used perspective to create the illusion of deep space?

What kinds of colors has he used? Don't just name colors but think about their values and intensities. What kind of color scheme has he used, and how does it affect the work? Has he used natural-looking colors, or has he used colors that express his own feelings? How does that affect the work?

Does Homer use real-looking or invented textures? Can you see the texture of the paint and the brush strokes, or are they hidden?

Name the kinds of rhythm he has used? Does he use rhythm to create a feeling of movement? Which elements are used to create rhythms?

What kind of balance has he used to organize this work? What is the effect of this type of balance?

How has Homer used proportion? Is it accurate or distorted? Is scale important in this work? Look at the ratio of the length to the width of this work? Does it relate to the Golden Mean? If you divide the work so that the left part is a square, where does the dividing line cross the boat and the figure?

How has Homer achieved a unified effect in this painting? Has he made any elements appear harmonious by repeating them or presenting them in a closely related manner? Has he introduced variety by contrasting any elements?

Has Homer used the principle of emphasis to create unity? If so, did he create emphasis through dominance of one element, or has he emphasized one area of the work by creating a focal point to attract your attention? If there is a focal point, where is it? Which of the following techniques has he used to create the focal point: contrast, isolation, convergence, clustering, location, or the unusual?

Interpretation: What Is Happening? What Is the Artist Trying Say?

Now it is time for you to guess the meaning of this work. Don't just repeat the story you unraveled during description. This painting is expressing much more than a simple story. What feelings or emotions is Homer communicating? Use the information you collected during analysis to help you interpret this work.

Write a paragraph explaining your interpretation of *Gulf Stream*.

Judgment: What Do You Think of the Work?

Now it is time to express your reactions to this painting. Do you like it? Why or why not? Is the work unified? Be sure to defend your reasons by using one of the three theories of art that you read about in Chapter 2.

A B O U T   T H E   A R T I S T

Winslow Homer

Figure 12.39 Winslow Homer, American, 1836–1910.

Courtesy of Bowdoin College Museum of Art, Brunswick, Maine.

Winslow Homer was a truly American artist. He turned his back on the subjects and themes popular with the European artists of his time. He didn't want to paint scenes from the Bible or mythology. Instead, he became one of the first artists to use the reality of America as his subject.

Homer fell in love with nature at an early age. He rose early, grabbed his fishing pole, and spent entire days fishing. He loved to explore the ponds, creeks, meadows, and woods. This love of the outdoors showed up later in his paintings.

When Winslow Homer was nineteen, his father read a newspaper ad that said "Boy wanted. Apply to Bufford, lithographer. Must have taste for drawing." Since Homer had that "taste for drawing," his father signed the papers that apprenticed Winslow to the printmaker until the age of twenty-one.

At age twenty-one Homer became an illustrator. He moved to New York and worked for *Harper's Weekly*, the greatest news magazine of the time. He did the job that a photographer does today. He drew pictures of events and people to illustrate the magazine.

When the Civil War broke out, Homer continued to make illustrations for *Harper's*. He traveled to the battlegrounds to sketch scenes of the troops. After the war he decided to learn to paint.

Winslow Homer's family had a profitable real-estate business, and he received a share of the profits. With this money he was able to do what most artists can only dream about. He built a studio atop a lonely cliff in Maine, where he could paint his favorite subject, the sea.

Winslow Homer developed a new way of using watercolors. Up to that time, artists had used watercolors to tint drawings. They used white paint to make the light values. But Homer used the white paper for white. He used it so much that the whiteness from the paper was sometimes the most important element in his work.

When *Gulf Stream* was first shown, people were shocked that the artist could have been present during such a horrible event. In truth, he painted this work in his Maine studio. It was based on sketches he had made in the tropics.

Homer received so many complaints about the subject of this work that he published an explanation. He informed the public that the man was rescued by a passing ship, returned to his home, and lived happily ever after.

Homer was able to paint until he was 73 years old. Then, in 1910, he became blind. Soon afterward he died.

Chapter 12 Review: Talking about Art

USING THE LANGUAGE OF ART

For each new art term below, choose a work of art from this chapter. Then write a sentence about that work using the new term correctly in the sentence.

contrast   harmony
dominant   subordinate
emphasis   unity
focal point   variety

LEARNING THE ART ELEMENTS AND PRINCIPLES

1. Name the two major types of visual emphasis.
2. What do we call an element when it is made the most important element in a comparison?
3. What must an artist consider when creating a focal point?
4. Name the five ways in which artists create a focal point.
5. Name five techniques that artists use to create unity in a work of art.

INCREASING YOUR ART AWARENESS

1. List five examples of visual emphasis you see in your environment.
2. Look at Figure 8-1. Tell how the artist has used the art elements and principles to create a unified work of art. How has he used variety and emphasis to express his ideas and feelings?
3. Discuss all the layers of meaning in Figure 8-1. If you researched the allegorical (symbolic) content of this painting in Chapter 3, include those findings here.
4. Compare the treatment of the clothing and jewelry you see in Figures 6-11 and 11-4. What techniques were used to create emphasis and unity in these portraits?
5. Compare the bronzes of different styles in Figures 6-16 and 12-13. How would you rate each in terms of unity?

UNDERSTANDING ART CULTURE AND HERITAGE

1. Give the title of the oldest work of art in this chapter. Name the artist.
2. Make a time line covering the art periods you learned about in Chapter 3. List two typical or important artworks for each period. Give reasons for your choices.
3. Place a star on the time line (from number 2) by what you consider the five *most* important works. Why did you choose them?
4. Give three examples of new inventions or technologies that have changed the form of art over the centuries. Name artworks that resulted from these inventions.
5. Discuss the different ways religious beliefs have influenced the art of Western and non-Western cultures. Give at least five examples from works of various cultures shown in this book.

JUDGING THE QUALITY OF ART

Gilbert Stuart, who painted *The Skater* (Figure 12-1), is best known for his portrait of George Washington. In fact, he made his fortune painting copies of his original Washington portrait over and over and selling the copies for $100 each.

Imagine that you are Gilbert Stuart just about to meet George Washington for the first time. You have brought *The Skater* with you to help you convince the President that he should let you paint his portrait. Use the four steps of art criticism to explain the qualities of *The Skater* to Washington. During analysis, emphasize the methods you have used to achieve unity in this work.

LEARNING MORE ABOUT ART

Research the change in style of any one kind of household object or piece of furniture through the ages. Then draw the changing forms of this object at correct points along your time line to show how styles of manufactured objects have changed.

As you read and talk about art and produce your own works, you may wish to examine the work of a particular artist. In these cases the following table will help you.

Listed below, in alphabetical order, are the names of the artists whose works appear in *ArtTalk*. Phonetic spellings are given for difficult names you may not know how to pronounce correctly. In these phonetic spellings, accented syllables are indicated by *italic*. Following the artist's name is the artist's nationality, life span, and style (if identifiable). Also listed are the titles of the artists' works that appear in *ArtTalk* and the page numbers on which they appear.

Albers, Joseph, German, 1888–1976, minimal/op
Homage to the Square: Glow, 259

Albright, Ivan, American, 1897–1983, realist
Into the World There Came a Soul Named Ida (The Lord in His Heaven and I in My Room Below), 184

Anuszkiewicz (an-*nus*-ku-witz), **Richard,** American, 1930– , optical
Iridescence, 150

Aron, Gunther, American born in Germany, 1923– , sculptor
Menorah for Synagogue, 189

Arp, Jean, Alsatian, 1888–1966, surrealist
Torso Fruit, 127

Aubin, Barbara, American, 1928– , collage
I Dreamed I Saw a Pink Flamingo in the Salle de Bain, 337

Bak, Brunislaw, American born in Poland, 1922–81
Holocaust, 140
Interpenetrations in Red, 312

Bak, Hedi, American born in Germany, 1924–
Grand Canyon #2, 178

Balla, Giacomo, Italian, 1871–1958, futurist
Dynamism of a Dog on a Leash, 226
Swifts: Paths of Movement + Dynamic Sequences, 223

Street Light, 224

Barlach (*bahr*-lock), **Ernst** (airnst), German, 1870–1938, expressionism
Singing Man, 325

Barnet, Will, American, 1911–
Kiesler and Wife, 251

Bayless, Florence, American, craftsperson
Family, 300
Thai Silk Shirt and Vest, 321

Bellows, George, American, 1882–1925, realist
Both Members of This Club, 146

Benton, Thomas Hart, American, 1889–1975, regionalist
I Got a Girl on Sourwood Mountain, 72

Bishop, Isabel, American, 1902– , realist-New York scene
Bootblack, 333
Two Girls, 287

Boccioni (bought-she-*oh*-nee), **Umberto** (oom-*bair*-toe), Italian, 1882–1916, furturist
Unique Forms of Continuity in Space, 228

Bonheur (bahn-*err*), **Rosa,** French, 1822–99, romantic realism
The Horse Fair, 214

Botticelli (bought-tee-*chel*-lee), **Sandro,** Italian, 1444–1510, Renaissance
The Adoration of the Magi, 114

Brancusi (bran-*coo*-see), **Constantin** (*con*-stan-tin), Rumanian, 1876–1957, abstract
Torso of a Young Man, 121

Brandt, Marianne, German, 1893– , Bauhaus School
Teapot, 19

Bulfinch, Charles, 1763–1844, American, architect
House of Representatives chamber ceiling, State House, Boston, 250

Burchfield, Charles, American, 1893–1967, expressionist
October Wind and Sunlight in the Woods, 212

The books listed below will help you improve your skills and expand your understanding of the visual arts.

Ball, Carlton, and Lovoos, Janice. *Making Pottery Without a Wheel: Texture and Form in Clay.* New York: Van Nostrand Reinhold Company, 1965. Many illustrations and directions that will assist you in clay hand-building techniques.

Barford, George. *Understanding Modern Architecture.* Worcester, Massachusetts: Davis Publishing Co., 1986. Will help you understand your architectural heritage and how it affects today's buildings.

Bevlin, Marjorie Elliot. *Design Through Discovery,* 3rd ed. New York: Holt, Rinehart and Winston, 1977. Based on the idea that design is order. Gives you a different slant on the basic design concepts, materials, media, and environmental design.

Brommer, Gerald F. *Discovering Art History.* Worcester, Massachusetts: Davis Publishing Co., 1981. A survey of art history that includes non-Western cultures.

Brommer, Gerald F. *Drawing: Ideas, Materials, Techniques.* Worcester, Massachusetts: Davis Publishing Co., 1978. Offers many exciting ideas about drawing.

Brommer, Gerald F., and Gatto, Joseph A. *Careers in Art: An Illustrated Guide.* Worcester, Massachusetts: Davis Publishing Co., 1984. A thorough overview of the careers in visual art, with specific information about each field, including educational requirements.

Brommer, Gerald F., and Horn, George F. *Art in Your Visual Environment,* 2nd ed. Worcester, Massachusetts: Davis Publishing Co., 1985. Full of pictures that will give you ideas for making art.

Edwards, Betty. *Drawing on the Right Side of the Brain.* Boston: Houghton Mifflin Company, 1979. Concentrates on the drawing exercises. Will definitely improve your skills.

Feldman, Edmund B. *Varieties of Visual Experience,* 2nd ed. Englewood Cliffs, New Jersey: Prentice-Hall, 1981. An advanced book about visual art. Presents deeper insight into the functions, structure, media, and meaning of visual art.

Laliberte, Norman, and McIlhaney, Sterling. *Banners and Hangings.* New York: Van Nostrand Reinhold Company, 1966. Full of ideas that will inspire you to try a banner of your own.

Lauer, David A. *Design Basics.* New York: Holt, Rinehart and Winston, 1979. Another good design resource. Will expand your understanding of design concepts.

Mittler, Gene A. *Art in Focus.* Peoria, Illinois: Bennett & McKnight Publishing Co., 1986. An art history that helps you use art criticism as well as an historical method to study art. Also contains studio activities.

Mueller, Mary Korstad, and Pollack, Ted G. *Murals: Creating an Environment.* Worcester, Massachusetts: Davis Publishing Co., 1979. A resource book for the mural activity in Chapter 12.

Nelson, Glenn C. *Ceramics,* 3rd ed. New York: Holt, Rinehart and Winston, Inc., 1983. An advanced resource book with illustrations that will give beginning potters new ideas.

Nicolaides, Kimon. *The Natural Way to Draw.* Boston: Houghton Mifflin, 1941. The original "how to" draw book, with specific instructions and examples of both master artists and student drawings.

Nigrosh, Leon. *Claywork: Form and Idea in Ceramic Design,* 2nd ed. Worcester, Massachusetts: Davis Publishing Co., 1986. Excellent, well-illustrated directions for both hand-building and wheel techniques, plus suggestions for surface decorations and formulas for glazes.

Phillips, May Walker. *Step-by-Step Macrame.* New York: Golden Press, 1970. You can really teach yourself macrame techniques by following the clear, well-illustrated directions.

Rainey, Sarita. *Weaving Without a Loom.* Worcester, Massachusetts: Davis Publishing Co., 1966. Explains weaving procedures that can be carried out on looms that you can improvise.

Rhodes, Danuel. *Clay and Glazes for the Potter.* Radnor, Pennsylvania: Chilton Book Co., 1974. For the student interested in science. Explains the origins and chemical make-up of clay and the chemical formulas for glazes.

Sivin, Carole. *Maskmaking.* Worcester, Massachusetts: Davis Publishing Co., 1986. Many illustrations that will give you ideas for the mask-making activity in Chapter 11.

Znamierowski, Nell. *Step-by-Step Weaving.* New York: Golden Press, 1967. You can learn many weaving procedures by following the directions in this book.

This section contains the important words and phrases used in *ArtTalk* that may be new to you. You may want to refer to this list of terms as you read the chapters, complete the exercises, and prepare to create your own works of art. You can also use the Glossary to review what you have learned in *ArtTalk*. It will help you to know that the terms used in the glossary definitions that are themselves defined elsewhere in the Glossary are in *italic*.

abstract art   Twentieth-century art containing shapes that simplify shapes of real objects to emphasize form instead of subject matter.

Abstract Expressionism   Painting style developed after World War II in New York City that stressed elements and principles of art as subject matter and emotion rather than planned design (Figure 3-19). Abstract Expressionism is also called *action painting* because artists applied paint freely to huge canvases.

academies   Art schools that developed in western Europe after the French Revolution. They replaced the *apprentice* system.

acrylic paint   *Pigments* mixed with an acrylic vehicle. Available in different degrees of quality: artists' and school acrylics. School acrylics are less expensive than the professional acrylics, can be washed out of brushes and clothes, and are nontoxic.

Action Painting   See *Abstract Expressionism*

active   Expressing movement. Diagonal and zigzag lines (Figures 5-23, 5-24) and diagonally slanting shapes and forms (Figure 6-43) are active. Opposite of *static*.

aesthetic (es thet′ ik) **experience**   Deep involvement or intense reaction to a work of art.

aesthetic (es thet′ ik) **judgment**   Values used in judging a work of art involving reasons for finding a work of art beautiful or satisfying.

afterimage   Weak image of *complementary color* created by a viewer's brain as a reaction to prolonged looking at a color. After staring at something red, the viewer sees an afterimage of green.

Age of Faith   See *Middle Ages*.

air brush   Atomizer operated by compressed air used for spraying on paint.

alternating rhythm   Visual rhythm set up by repeating *motifs* but changing position or content of motifs or spaces between them (Figures 9-17, 9-18).

analogous (ə nal′ ə gəs) **colors**   Colors that contain a common hue and are found next to each other on the *color wheel* (Figure 7-19). Violet, red-violet, and red are analogous colors. Analogous colors can be used as a *color scheme*.

animation   Moving cartoons used in films and television (Figure 4-10). A series of drawings are photographed, and the figures seem to move when they are projected one after another.

appliqué (ap′ lə kā′)   Technique of attaching fabric shapes to fabric background by gluing or sewing.

apprentice   Student artist. In the *Middle Ages*, apprentices learned from master artists in *craft guilds*.

approximate symmetry   Balance that is almost *symmetrical* (Figure 10-8). This type of symmetry produces the effect of stability, as formal balance does, but small differences make the arrangement more interesting.

arbitrary color   Color chosen by an artist to express his feelings (Figure 7-33). Opposite of *optical color*.

arch   Curved stone structure supporting weight of material over an open space. Doorways and bridges use arches.

architecture   Art form of designing and planning construction of buildings, cities, and bridges.

armature   Framework for supporting material used in sculpting.

Armory Show   First large exhibition of modern art in America. It was held in the 69th Regiment Armory building in New York City in 1913. The *Ashcan School* artists, who were influenced by modern European art, helped organize this exhibit.

art   The use of skill and imagination to produce beautiful objects.

art criticism   Skill of studying, understanding, and judging a work of art. It has four stages: description, analysis, interpretation, and judgment.

artistic style   Way of expression shared by an individual artist or a group of artists.

Ashcan School   Group of American artists working in the early twentieth century who used city people and city scenes for subject matter (Figure 7-13). Originally called "The Eight," they helped to organize the *Armory Show*.

assemblage (ə sem′ blij)   Three-dimensional work of art consisting of many pieces assembled together.

asymmetrical (ā′ sə met′ ri k'l) **balance**   Another

name for *informal balance*, in which unlike objects have equal *visual weight* or eye attraction.

atmospheric perspective Effect of air and light on how an object is perceived by the viewer (Figure 6-31). The more air between the viewer and the object, the more the object seems to fade. A bright object seems closer to the viewer than a dull object.

background Part of the picture plane that seems to be farthest from the viewer.

balance Principle of design that deals with arranging visual elements in a work of art equally. If a work of art has visual balance, the viewer feels that the elements have been arranged in a satisfying way. Visual imbalance makes the viewer feel the elements need to be rearranged. The two types of balance are *formal* (also called *symmetrical*) and *informal* (also called *asymmetrical*).

barbarians Non-Greek-speaking peoples in the ancient world. Barbarians conquered Rome in 476 A.D. and ended the rule of Rome over the civilized world.

Baroque (bə rōk′) Artistic style developed after the Reformation in the seventeenth century. Artists used movement of forms and figures toward the viewer, dramatic lighting effects, contrast between dark and light, ornamentation, and curved lines to express energy and strong emotions.

bas-relief (bä′ rə lēf′) Sculpture in which areas project slightly from a flat surface. Bas-relief is also called *low relief*.

blending Technique of *shading* through smooth, gradual application of dark value.

block Piece of engraved wood or linoleum inked to make a print.

brayer Roller with a handle used to apply ink to a surface (Figure 5-48).

buttress Projecting brick or stone structure that supports an arch or *vault*. A *flying* buttress is connected with a wall by an arch. It reaches over a side aisle to support the roof of a *cathedral*.

Byzantine (biz′ ′n tēn′) Artistic style that developed around the city of Constantinople (now Istanbul, Turkey) in the eastern Roman Empire. The style blended Roman, Greek, and Oriental art. It featured the rich use of color, especially gold; flat, stiff figures; and religious themes (Figure 3-6).

calligraphic (kal′ ə graf′ ik) **lines** Flowing lines made with brush strokes similar to Oriental writing (Figures 5-32, 5-33).

calligraphy (kə lig′ rə fē) An Oriental method of beautiful handwriting using a brush (Figure 5-34).

canvas Rough cloth on which an oil painting is made.

caricature (kar′ə kə chər) Humorous drawing that exaggerates features of a person to make fun of or criticize him or her. Caricatures are often used in editorial cartoons.

carving Shaping wood, stone, or marble by cutting and chipping.

catacombs Rock tunnels under the city of Rome that early Christians used as meeting places. Paintings on catacomb walls used secret symbols since Christianity was illegal until the fourth century.

cast Shaped by pouring melted material into a mold and letting it harden.

cathedral Main church in a district (Figure 3-7).

central axis Imaginary central line that divides a composition in half. The central axis is used to measure *visual weight* in a work of art. It can be vertical (balance between sides is measured) or horizontal (balance between top and bottom is measured).

ceramics Art of making objects with *clay* to produce pottery and sculpture. Pottery is *fired* in a *kiln* to make it stronger.

characters Chinese or Japanese line drawings that stand for letters, ideas, objects, or verbal sounds. They are formed by *calligraphic lines*.

chiaroscuro (kē är′ ə skyoor′ ō) Method of arranging light and shadow in two-dimensional art to create the illusion of three-dimensional form (Figure 6-1). This technique was introduced by Italian artists during the Renaissance and used widely by Baroque artists. Chiaroscuro is also called *modeling* and *shading*.

cityscape Painting or drawing in which a city is the main feature.

Classical Referring to the art of ancient Greece and Rome. The Greeks created art based on the ideals of perfect proportion and logic instead of emotion. The Romans adapted Greek art and spread it throughout the civilized world.

clay Stiff, sticky kind of earth that is used in ceramics. It is wet, and it hardens after drying or heating.

clustering Technique for creating a *focal point* by grouping several different shapes closely together (Figure 12-24).

coil Long roll joined into a circle or spiral. Clay coils are used to make pottery.

collage (kə läzh′) Two-dimensional work of art consisting of many pieces pasted onto a surface.

color Element of art derived from reflected light. The sensation of color is aroused in the brain by response of the eyes to different wavelengths of light. Color has three properties: *hue*, *value*, and *intensity*.

Color Field Painting Twentieth-century style of

painting using flat areas of color. Artists creating color field paintings are not trying to express emotion or use a precise design.

color scheme   Plan for organizing colors. Types of color schemes include *monochromatic, analogous, complementary, triad, split complementary, warm,* and *cool.*

color spectrum   Band of colors produced when white light passes through a *prism* and is broken into separate wavelengths. Colors always appear in the same order, by wavelength, from longest to shortest: red, orange, yellow, green, blue, violet. A rainbow displays the spectrum.

color triad   Three colors spaced an equal distance apart on the *color wheel* (Figure 7-23). The primary color triad is red, yellow, and blue; the secondary color triad is orange, green, and violet. A color triad is a type of *color scheme.*

color wheel   A tool for organizing colors that shows the *spectrum* bent into a circle (Figure 7-8).

compass   Instrument used for measuring and drawing arcs and circles.

complementary colors   Two colors opposite one another on the *color wheel* (Figure 7-15). A complement of a color absorbs all the light waves the color reflects and is the strongest contrast to the color. Mixing a hue with its complementary color dulls it. Red and green are complementary colors. Complementary colors can be used as a *color scheme.*

composition   Arrangement of elements in a work of art.

content   Message the artist is trying to communicate in a work of art. The content can relate to the subject matter or be an idea or emotion. *Theme* is another word for content.

continuation   Technique for creating *unity* by arranging shapes so that the line or edge of one shape continues a line or edge of the next (Figure 12-25).

contour drawing   Drawing in which only *contour lines* are used to represent the subject matter (Figure 5-29). Artists keep their eyes on the object they are drawing and concentrate on directions and curves.

contour lines   Lines creating boundaries that separate one area from another (Figure 5-28). Contour lines define edges and surface ridges of objects and figures.

contrast   Technique for creating a *focal point* by using differences in elements (Figure 12-7).

convergence   Technique for creating a *focal point* by arranging elements so that many lines or shapes point to one item or area (Figure 12-9).

cool colors   Blue, green, and violet (Figure 7-27). Cool colors suggest coolness and seem to recede from a viewer. Cool colors can be used as a *color scheme.* Opposite of *warm colors.*

craft guilds   Groups of artists working in western European towns in the Middle Ages. Master artists taught *apprentices* their skills.

crafts   Art forms creating works of art that are both beautiful and useful. Crafts include printmaking, weaving, fabric design, ceramics, and jewelry making.

crayons   *Pigments* held together with wax and molded into sticks.

credit line   Information identifying a work of art. A credit line usually includes the artist's name, the title of the work, year completed, medium used, size (height, width, and depth), location (gallery, museum, or collection and city), donors, and date donated.

crewel   Loosely twisted yarn used in embroidery.

crosshatching   Technique of *shading* using two or more crossed sets of parallel lines (Figure 5-37).

Cubism   Twentieth-century art movement in which subject matter was separated into cubes and other geometric forms (Figure 3-14). Three-dimensional objects were pictured from many different points of view at the same time.

culture   Behaviors, customs, ideas, and skills of a group of people. Studying art objects produced by a group of people is one way to learn about a culture.

curved lines   Lines that are always bending and change direction gradually (Figure 5-10).

Dadaists (dä′ dä ists)   Early twentieth-century artists using fantastic and strange objects as subject matter.

Dark Ages   See *Middle Ages.*

decalcomania   The technique of creating random texture patterns by pulling apart canvases between which blobs of paint have been squeezed.

dense   Compact; having parts crowded together. Dense materials are solid and heavy. Opposite of *soft.*

design   Plan, organization, or arrangement of elements in a work of art.

De Stijl (də stīl)   Dutch for "the style." A painting style developed by Mondrian in Holland in the early twentieth century that uses only vertical and horizontal lines; black, white, and gray; and the three primary colors.

diagonal lines   Lines that slant (Figure 5-9).

dimension   Amount of space an object takes up in one direction. The three dimensions are length, width, and depth.

distortion   Stretching an object or figure out of normal shape to communicate ideas and feelings.

Divine Proportion   See *Golden Mean.*

dome   Hemispherical *vault* or ceiling over a circular

opening. A dome rises above the center part of a building.

dominant element Element of a work of art noticed first. Elements noticed later are called *subordinate*.

dye *Pigments* dissolved in liquid. Dye sinks into a material and stains it.

dynamism Term used by the *Futurists* to refer to the forces of movement.

elements of art Basic visual symbols artists use to create works of visual art. The elements of art are *line, shape, form, space, value, color,* and *texture.*

embroidery Decorating fabric with stitches.

emotionalism Idea that art should communicate emotion. One of the three theories of art, the others being *formalism* and *imitationalism.*

emphasis Principle of design that stresses one element or area in a work of art to make it attract the viewer's attention first. The element noticed first is called *dominant;* the elements noticed later are called *subordinant.*

engraving Method of cutting a design into a material, usually metal, with a sharp tool. A print can be made by inking an engraved surface.

exaggeration Increasing or enlarging an object or figure or one of its parts to communicate ideas and feelings.

Expressionism Twentieth-century art movement in which artists tried to communicate emotions through art by distorting reality.

fabric Material made from fibers. Cloth and felt are fabrics.

Fauves (fōvs) French for "wild beasts." A group of early twentieth-century painters who used brilliant colors and bold distortions in an uncontrolled way. Their leader was Henri Matisse.

Federal Arts Project Government program established during the Depression to create jobs for American artists.

fiber Thin, threadlike linear material that can be woven or spun into fabric.

fiberfill Lightweight, fluffy filling material made of synthetic fibers.

figure Human form in a work of art.

fine art Works of art made to be enjoyed, not used, and judged by the theories of art. Opposite of *functional art.*

fire To apply heat to harden pottery.

flowing rhythm Visual rhythm created by repeating wavy lines (Figures 9-21, 9-22).

focal point Area of a work of art that attracts the viewer's attention first (Figure 12-5). Focal points are created by *contrast, location, isolation, convergence,* and use of the *unusual.*

foreground Part of the picture plane that appears closest to the viewer. The foreground is usually at the bottom of the picture.

foreshortening Method of drawing or painting an object or person so that it seems to go back into space (Figure 11-19). This method reproduces proportions a viewer actually sees, which depend on the viewer's distance from the object or person.

form 1. Artist's way of using elements of art, principles of design, and media. 2. Element of art that is three-dimensional and encloses space. Like a *shape,* a form has length and width, but it also has depth. Forms are either *geometric* or *free-form.*

formal balance Way of organizing parts of a design so that equal or similar elements are placed on opposite sides of a *central axis* (Figures 10-3, 10-4, 10-5). Formal balance suggests stability. *Symmetry* is a type of formal balance. Opposite of *informal balance.*

formalism Idea that art should emphasize principles and elements of art such as *texture, color,* or *line.* One of the three theories of art, the others being *emotionalism* and *imitationalism.*

found materials Natural objects (such as stones or leaves) and ordinary, manufactured objects (such as coins, keys, wire, or paper plates) found by chance that can be used to create a work of art.

free-form shapes/forms Irregular and uneven shapes or forms (Figure 6-5). Their outlines are curved or angular, or both. Free-form shapes and forms are often natural. Opposite of *geometric shapes/forms.*

freestanding Work of art surrounded by *negative space* (Figure 6-16). A three-dimensional work of art is freestanding. Opposite of *relief.*

frottage A method of reproducing textures by rubbing crayon on paper over a textured surface such as tree bark; or, scraping across a freshly painted canvas.

functional art Works of art made to be used instead of only enjoyed. Objects must be judged by how well they work when used. Opposite of *fine art.*

Futurists Early twentieth-century Italian artists who arranged angular forms to suggest motion (Figure 9-28). They called the forces of movement *dynamism.*

gallery Place for displaying or selling works of art.

genre painting Paintings that have scenes from everyday life as their subject matter.

geometric shapes/forms Precise shapes or forms that can be defined using mathematical formulas (Figures 6-4, 6-7). Basic geometric shapes are the circle, the square, and the triangle. Basic geometric forms are the cylinder, the cube, and the pyramid. Opposite of *free-form shapes/forms.*

German Expressionism   Early twentieth-century artistic style expressing negative emotions (Figure 3-13).

gesture drawing   Line drawing done quickly to capture movement of the subject's body (Figure 5-30).

glaze   In ceramics, a thin, glossy coating fired into pottery. In painting, a thin layer of transparent paint.

Golden Mean   Perfect ratio (relationship of parts) discovered by Euclid, a Greek Philosopher (Figure 11-5). Its mathematical expression is 1 to 1.6. It was also called the *Golden Section* and the *Golden Rectangle* (Figure 11-6). The Golden Rectangle has longer sides a little more than half again as long as the shorter sides. This ratio was rediscovered in the early sixteenth century and named the *Divine Proportion.*

Gothic   Artistic style developed in western Europe between the twelfth and sixteenth centuries. Gothic *cathedrals* used pointed arches and flying *buttresses* to emphasize upward movement and featured *stained glass* windows. Sculpture and painting showed humans realistically.

gouache (gwäsh)   Pigments ground in water and mixed with gum to form *opaque* watercolor. Gouache resembles school tempera or poster paint.

grattage   The technique of scratching into wet paint with a variety of tools, such as forks, razors, and combs for the purpose of creating different textures.

grid   Pattern of intersecting vertical and horizontal lines (Figure 9-14).

ground   See *negative spaces.*

hard-edge   In two-dimensional art, shapes with clearly-defined outlines. Hard-edge shapes look dense. Opposite of *soft-edge.*

harmony   Technique for creating *unity* by stressing similarities of separate but related parts (Figure 12-17).

hatching   Technique of *shading* with a series of fine parallel lines.

hieroglyphics (hī′ ə rə glif′ iks)   Picture writing used by ancient Egyptians.

high-key painting   Painting using many *tints* of a color (Figure 7-12). Opposite of *low-key painting.*

highlights   Small white areas in a drawing or painting. Highlights show the surfaces of the subject that reflect the most light. They are used to create the illusion of form. Opposite of *shadows.*

high relief   Sculpture in which areas project far out from a flat surface.

high-resolution   Producing a sharp image.

hologram (häl′ ə gram′)   Photograph taken without lenses by exposing a photographic plate near an object lit by a laser beam. A hologram is a three-dimensional image.

horizon   Point at which earth and sky seem to meet.

horizontal lines   Lines parallel to the horizon (Figure 5-8). Horizontal lines lie flat and are parallel to the bottom edge of the paper or canvas.

hue   Name of spectral color. Hue is related to the wavelength of reflected light. The primary hues are red, yellow, and blue; they are called *primary* because they cannot be made by mixing other hues together. The secondary hues, made by mixing two primary hues, are orange, violet, and green. Hue is one of the three properties of color.

Hyper-realism   See *New Realism.*

imitationalism   Idea that art should imitate what the viewer sees in the real world. One of the three theories of art, the others being *emotionalism* and *formalism.*

implied lines   Series of points or shapes that the viewer's eyes connect. Implied lines are suggested, not real.

impression   Mark or imprint made by pressure.

Impressionism   Style of painting started in France in the 1860s (Figure 3-11). It emphasized the effect of sunlight on objects and used small dabs of pure color that are blended by the viewer's eyes to imitate reflected light.

informal balance   Way of organizing parts of a design so that unlike objects have equal *visual weight* or eye attraction (Figure 10-15). *Asymmetry* is another term for informal balance. Opposite of *formal balance.*

intensity   Brightness or dullness of color. A pure hue is called a high-intensity color. A dulled hue (a color mixed with its complement) is called a low-intensity color. Intensity is one of the three properties of color.

intermediate color   A color made by mixing a primary color with a secondary color. Red-orange is an intermediate color.

invented texture   A kind of *visual texture* that does not represent a real texture but creates a sensation of one by repeating lines and shapes in a two-dimensional pattern (Figure 8-4). Opposite of *simulated texture.*

isolation   Technique for creating a *focal point* by putting one object alone to emphasize it (Figure 12-8).

kiln   Furnace in which *clay* is fired in order to harden it. A kiln may be electric, gas, or wood-burning.

kinetic sculpture   A work of art that moves due to the real forces of air currents and gravity (Figure 9-31).

landscape   Painting or drawing in which natural land scenery, such as mountains, trees, rivers, or lakes, is the main feature.

layout   Arrangement of type and illustration on a printed page, computer, or television screen.

line   Element of art that is a continuous mark made on a surface with a pointed, moving tool. Although lines can vary in appearance (they can have different lengths, widths, textures, directions, and degree of curve), they are considered one-dimensional and are measured by length. A line is also considered the path of a dot through space and is used by an artist to control the viewer's eye movement. There are five kinds of lines: *vertical, horizontal, diagonal, curved,* and *zigzag.*

linear perspective   Technique of using lines in drawing and painting to create the illusion of depth on a flat surface. In one-point linear perspective, all receding lines meet at a single point. In two-point linear perspective, different sets of lines meet at different points (Figure 6-32, 6-33).

location   The technique of using placement of elements to create a *focal point* (Figure 12-10). Items near the center of a work of art are usually noticed first.

loom   Machine or frame for weaving.

low-key painting   Painting using many *shades* or dark values of a color (Figure 7-13). Opposite of *high-key painting.*

low-relief   See *bas-relief.*

Lucite ($\overline{loo}'$ sīt)   Trademark for an acrylic plastic molded into transparent sheets, tubes, or rods.

Mannerism   European sixteenth-century artistic style featuring highly emotional scenes and distorted figures.

manufactured shapes/forms   Shapes or forms made by people either by hand or using machines. Opposite of *natural shapes/forms.*

mat   To frame a picture or drawing with a cardboard border.

matte (mat) **surface**   Surface that reflects soft, dull light (Figure 8-11). Paper has a matte surface. Opposite of *shiny surface.*

medallion   Round, medal-like decoration (Figure 10-34).

medieval (mē dē' v'l)   Related to the *Middle Ages.*

media   See *medium.*

medium   Material such as paint, glass, metal, or fibers used to make an art object. Plural is *media.*

Mexican muralists   Early twentieth-century artists whose paintings on walls and ceilings used solid forms and powerful colors to express their feelings about the Mexican Revolution. Also called *Mexican Expressionists.*

Middle Ages   Period of roughly one thousand years from the destruction of the Roman Empire to the *Renaissance.* Culture centered around the church. The Middle Ages are also called the *Dark Ages* (because few new ideas developed) and the *Age of Faith* (because religion was a powerful force).

middle ground   Area in a picture between the *foreground* and the *background.*

mobile (mō' bēl)   Moving sculpture in which shapes are balanced and arranged on wire arms and suspended from the ceiling to move freely in the air currents (Figure 3-17).

modeling   See *chiaroscuro.*

modular (mäj' ə lər) **sculpture**   *Freestanding* sculpture that joins *modules* (Figures 9-33, 9-34).

module (mäj' $\overline{oo}$l)   Three-dimensional *motif.*

monk's cloth   Heavy cloth with a basket weave, often used for curtains.

monochrome   One color. A monochromatic *color scheme* uses only one hue and all values of it for a unifying effect (Figure 7-18).

mortar and pestle   Ceramic bowl and tool for grinding something into a powder.

mosaics   Pictures made with small cubes of colored marble, glass, or tile and set into cement.

motif (mō tēf')   Unit repeated in visual rhythm (Figure 9-6). Units in a motif may or may not be an exact duplicate of the first unit.

movement   Principle of design that deals with creating the illusion of action or physical change in position. Artists often use visual movement to control the way a viewer looks at a work of art.

mural   Painting on a wall or ceiling.

natural shapes/forms   Shapes or forms made by the forces of nature. Opposite of *manufactured shapes/forms.*

negative spaces   Empty spaces surrounding shapes and forms (Figures 6-10, 6-11). The shape and size of negative spaces affect the interpretation of *positive spaces.* Negative spaces are also called *ground.*

Neoclassicism (nē' ō klas' ə siz'm)   New classic. French artistic style developed in the nineteenth century after the *rococo* style. It used *classical* features and was unemotional and realistic.

neutral colors   Black, white, and gray. Black reflects no wavelengths of light, white reflects all wavelengths of light, and gray reflects all wavelengths of light equally but only partially.

New Realism   Twentieth-century American artistic style in which subjects are portrayed realistically (Figure 3-20). Also called *Hyper-realism*, *Photo-realism*, and *Super-realism*.

oil paint   slow-drying paint made by mixing *pigments* in oil and usually used on *canvas*.

opaque (ō pāk′)   Quality of a material that does not let any light pass through. Opposite of *transparent*.

Op Art   Optical art. Twentieth-century artistic style in which artists tried to create the impression of movement on the surface of paintings with hard edges, smooth surfaces, and mathematical planning.

optical color   Color perceived by the viewer due to the effect of atmosphere or unusual light on the actual color (Figures 7-34, 7-35). Opposite of *arbitrary color*.

paint   *Pigments* mixed with oil or water. Pigment particles in paint stick to the surface of the material.

palette   Tray for mixing colors of paints.

papier-mâché (pā′ pər mə shā′)   French for "mashed paper." Modeling material made of newspaper and liquid paste and molded over a supporting structure called the *armature*.

parallel lines   Lines that move in the same direction and always stay the same distance apart.

pastels   *Pigments* held together with gum and molded into sticks.

paste-up   Model of a printed page. It is photographed for the purpose of making a plate for the printing process.

pattern   Two-dimensional decorative visual repetition (Figure 9-7). A pattern has no *movement* and may or may not have *rhythm*.

perspective   Method used to create the illusion of depth on a two-dimensional surface. It was developed during the Renaissance by architect Filippo Brunelleschi. Perspective is created by overlapping, size variations, placement, detail, color, and converging lines.

photogram   Image on blueprint paper developed by fumes from liquid ammonia (Figure 6-51).

Photo-Realism   See *New Realism*.

picture plane   The surface of a painting or drawing.

pigments   Finely ground, colored powders that form paint or dye when mixed with a liquid, called the *vehicle*. Pigments are also used to make *crayons* and *pastels*.

plaster   Mixture of lime, sand, and water that hardens on drying.

point of view   Angle from which the viewer sees an object (Figure 6-18). The shapes and forms a viewer sees depend on his or her point of view.

polymer medium   Liquid used in acrylic painting as a thinning or finishing material.

Pop Art   Artistic style used in the early 1960s in America featuring subject matter from popular culture (mass media, commercial art, comic strips, advertising).

portrait   Image of a person, especially the face and upper body.

positive spaces   Shapes or forms in two and three-dimensional art (Figures 6-10, 6-11). Empty spaces surrounding them are called *negative spaces* or *ground*.

Post-Impressionism   French painting style of the late nineteenth century that used basic structures of art to express feelings and ideas (Figure 3-12). The Post-Impressionism movement, which immediately followed *Impressionism*, was led by Paul Cézanne, Vincent van Gogh, and Paul Gauguin.

prehistoric   Period before history was written down.

principles of design   Rules for using the elements of art to produce certain effects based on how viewers react to visual images. The principles of design are *rhythm*, *movement*, *balance*, *proportion*, *variety*, *emphasis*, and *unity*.

print   *Impression* created by an artist made on paper or fabric from a *printing plate*, *stone*, or *block* and repeated many times to produce identical images.

printing plate   Surface containing the *impression* transferred to paper or fabric to make a print (Figure 5-47).

printmaking   Art form of making *prints*.

prism   Wedge-shaped piece of glass that bends white light and separates it into spectral hues.

profile   Side view of a face.

progressive rhythm   Visual rhythm that changes a *motif* each time it is repeated (Figure 9-24).

proportion   Principle of design concerned with the size relationships of one part to the whole and one part to another.

protractor   Semicircular instrument used to measure and draw angles.

proximity   Technique for creating unity by limiting *negative spaces* between shapes (Figure 12-23).

pyramids   Tombs of Egyptian pharaohs, who were rulers worshipped as gods.

radial balance   Type of balance in which forces or elements branch out from a central point, the axis, in a circular pattern (Figures 10-10, 10-11).

random rhythm   Visual rhythm in which a *motif* is

repeated in no apparent order, with no regular spaces.

rasp   File with sharp, rough teeth used for cutting into a surface.

Realism   Mid-nineteenth-century artistic style in which artists turned away from the style of Romanticism to paint familiar scenes and ordinary people.

Realists   Artists in the nineteenth century who portrayed political, social, and moral issues (Figure 3-10).

real texture   Texture that can be perceived through touch. Opposite of *visual texture*.

recede   To move back or become more distant.

Reformation   Religious revolution in western Europe in the sixteenth century. It started as a reform movement in the Catholic Church and led to the beginnings of Protestantism.

regular rhythm   Visual rhythm achieved through repeating identical *motifs* using the same intervals of space between them (Figure 9-13).

relief   Work of art in which forms project from a flat surface into *negative space* (Figure 6-17). Opposite of *freestanding*.

Renaissance (ren′ ə säns′)   French for "rebirth." Revival of cultural awareness and learning in the fourteenth and fifteenth centuries, especially in Italy (Figure 3-8). Interest in *Classical* art was renewed. Important Renaissance artists are Leonardo da Vinci, Michelangelo, and Raphael.

repetition   Technique for creating *rhythm* and *unity* in which a *motif* or single element appears again and again (Figure 12-21).

reproduction   Copy of a work of art.

rhythm   Principle of design that repeats elements to create the illusion of movement. Visual rhythm is perceived through the eyes, and is created by repeating *positive spaces* separated by *negative spaces*. There are five types of rhythm: *random*, *regular*, *alternating*, *flowing*, and *progressive*.

Rococo (rə kō′ kō)   Eighteenth-century artistic style that began in the luxurious homes of the French aristocracy and spread to the rest of Europe. It featured delicate colors and graceful movement.

Romanesque (rō′ mə nesk′)   Style of architecture and sculpture developed during the Middle Ages in western Europe. *Cathedrals* became bigger and featured heavy walls, rounded *arches* and *vaults*, and sculptural decorations.

Romanticism   Early nineteenth-century artistic style that was a reaction against *Neoclassicism*. It featured dramatic scenes, bright colors, loose compositions, and exotic settings. It also emphasized the feelings and personality of the artist.

rough texture   Irregular surface that reflects light unevenly (Figure 8-9). Opposite of *smooth texture*.

rubbing   Technique for transferring textural quality of a surface to paper by placing paper over the surface and rubbing the top of the paper with crayon or pencil (Figure 8-5).

safety labels   Labels identifying art products that are safe to use or that must be used with caution.

scale   Size as measured against a standard. Scale can refer to an entire work of art or to elements within it.

score   To make neat, sharp creases in paper using a cutting tool.

sculpture   Three-dimensional work of art created out of wood, stone, metal, or clay by carving, welding, casting, or modeling.

seascape   Painting or drawing in which the sea is the subject.

shade   Dark *value* of a hue made by adding black to it. Opposite of *tint*.

shading   See *chiaroscuro*.

shadows   Shaded areas in a drawing or painting. Shadows show the surfaces of the subject that reflect the least light and are used to create the illusion of form. Opposite of *highlights*.

shape   Element of art that is two-dimensional and encloses space. While a *form* has depth, a shape has only length and width. Shapes are either *geometric* or *free-form*.

shiny surface   Surface that reflects bright light (Figure 8-12). Window glass has a shiny surface. Opposite of *matte surface*.

sighting   Technique for determining the proportional relationship of one part of an object to another (Figure 11-18).

silhouette (sil′ oo wet′)   Outline drawing of a shape. Originally a silhouette was a *profile* portrait, filled in with a solid color (Figure 6-3).

simplicity   Technique for creating *unity* by limiting the number of variations of an element (Figures 12-19, 12-20).

simulated texture   A kind of *visual texture* that imitates real texture by using a two-dimensional pattern to create the illusion of a three-dimensional surface (Figure 8-3). A plastic table top can use a pattern to simulate the texture of wood. Opposite of *invented texture*.

sketch   Quick, rough drawing without much detail that can be used as a plan or reference for later work.

slip   Creamy mixture of *clay* and water used to fasten pieces of clay together.

smooth texture   Regular surface that reflects light

evenly (Figure 8-10). Opposite of *rough texture*.

soft edge   In two-dimensional art, shapes with fuzzy, blurred outlines. Soft-edge shapes look soft. Opposite of *hard-edge*.

soft sculpture   Sculpture made with fabric and stuffed with soft material (Figure 6-50).

solvent   Liquid that dissolves another liquid.

space   Element of art referring to the emptiness or area between, around, above, below, or within objects. Shapes and forms are defined by space around and within them.

spectral colors   Red, orange, yellow, green, blue, violet.

split complementary colors   One hue and the hues on each side of its complement on the *color wheel* (Figure 7-24). Red-orange, blue, and green are split complementary colors. Split complementary colors can be used as a *color scheme*.

stained glass   Colored glass cut into pieces, arranged in a design, and joined with strips of lead.

static   Inactive; motionless. Vertical and horizontal lines (Figure 5-21, 5-22) and horizontal shapes and forms (Figure 6-44) are static. Opposite of *active*.

still life   Painting or drawing of inanimate (non-moving) objects.

stippling   Technique of *shading* using dots.

stitchery   Technique for decorating fabric by stitching fibers onto it.

Stone Age   Period of history during which stone tools were used.

storyboards   Still drawings that show a story's progress for *animation*. Storyboards are an outline for the development of a film.

subject   What is represented in a work of art. The subject is the part of the work that the viewer can recognize.

subordinate element   Element of a work of art noticed after the *dominant element*.

Super-Realism   See *New Realism*.

Surrealism   Twentieth-century artistic style in which dreams and fantasy were used as subject matter (Figure 3-15).

symbol   Visual image that stands for or represents something else.

symmetrical balance   Type of *formal balance* in which two halves or sides of a design are identical (Figure 10-6).

synthetic   Made by chemical processes rather than natural processes.

tapestry   Fabric wall hanging that is woven, painted, or embroidered.

tempera   Paint made by mixing *pigments* with egg yolk (egg tempera) or another liquid. School poster paint is a type of tempera.

texture   Element of art that refers to how things feel or how they look like they might feel on the surface. Texture is perceived by touch and sight. Objects can have *rough* or *smooth textures* and *matte* or *shiny surfaces*.

tint   Light *value* of a hue made by mixing the hue with white. Opposite of *shade*.

tonality   Arrangement of colors in a painting so that one color dominates the work of art (Figure 7-37).

transparent   Quality of a material that allows light to pass through. Opposite of *opaque*.

trompe-l'oeil (trônp lö′ y′)   French for "trick of the eye." Style of painting in which painters try to give the viewer the illusion of seeing a three-dimensional object, so that the viewer wonders whether he is seeing a picture or something real.

undercut   A cut made below another so that an overhang is left.

unity   Principle of design that allows the viewer to see a combination of elements, principles, and media as a whole. Unity is created by *harmony, simplicity, repetition, proximity,* and *continuation*.

unusual   Technique for creating a *focal point* by using the unexpected (Figure 12-11).

value   Element of art that deals with darkness or lightness. Value depends on how much light a surface reflects. Value is also one of the three properties of color.

vanishing point   Point on the horizon where receding parallel lines seem to meet (Figure 6-32).

variety   Principle of design concerned with difference or contrast.

vault   Arched roof, ceiling, or covering made of brick, stone, or concrete.

vehicle   Liquid, like water or oil, that pigments are mixed with to make *paint* or *dye*.

vertical lines   Lines that are straight up and down (Figure 5-7). Vertical lines are at right angles to the bottom edge of the paper or canvas and the horizon, and parallel to the side of the paper or canvas.

viewing frame   A piece of paper with an area cut from the middle. By holding the frame at arm's length and looking through it at the subject, the artist can focus on the area of the subject he or she wants to draw or paint.

visual arts   The arts that produce beautiful objects to look at.

visual texture   Illusion of a three-dimensional surface based on the memory of how things feel. There are two types of visual texture: *invented* and *simulated*. Opposite of *real texture*.

visual weight   Attraction that elements in a work of art have for the viewer's eyes. Visual weight is affected by size, contour, intensity of colors, warmth and coolness of colors, contrast in value, texture, and position.

warm colors   Red, orange, and yellow (Figure 7-25). Warm colors suggest warmth and seem to move toward the viewer. Warm colors can be used as a *color scheme*. Opposite of *cool colors*.

warp   In *weaving*, lengthwise threads held in place on the loom and crossed by *weft* threads.

watercolor paint   Transparent *pigments* mixed with water.

weaving   Art of making fabric by interlacing two sets of parallel threads, held at right angles to each other on a *loom*.

weft   In *weaving*, crosswise threads that are carried back and forth across the *warp* threads.

yarn   Fibers spun into strands for *weaving*, knitting, or making thread.

zigzag lines   Lines formed by short, sharp turns (Figure 5-11). Zigzag lines are a combination of diagonal lines. They can change direction suddenly.